PRACTICES OF SURPRISE IN AMERICAN LITERATURE AFTER EMERSON

Practices of Surprise in American Literature After Emerson locates a paradoxical question – how does one prepare to be surprised? – at the heart of several major modernist texts. Arguing that this paradox of perception gives rise to an American literary methodology, this book dramatically reframes how practices of reading and writing evolved among modernist authors after Emerson. Whereas Walter Benjamin defines modernity as a "series of shocks" inflicted from without, Emerson offers a countervailing optic that regards life as a "series of surprises" unfolding from within. While Benjaminian shock elicits intimidation and defensiveness, Emersonian surprise fosters states of responsiveness and spontaneity whereby unexpected encounters become generative rather than enervating. As a study of how such states of responsiveness were cultivated by a post-Emerson tradition of writers and thinkers, this project displaces longstanding models of modernist perception defined by shock's passive duress and proposes alternate models of reception that proceed from the active practice of surprise.

KATE STANLEY is Assistant Professor of English at the University of Western Ontario. She received her Ph.D. from Columbia University in 2013. Her contributions to the study of American literature, modernism, pragmatism, and pedagogy have appeared or are forthcoming in *Modernism/modernity*, *American Literary History*, *Criticism*, *Henry James Review*, and *Women's Studies Quarterly*.

(*Continued after the Index*)

PRACTICES OF SURPRISE IN AMERICAN LITERATURE AFTER EMERSON

KATE STANLEY

The University of Western Ontario

CAMBRIDGE
UNIVERSITY PRESS

CAMBRIDGE
UNIVERSITY PRESS

University Printing House, Cambridge CB2 8BS, United Kingdom

One Liberty Plaza, 20th Floor, New York, NY 10006, USA

477 Williamstown Road, Port Melbourne, VIC 3207, Australia

314–321, 3rd Floor, Plot 3, Splendor Forum, Jasola District Centre,
New Delhi – 110025, India

79 Anson Road, #06–04/06, Singapore 079906

Cambridge University Press is part of the University of Cambridge.

It furthers the University's mission by disseminating knowledge in the pursuit of
education, learning, and research at the highest international levels of excellence.

www.cambridge.org
Information on this title: www.cambridge.org/9781108426879
DOI: 10.1017/9781108551236

© Kate Stanley 2018

First published 2018

Printed and bound in Great Britain by Clays Ltd, Elcograf S.p.A.

A catalogue record for this publication is available from the British Library.

ISBN 978-1-108-42687-9 Hardback

For RJK

Contents

Acknowledgments

Throughout the extended process of writing this book, the drawing by John Cage that now serves as its cover provided me with a kind of touchstone, an image of the looping movement of surprise so evocatively described by Emerson's "Circles," and so diversely enacted by the subsequent subjects of my study. In approaching the final and foremost task of thanking those who made the book possible, it strikes me that the decade-long process used by Cage in producing the cover image (part of his Ryoanji series) might also provide an apt figure for the long, entwining process of writing and revising these pages. While Cage's experimental aesthetics may seem far afield of a scholarly monograph's conventions, as I beheld the Ryoanji drawings I nonetheless experienced an unexpected sense of overlap—Cage's visual investigations seeming to describe my procedural methods and subjects too.

For Cage, art is not a product of spontaneous inspiration; rather, an inchoate idea takes shape through a prescribed set of steps repeated again and again. Cage's first foray into the visual arts was prompted by a question that occurred to him in 1962, during his visit to a sixteenth-century Buddhist rock garden at the Ryoanji Temple near Kyoto: was the arrangement of the temple's fifteen boulders produced by an exacting process of calculation, or by chance? In undertaking his Ryoanji series, Cage sought to bypass the either/or provenance posed by this question by designing a framework of calculated chance. Numbering fifteen stones and seventeen pencils of various thicknesses, and marking off a sixty-four by sixty-four grid, Cage established four basic questions for determining the placement of stones on the page: Which pencil? Which stone? Which horizontal position (between one and sixty-four)? And which vertical position? To generate four numbers as responses to these questions, Cage initially used the *I Ching*, then later a computer program designed by his assistant. This procedure, according to one Cage critic, "was in equal measures pragmatic and poetic." For me this comment in turn recalls the work of

Richard Poirier, for whom pragmatism becomes indistinguishable from poetry at the very point where the programmatic and the improvisational converge. As such, if any affinities exist between the aesthetic procedures that produced Cage's Ryoanji series and the institutional procedures that produced this monograph, they would be located in similar points of convergence, between the repetitions of intellectual rigor and the spontaneity of intellectual discovery.

This book would not exist without the teachers, colleagues, family, and friends who sustained me through the most unvarying scholarly tasks and nurtured my appetite and appreciation for surprise at every stage. Adam Frank set me on the academic path and has mentored me with wisdom along the way. From my first tentative inquiry about graduate school, Marianne Hirsch has been a true champion of my every effort and a true support through every challenge. From Eve Kosofsky Sedgwick I learned the steadfast merits of proceeding provisionally. By directing me to a key passage in "Circles," Ross Posnock provided the first root of this project and has supplied apt citations and suggestions with perfect timeliness ever since. Sarah Cole responded with incisive insight to countless drafts of dissertation chapters. Katherine Biers and the members of Columbia's Americanist Colloquium brought structural aid to my unwieldy ideas, and Sharon Marcus gave practical counsel for finishing and publishing. I'm grateful to Branka Arsić, Steven Meyer, and Joan Richardson for their intellectual nourishment and for variously modeling the kind of committed scholar I aspire to be. I've received formative tutelage in the practices of thinking pragmatically from Nick Gaskill and Lisi Schoenbach. Brian Glavey and Jane Thrailkill offered exceptionally thorough and receptive readings of the manuscript as a whole.

It's difficult to imagine a more hospitable place to work than the University of Western Ontario. No one has worked harder to extend that hospitality than Bryce Traister and Alison Conway, extraordinary advocates and generous friends. In welcoming me into their family, Anne Schuurman and Zoë Sinel, as well as Isabel and Sofie, truly made Ontario feel like home. Josh Schuster, Thy Phu, and the members of Western's Americanist Reading Group created the special alchemical conditions from which dissertations emerge, somehow, as books. I discovered that this work was at heart about pedagogy while learning to teach from my inspiring students and colleagues, including Madeline Bassnett, Jonathan Boulter, Joel Faflak, Patti Luedecke, David Huebert, Alyssa MacLean, Zeinab McHeimech, Mary Helen McMurran, Matthew Rowlinson, Peter Schwenger, Kim Solga, Sam Shearman, and Thomas Sorenson.

My research received helpful support from Western and from the Social Sciences and Humanities Research Council of Canada. The editors and referees at *American Literary History* and *Henry James Review* substantially refined essays that would become Chapters 1 and 2. Portions of those chapters were published previously in *American Literary History* 28.3 (2016): 455–483 and *Henry James Review* 34.1 (2013): 16–32 (Reprinted with permission by Johns Hopkins University Press). I benefited enormously from the scrupulous insights offered by my readers at Cambridge University Press. My thanks to Ray Ryan and everyone at CUP who ushered the book through production and publication.

The companionship of beloved friends has to an inexpressible degree improved the quality of these pages and the happiness of these years. I am thankful for you, Saskia Cornes, Anne Diebel, Kim Duff, Colleen Derkatch, Jess Fenn, Laura Fisher, Lisa Kerr, Anjuli Raza Kolb, Heather Latimer, Joe North, Elliot Paul, Sherally Munshi, Sonali Thakkar, Miriam Torchinsky, and Colin Webster. Thanks especially to Alicia DeSantis for teaching me that criticism can be an act of love. Without Emily Muller I would doubtless still be spinning my wheels. Bottomless love and appreciation to my family—Roslyn Boniface, Ali Boniface, Lynne Pomfret, Jesse Stanley, Peter Stanley, and, of course, Benjamin—who reminds me each day what matters most. While writing this book, my family expanded to include the Kadyschuks; my deepest thanks to Ron and Barb for so warmly embracing me and this work.

This book is for Royden, who makes living and writing the happiest collaboration.

Abbreviations

Quotations from the following works are identified by abbreviated title and page number.

A	Henry James, *The American*
AM	Henry James, *The Ambassadors*
AN	Henry James, *The Art of the Novel*
EAL	Ralph Waldo Emerson, *The Early Lectures of Ralph Waldo Emerson, 1833–1836*
EL	Ralph Waldo Emerson, *Essays and Lectures*
EJ	Ralph Waldo Emerson, *Emerson in His Journals*
FT	Marcel Proust, *Finding Time Again*
G	Marcel Proust, *The Guermantes Way*
GB	Henry James, *The Golden Bowl*
HTW	Gertrude Stein, *How to Write*
M	Walter Benjamin, "On Some Motifs in Baudelaire"
N	Gertrude Stein, *Narration*
OR	Marcel Proust, *On Reading*
PP	William James, *The Principles of Psychology, Vol.1*
PPII	William James, *The Principles of Psychology, Vol.2*
Q	Nella Larsen, *Quicksand*
S	John Cage, *Silence*
WI	William James, *Writings, 1878–1899*
WII	William James, *Writings, 1902–1910*
WL	Gertrude Stein, *Writings and Lectures, 1911–1945*

Introduction
Through Emerson's Eye

Experience ... has a way of boiling over, and making us correct our present formulation.

William James

I begin by returning to a well-trod tract of literary ground, "crossing a bare common, in snow puddles, at twilight, under a clouded sky," alongside Ralph Waldo Emerson. Without warning, this unremarkable scene is interrupted: in a vivid rush, Emerson is seized by a sense of "perfect exhilaration." A state of mind as undistinguished as the evening is suddenly overtaken by a gladness verging "on the brink of fear." Most strikingly, this influx of elation seems to appear from nowhere; Emerson emphasizes the bareness of the common and the absence of any triggering sense "of special good fortune."[1] Freed from the scripted constraint of causal logic or predictability, Emerson feels the full force of an unpresaged experience that takes him by surprise.

I recall anew this famous scene because it underlines two vital challenges – one to composition, one to reception – facing a writer like Emerson, who aims to seize his readers with a force akin to what surprised him on the common. The primary compositional problem Emerson faces is belatedness, the lag between life and its mimetic inscription. His sudden sense of exaltation hinges wholly on immediacy, yet his written account of the striking feeling must unfold over time and can only be reported after the fact. To even begin to reflect on the moment is to evaluate retrospectively an event that has passed. Emerson's first articulation of his experience on the common, a journal entry from the spring of 1835, is already belated, an interpretation subsequent to the experience; when he revises that initial impression a year later for the opening of *Nature* (1836), Emerson is at even further temporal remove from the suddenness of that seizing moment. For an author seeking to capture in writing what he describes as "an everlasting Now," these temporal delays in relaying the

I

sensation have the potential to derail the compositional process completely, precluding all efforts to accurately transmit the immediacy of his
experience to a receptive reader.[2]

Let's say Emerson addresses the challenge posed by belatedness: he
develops methods for employing composition itself to access his initial
experience of surprise and to approximate its effects on the page, where it
can in turn surprise his readers. Even if Emerson succeeds in seizing readers
in their initial encounter with his work, the question remains whether the
same passage can retain a capacity to surprise upon rereading, under
repetitive circumstances of reception. Michael Clune states this problem
succinctly: "Time poisons perception."[3] If richness and vivacity were
diminished with each instance of exposure, this problem of familiarity
would seem insurmountable in the reception of something as widely cited
and circulated as Emerson's bare common scene. The very ubiquity of
what Harold Bloom declares "the central passage in American literature" –
reproduced on greeting cards and calendars as often as it is anthologized –
would effectively threaten to cancel out its startling force.[4]

The inescapable ubiquity of the scene may in fact assure many readers
that they already know what to expect in the sentences that come next in
Nature:

> Standing on the bare ground, – my head bathed by the blithe air, and
> uplifted into infinite space, – all mean egotism vanishes. I become
> a transparent eyeball; I am nothing; I see all; the currents of the Universal
> Being circulate through me . . . (*EL*, 10)

Given *Nature*'s omnipresence on high school and university curricula, this
luminously strange figure of transparency may suffer an unavoidable
weakening of voltage beneath classroom fluorescents and study lamps
that wane as conduits of Universal Being. Recurrent exposure to the
passage may foster a more intimate understanding, but overfamiliarity
can just as easily dim its radiant peculiarity. To raise a dictum likewise
fatigued by overcitation, is it possible to "Make it New," or more precisely,
when returning again and again to scenes of literary surprise, to "Make it
New Again?"

This book establishes the centrality of Emersonian surprise to
a transatlantic tradition of writers who extend the newness-making imperative of modernism's defining credo by adding the dimension of reiteration:
by emphasizing "again," by making newness a routine rather than a feat,
these writers push beyond the one-off or short-lived forms of aesthetic
novelty invoked by Pound's motto and address the evanescence and long-

term obsolescence of such forms. The historical ubiquity of the credo itself exemplifies how easily a rousing call for revolutionary newness becomes a tired catchphrase.[5] Recognition of how the thrill of immediacy can evaporate as ephemera or calcify into cliché is what motivates Emerson and literary modernists working in his wake to distinguish between newness that is fleeting and what Emerson describes as "perpetual surprise."[6]

How might an experience as impermanent as a sudden startle be renewed and potentially sustained – for a writer and for a reader? As I argue, questions like this stimulate formal experiments among some of Emerson's most responsive readers and give rise to a range of modernist hallmarks – including Baudelaire's flashes of *correspondance*, Proust's *mémoire involontaire*, Henry James's scenes of recognition, Nella Larsen's depictions of double consciousness, and Gertrude Stein's break from narrative form. These aesthetic innovations at the level of verb tense, grammatical mood, or scenic and syntactical structure all recall that the verb "to innovate" is rooted in the Latin *innovare*, which means not *new* or *form* but to *renew* or *reform*.[7] As I will demonstrate in the chapters that follow, renovations of narrative time and consciousness were for each of these writers spurred and guided by a twofold Emersonian insight. First, familiarity and belatedness can act as instigators rather than inhibitors of aesthetic surprise. And second, recasting apparent impediments as catalysts for unexpected encounters requires preparation and practice.

The Paradox of Preparation

How does one prepare to be surprised? "Surprises" are generally understood as events which preempt poise, events for which one is the opposite of prepared. To ready oneself for surprises would then seem to suggest transforming volatile phenomena into regular, even routinized experiences – to disarm their unpredictability and contain their impact. In other words, the task of preparing to be surprised is easily inverted into the task of preparing *not* to be surprised. I claim that Emerson provides a set of major modernist writers and intellectuals with practical strategies for avoiding such an inversion at transitional moments in their life and work. In reconstructing the practices that Emerson establishes, I revise two influential critical narratives that would assert the irreconcilability of preparation and surprise.

First, I contest a narrative that too readily casts Emerson as the primary literary inheritor and disseminator of a Puritan legacy of preparationism. According to this story, most forcefully narrated by the Americanist critic

Sacvan Bercovitch, Emerson perpetuates the literary equivalent of prepara-
tionist perception: an overvigilant, appropriative gaze that kills the surprise
of spontaneous grace by working unceasingly toward its acquisition.
By recasting Emerson's perceptual practices as powerful tools for cultivating spontaneity, I also recast Emerson's central role in the Bercovitchean
story of Puritan inheritance and in turn reframe the model of receptivity
taken up by writers working in an Emersonian lineage. Second, I contest
Emerson's omission in a narrative of modernist shock that has occluded the
importance of surprise by overlooking Emerson's crucial transatlantic
influence. The pervasive paradigm of modernism, derived from Walter
Benjamin, subsumes surprise into shock, making no distinction between
the two affects, so that all sudden and seizing experiences must be pre-
empted by perceptual defenses that are protective, but also deadening.
While for scholars committed to these standing narratives Emerson epitomizes a provincial romanticism that has little relevance for the study of
modernism, I follow the injunction of Baudelaire – Benjamin's shock poet
par excellence – who claims the sage of Concord as a defining figure of
transatlantic modernity. In my consideration, Emerson's strategies for
embracing the unexpected similarly enable writers on both sides of the
Atlantic to open themselves to the surprises of modernity.

   In considering how surprise can paradoxically be facilitated by preparation and in tracing the influence of this paradox back to Emerson, I follow
William James and John Dewey, both of whom invoke the famous figure
of Emerson's transparent eyeball as a practical model for the "surprise of
reception."[8] Only when one is receptive to surprises, they observe, are
perceptual breakthroughs possible and then aesthetically or pedagogically
repeatable. James and Dewey each notably refer to Emerson's bare common episode in lectures they devote to educational reform. The opening
scene of *Nature* would first serve as the touchstone for a series of talks James
delivered to teachers and students with the goal of putting his principles of
psychology to practical use in the classroom.[9] Education is only useful,
James insists, insofar as it enriches daily life. Several decades later, Dewey
would invoke the same scene in a talk that inaugurated an annual Harvard
lecture series named to honor the lifelong interlocutor he found in James
(who taught in the university's psychology and philosophy departments
until his death in 1910). Both lectures were influential in their time and
have maintained a remarkable critical durability, recorded in two volumes
that have never gone out of print: James's *Talks to Teachers on Psychology;
and Talks to Students on Some of Life's Ideals* (1899), and Dewey's *Art as
Experience* (1934).

Together, these lectures suggest that Emersonian surprise might serve as the antidote for modern perceptual experience, which for shock-oriented critics since the turn of the century has been threatened and limited by crisis and closure. By reading Emerson, both James and Dewey find themselves equipped to face two saboteurs of surprise: the Puritan forms of preconception that Bercovitch blames for American blindness and the sense of inauthentic belatedness that Benjamin identifies as the defining condition of urban modernity. As I will suggest, James and Dewey formalize the perceptual practices they learn from Emerson, first as a method of psychological investigation – the act of introspection – and later as what they would call "the method of pragmatism."[10]

Ancestral Blindness

Writing to an audience of psychologists at the beginning of his career, William James attributes the problem of preconception to physiology. In *The Principles of Psychology* (1890), he focuses on the adaptive function of "anticipatory preparation."[11] Quoting the German physiologist Wilhelm Wundt in his chapter on attention, James initially sets surprise in opposition to "anticipatory preparation": "The surprise which unexpected impressions give us is due essentially to the fact that our attention, at the moment when the impression occurs, is not accommodated for it" (*PP*, 440). If one's goal is to optimize response speed to sensory stimuli, as it was for Wundt, the most efficient form of preparation is what James calls "preperception." To perceive something, James asserts, is to call forth a preexisting idea or image of that thing. "The *preperception*," he estimates, is "half of the perception" (*PP*, 442). Framed by Wundt's concern with perceptual accommodation, James at first presents this startling claim as evidence of effective adaptation. However, he goes on to admit that the operations of preperception are double-edged. On the one hand, preperception provides ideational and sensory preparation, without which we would move through life in a state of perpetual disorientation. On the other hand, the experience of losing one's bearings, of exceeding previous frames of reference, is what facilitates discovery. As James worries, adept preperceivers "have no eyes but for those aspects of things which they have already been taught to discern" (*PP*, 443). It is not until James begins to consider the practical implications of his psychology of perception that he envisions how certain kinds of perceptual preparation might facilitate rather than foreclose the experience of surprise.

Two years after the publication of *Principles*, James puts his psychological insights to work in a pedagogical context. In his lectures on education, teachers are tasked with awakening "spontaneous attention" by knitting "novelties on to things of which [students] already have preperceptions" (*PP*, 447). This is to say that James advocates pedagogical practices that foster discovery by enmeshing the unexpected with what is already known. The classroom is framed as a practice ground that prepares students to have their perceptual paradigms continually unsettled. Addressing teachers, James advises: "Prepare yourself in the *subject so well that it shall be always on tap*; then in the class-room trust your spontaneity and fling away all farther care."[12] Here James overturns his earlier model of preparation; in order to learn, a thoroughly prepared perceptual apparatus must be receptive rather than defensive. As veteran teachers (similar to, say, proficient musicians) might attest, from a state of adaptive preparation and adept responsiveness, unforeseen spontaneity and inspiration can spring forth readily, even under the most familiar and reiterative circumstances. The goal of education, as James frames it, is to programmatically cultivate such spontaneity as a lifelong habit.

While James's *Talks to Teachers* focuses on the pedagogical challenges posed by his psychology of perception, his *Talks to Students* addresses a set of perceptual pitfalls he attributes to a specifically American inheritance. As James suggests, his countrymen have inherited from their Puritan predecessors "an ancestral blindness," a hardened insensibility to objects and others who threaten preconceived certainties (*WI*, 865). In the opening lecture of the series, James identifies "ancestral intolerances" as the source of "bad models" of perception he observes to be prevalent around him. He writes, "We, here in America, through following a succession of pattern-setters, whom it is not impossible to trace, and through influencing each other in a bad direction, have at last settled down collectively into . . . our own characteristic national type" (*WI*, 832). Unimpressed, James blames the Puritans for bestowing "bad habits" of perception that have resulted in the "defective training of our people" (*WI*, 832, 834). His condemnation of this "national type" is thus a withering diagnosis of his fellow Americans who have grown "stone-blind and insensible" toward "creatures and people different from ourselves" (*WI*, 832, 841).

In his first lecture to students, James's focus on an "over-contracted" field of American perception seems to dovetail with Bercovitch's account of the narrowing of national vision (*WI*, 831). As Bercovitch argues in the recently reissued *The Puritan Origins of the American Self* (1975/2011), a direct line can be drawn between the Puritans' appropriative view of the "New World" and the acquisitive cultural desire exemplified by Emerson's trope of transparent vision. This critical narrative marks the Emersonian Eye as the apotheosis of an expansionist ideology of exceptionalism. Bercovitch's seminal account has generated several decades' worth of scholarship so consistent in its condemnation of America's "self-serving blindness" that Elisa New has described this scholarly strain as a "genre" unto itself.[13] According to this Americanist narrative, which New dubs "vision with a vengeance," Emerson's expressed desire to "enjoy an original relation to the Universe" extends the origin story established by his New England ancestors: the myth of a nation divinely elected to realize its Manifest Destiny.[14] When American vision is projected as an agonistic force, the transparent eyeball annexes its purview to individualist and imperial interests. The Emersonian Eye, for this genre of criticism, is defined by a nationalist myopia.[15]

In his second lecture, James's approach to the Puritans' perceptual legacy veers away from the proto-Bercovitchean narrative; "On a Certain Blindness in Human Beings" – James's favorite of all his talks – presents the Emersonian Eye as a corrective to America's "ancestral blindness" rather than its exacerbation. Against those who would position Emerson as epitomizing the myopic closure of the American eye, James recovers the means by which Emerson in fact aims to correct such closure. James attributes to Emerson's words a startling force capable of breaking through a "hard externality," which too easily overtakes the "responsive sensibilities" that make life "worth living" (*WI*, 847, 856). Emerson's essays are eye-opening for James in the sense that they help him dissolve a cataract of heedlessness and recover a responsive and edifying acuity.

Attesting that narrow forms of nationalism and individualism have "been preached long enough in our New England," James looks to Emerson for better models (*WI*, 839). While inherited habits incline the "American character" toward grasping, James invokes the bare common passage to exemplify "the capacity of the soul *to be grasped*, to have its life-currents absorbed by what is given" (*WI*, 834, 855, emphasis added). Where the Puritans preached unrelenting vigilance, Emerson's essay delivers "the gospel of relaxation" (*WI*, 835). James names the watchword of this gospel: "*Unclamp*" (*WI*, 836). Instead of holding the visual field captive to a mastering gaze, Emerson exemplifies "esthetic surrender"; the eye relinquishes its capacity to seize objects of view so that it might itself be seized.[16] In this receptive state of surrender, the "I" disperses into the process of vision: "I am nothing; I see all" (*EL*, 10).

As James suggests, Emerson's prose has the potential to prepare readers to be similarly seized. In the scenes of reading that James describes, "this higher vision comes over a person suddenly; and . . . makes an epoch in his history" (*WI*, 848). While James emphasizes suddenness in this formulation, he makes clear that the spontaneous arrival of a "new perspective" is made possible by an established reading practice, one which allows the familiarity of one's own consciousness to commingle with another unfamiliar consciousness over the course of life (*WI*, 847). "We are trained to seek the choice, the rare, the exquisite exclusively, and to overlook the common," James observes, but Emerson's prose offers a new kind of training that instills "the individual fact and moment . . . with absolute radiance."[17] James locates Emerson's power of "transfiguration" – his capacity to transform the world into something "still new and untried" – in the processual aspect of his literary language (*WII*, 1125, 1121). James's lifelong engagement with Emerson's writing underscores the time it takes time to clear obscured vision; the "great cloud-bank of ancestral blindness weighing down upon us" lifts so imperceptibly that when formerly "invisible things" are revealed, it can come as a surprise (*WI*, 862, 849). Through this protracted process of reading, one gains gradual access to perceptions that are not preperceived: "Our self is riven and its narrow interests fly to pieces, then a new centre and a new perspective must be found" (*WI*, 847).

As I will elaborate in Chapter 1, Emerson's own account of his Puritan inheritance radically reframes his politics of perception and his corresponding vision of nationhood. Drawing a line from his ancestors to himself, Emerson reinvents Puritan methods of preparing the unregenerate soul for the surprise of spontaneous grace. As Emerson observes, the Puritans' overvigilant preparations for receiving grace left them finally unreceptive to the spontaneous spiritual encounters they sought. In my reading, Emerson's recurrent emphasis on cultivating receptivity represents his ongoing effort to correct the misapprehensions of his forebears. Revising free grace into a guiding principle of surprise, Emerson establishes an American lineage that privileges literature as the domain where the unfulfilled Puritan promise of spiritual plenitude and perceptive revelation might be redeemed. *Practices of Surprise* charts the development of this post-Emerson tradition through writers united by a common commitment to creating the conditions for "perpetual surprise" – a renewable receptivity to unexpected encounters.

The Challenge of Modernity

Where William James recalls Emerson to negotiate perceptual problems rooted in the past, John Dewey looks to Emerson to meet the perceptual demands of the present. For Dewey, the task of realizing the redemptive receptivity James finds in Emerson became freshly charged, but also newly challenged, by "the dislocations and divisions of modern life."[18] *Art as Experience* argues that a variety of "forces at work" – industrial, technological, psychological – have bifurcated perception: "Modern society operate[s] to create ... a chasm between ordinary and esthetic experience."[19] As Dewey worries, the ever-increasing speed and density of stimulation has likewise asserted debilitating discontinuities between inner and outer life.

Dewey points to the bare common passage in his introduction to suggest how modern audiences might begin to bridge these gulfs and fill the blind spots they generate. In Dewey's reading, Emerson's writing invites a "spontaneous and uncorked esthetic response," which draws out the "natural continuity" between art and "normal processes of living"; Emerson's essays provide palpable evidence of the "immediate sensuous" reality of apparently "etherial things."[20] To recover these vital continuities between art and experience is to enrich one's perceptive faculties and expand one's perceptual field. However, Dewey's perpetual rereading of Emerson over the course of his life reveals that such enrichment and expansion rarely arrives in a single instant – as the eyeball episode might suggest when excerpted as a maxim – but rather develops gradually through ongoing practice.

Like James, Dewey receives from Emerson an extended "education of the human soul," which takes the form of attention training.[21] Emerson's approach to perceptual exercise helps James overturn his previous model of preperception; likewise, Emerson's antidote to preconception helps Dewey counteract the second major saboteur of surprise, belatedness, by affirming that a delayed response to disorientation may bring that disorientation into a sharper focus. As Dewey asserts, an artwork of "high esthetic value" often generates a "surprise that is disconcerting."[22] He describes the initial "seizure" of surprise like this: "The total overwhelming impression comes first ... there is an impact that precedes all definite recognition of what it is about."[23] Yet, rather than privileging the overwhelming immediacy of first impact, Dewey insists that the "disconcerting" moment "you are seized" cannot be isolated from the process of preparation and reflection that precedes and follows.[24] The surprise of reception, in short, "takes time."[25]

For Dewey, "the temporal aspect of perception" distinguishes true reception from "mere recognition," the latter of which simply confirms what is already known: "In no case can there be perception of an object except in a process developing in time. Mere excitations, yes; but not as an object perceived, instead of just recognized as one of the familiar kind."[26] Like James, Dewey places "preparation" at the heart of "aesthetic education"; spontaneous reception is not possible unless "channels of response are prepared in advance."[27] As I will show, Deweyan reception unfolds according to the strange temporality of Emersonian surprise. The prepared perceptual apparatus is open to spontaneous seizure, and then to the disconcerting experience of disorientation, and then to a reorienting process of reflection upon what happened in the immediate moment of encounter. Dewey concludes *Art as Experience* by suggesting that a writer like Emerson allows his readers to inhabit time differently: "Literature conveys the meaning of the past that is significant in present experience and is prophetic of the larger movement of the future. Only imaginative vision elicits the possibilities that are interwoven within the texture of the actual."[28]

Dewey's model of a preparatory process that renews and improves reception provides a powerful alternative to the Benjaminian discourse of defensive perception that has proved so influential in critical narratives of modernist experience. In his essay, "On Some Motifs in Baudelaire" (1939), Benjamin generalizes and amplifies Sigmund Freud's concept of shock – trauma undergone in wartime – into the defining structure of modernity.[29] Modern consciousness, in Freud's conception, must act as a "protective shield" against relentless psychological incursions generated by the "excessive energies at work in the external world."[30] The onslaught of war, urbanization, and technological change at the turn of the twentieth century all contribute to a "crisis of experience," and in the face of this assault, perceptual preparation is tasked with "protection against stimuli" (*M*, 161).[31] As Benjamin deduces, however, guarding oneself against unanticipated experiences comes at the high cost of a generally dulled receptivity to all new encounters. Modernity's assault on receptive consciousness leaves only two experiential possibilities in the modern era: shock and its counter, "shock defense" (*M*, 163).

While Benjamin defined modern experience as a "series of shocks," and many signature moments of literary modernism have since been understood to correspondingly register sensory inundation and psychological breakage, Benjamin's essay also tellingly collapses any difference between surprise and shock by using the terms synonymously (*M*, 175). He quotes the poet Paul Valéry, who argues that experiences "in the category of surprises . . . are evidence of an insufficiency in man" (quoted in *M*, 161). Valéry describes "surprises" as the sudden "impressions and sense perceptions" that overwhelm all immediate interpretive faculties, an influx that Benjamin then parses as "traumatic shocks" that must be "cushioned" or "parried" (*M*, 161, 162). Notably, where Valéry emphasizes the act of recollection that permits the "surprise" of this influx to be interpreted belatedly, Benjamin's paraphrase derives a more preemptive act of mitigation that would defend against the "shock" of this influx and filter its full force. This tendency for eliding the startle of surprise into the strain of shock, or for conflating the two terms of experience outright, may ultimately seem semantic. Yet with this book I want to demonstrate that a strong and nuanced affective distinction does meaningfully differentiate these terms across literary and critical history. Because my methods for establishing this distinction (as I will elaborate in the next section) are fundamentally pragmatist, I will argue that the divestment of surprise from shock is creatively, receptively, and pedagogically consequential, for it also marks the point where curiosity can divest from caution, where adaptation can divest from entrenchment, where iteration can divest from repetition.

While I set Emersonian surprise against Benjaminian shock in deliberately polemical terms in the opening pages of this introduction, it's worth pausing here to make explicit Benjamin's positioning in this project. In naming Benjamin as a foil for Emerson, I mean specifically to invoke the widespread critical use to which his foundational descriptions of shock have been put in modernist studies and in cultural studies more generally. "Motifs" is so frequently cited by cultural critics in part because it distills an exportable conceptual vocabulary for theorizing "modern times," and then models how readily that terminology might be applied to literature and film (*M*, 178). It is important to note, however, that when Benjamin derives Freud's framework of "shock experience" from *Beyond the Pleasure Principle* (1920), he issues a crucial caveat against taking this view of shock as definitive: "The following remarks based on [Freud's essay] are not intended to confirm it; we shall have to content ourselves with investigating the fruitfulness of this hypothesis in situations far removed from those which Freud had in mind when he wrote" (*M*, 162, 160). Many of Benjamin's readers have indeed affirmed the fruitfulness of Freudian shock for understanding situations far removed from his case studies of "war neuroses"; the diverse field of trauma studies has largely developed from this starting point.[32] Yet Benjamin frames "Motifs" as a preliminary investigation, rather than an absolute confirmation of the categorical applicability of Freud's paradigm of "traumatic shocks" (*M*, 161). As it turns out, Benjamin's investigation into the topic of shock will remain largely limited to this lone essay.[33]

Nevertheless, despite Benjamin's caveat of provisionality, the method of reading for shock that he models in "Motifs" continues to cast a long shadow of critical influence. Even the most trenchant critiques of Benjamin, which accuse him of "unduly extend[ing] the Freudian conception of shock," can have the effect of reinforcing his status as the figurehead for a narrative of shock modernism that ultimately received limited elaboration in his own work.[34] As such, if the significance of Freudian shock as a tool for analyzing modernist texts has been overextended, I would venture this owes less to Benjamin himself than to the unduly inexorable "Benjaminian tradition" that later literary critics have established. Benjamin's original experiment in reading for shock is hence the obligatory starting point for tracing the persistent and definitive appeal of shock-oriented methods – and also for alternately framing, as I will, a less prominent but equally persistent method of reading for surprise.

Benjamin's application of a Freudian framework to literary texts may be provisional, but it quickly accrues a sense of inevitability because of the causal relationship he draws between historical change and literary style. After first considering Henri Bergson's theory of involuntary memory, he ultimately prefers to mobilize Freud's theory of "shocks effects" because, he explains, the latter accounts more fully for the "historical determination" of experience (*M*, 157). Seeking sites of cultural application, Benjamin focuses on Baudelaire and Proust, whose signature styles exemplify for him how literature can register dramatic shifts in historically determined structures of experience. "Motifs" opens by situating these writers in "the inhospitable, blinding age of big-scale industrialism," defining this "modern age" in terms of historical rupture (*M*, 157, 194). In marking out the singularity of these "modern times," Benjamin also implicitly distinguishes modernism as an unprecedented period in cultural history (*M*, 178). One reason his shock-oriented narrative of modernity has gained such traction owes to how its method of historicizing enables a particular approach to periodization, one that defines modernism by an epochal break in cultural continuity, thus by demarcation establishing its uniqueness as an era and an object of study.

I want to underline that the broader account of modern life in Benjamin's oeuvre is richly complex and ultimately not solely reducible to the methods of reading for shock and for historicizing modernity that he models in "Motifs." And yet this essay has become the critical touchstone for equating shocks with bad surprises and for periodizing literary modernism as a break with everything that came before. The logic of shock and discontinuity so familiarly articulated in "Motifs" therefore offers a stark point of contrast for discerning what is distinctly alternative about Emerson's logic of "perpetual surprise." Whereas Benjamin defines modernity as a "series of shocks" inflicted from without by external and historically specific stimuli, Emerson had previously described a countervailing optic for regarding life as a "series of surprises" unfolding from within, in whatever place and whichever time one's experience occurs (*M*, 175; *EL*, 483). In drawing these contrasts, I am claiming neither that surprise ought to displace shock as the defining affect of modernity nor that Emerson provides a refutation or an antidote to traumatic experience. However, when "shock experience has become the norm," as it has in Benjamin's essay, subsequent modernist criticism tends to likewise normalize shock as the sole variety of experiential suddenness, consolidating a diversity of encounters into a single, and reductively negative, affect (*M*, 162). To cite just one example, in *Infancy and History: The Destruction of Experience* Giorgio Agamben likewise uses surprise and shock as synonyms, where both terms imply "a gap in experience"; crucially, Agamben here defines "experience" as an unremitting impression of continuity and certainty, "that which affords us protection from surprises."[35] This indicates a precarious vision of experience as something that can be undermined (even "destroyed") by its susceptibility to interruption and so must be insulated and defended. By this definition, surprise does not just threaten experience; it is even antithetical to experience, with the bursts of discontinuity or states of uncertainty it hastens seen to lie outside the purview of experience itself (*M*, 47).

In looking to Emerson for an alternate vision of this "gap in experience," I take a cue from Philip Fisher, who wonders if "that favorite modern aesthetic category, shock" might more productively be placed within the broader category of "the aesthetics of surprise and the sudden."[36] In Fisher's account, "surprise, the eliciting of notice," is the most capacious of the aesthetic categories and is also fundamentally neutral because it is "the very heart of what it means to 'have an experience' at all."[37] Marking and enabling experience (rather than obviating or impairing it), Fisher's conception of surprise as an essential aesthetic category here counters a Benjaminian shock reading, while aligning with psychological definitions of surprise as an essential affective category (as per Silvan Tomkins, whose appraisal of surprise I will outline in a moment and discuss further in Chapter 2). Pursuing aesthetic stakes alongside the affective stakes of countering shock modernism, this study examines the work of writers who seek narrative means for incurring and holding open the interval of surprise, in order to explore the temporal and perceptual dimensions of an encounter remarkable not as an injurious state of entropy that precludes meaning but as a neutral state of uncertainty that precedes interpretation. For Fisher, as for Emerson, the nature of surprise cannot be determined in advance; one's response to unexpected encounters depends as much on perceptual orientation as it does on the object of encounter, and modernity's range of responsive affects is equal in variety to modernity's range of surprising stimuli. Given the wealth of critical work addressing experiences that might be understood as bad surprises, this project follows Emerson in raising unexpected experiences that might be welcomed rather than warded off. Acknowledging the existence of "destructive shocks" which might indeed require "parrying and defence," Emerson's practice of surprise is ideally calibrated for adapting equally to the perilous and the tedious, providing protection from duress in "rugged crises" while remaining porous to discovery under "most ordinary circumstances."[38]

For Benjamin in "Motifs," then, "preparedness" means protection against the experience of sudden seizure (*M*, 161). By contrast, Dewey's preparatory practices foster states of responsiveness amid inundation whereby unexpected encounters can become generative rather than enervating. While Benjamin announces experiential crisis, Dewey asserts that the perceiver can be trained to strike openly perceptive postures in response to the challenges of modernity. For Dewey, Emerson's prose offers a particularly fertile training ground for this reconditioning of perception. To return once more to the bare common episode: even as Emerson is seized without warning, he is far from unprepared for what transpires in that moment. The bare common passage is so often isolated from the rest of *Nature* that it's easy to overlook that in the pages that follow, Emerson emphasizes the rigorous practices of attention he undertakes to render himself receptive to such an experience: moving from "superficial seeing" to an "attentive eye" requires "discipline" (the name of *Nature*'s pivotal fifth chapter) (*EL*, 10, 15, 26). "Interest surprises us," Emerson says, and through the "constant exercise" of letting attention take disorienting turns, the chance to "unlock a new faculty" is optimized (*EL*, 26, 25). The process becomes serial: new perceptive faculties discover untried channels of interest, which open further faculties, one surprising experience begetting another, such that life unfolds as "a series of surprises" – a phrase that recurs throughout Emerson's essays (*EL*, 413, 483).

The classic Emersonian ideal of moving through life with open eyes is accompanied by an equally expansive and pliant model of time, in contrast with the hermetic and hardened loop of shock. Benjamin's compulsion for returning to moments of rupture in the past has the effect of foreclosing the "prospective" dimension of surprise (*EL*, 552). Conversely, while Emerson is often thought to disavow the past, Dewey draws out the rhythmic fluctuations between "prospect or retrospect" that pattern Emerson's "everlasting Now," as his "loom of time" weaves the "warp and woof" of "past and future" into a shuttling temporal order.[39] Dewey values Emersonian surprise for the way it opens a vital (though always provisional) possibility: that the future can look different from what came before and that the past could have taken a different shape.[40]

Emersonian Pragmatism

This study builds on the work of Elisa New and Joan Richardson, who each reframe Dewey's relation to Emerson by drawing direct lines from Puritanism to pragmatism. In so doing, these two critics clear the channel through which I will put Emersonian pragmatism into contact with modernism. Reading *Art as Experience,* New notes Emerson's influence in Dewey's embrace of experiences of art-reception and art-making that depend on "the trained kind of discrimination, or selection"; aesthetic training, in Dewey's account, stimulates a "readiness for revelation."[41] New first traces Dewey's "esteem" for "disciplined" practices of revelatory perception back to "an older religious fealty" exemplified by his Puritan forebears; she then extends her claims for Deweyan aesthetics to the wider philosophical tradition of pragmatism, which she follows James in identifying as "one of the varieties of religious experience."[42]

New's narrative of the "reorientation of American sight" from the Puritans to the pragmatists has received scant critical elaboration, but Joan Richardson has authored several studies that deepen and extend the story.[43] Richardson argues that for Dewey, Emerson exemplifies "the human activity . . . [of] 'reception,'" which represents a "secular, naturalized grace."[44] This receptivity resembles the Puritan ideal of spontaneous grace insofar as it arrives without warning, yet relies on "the severe discipline of thought."[45] As Richardson observes, Dewey disciplines his thought through practices of reading and writing. More specifically, he seeks to integrate Emerson's transparent eyeball "into the everyday transparency of his style," a style which achieves novel insight "through deliberate and disciplined selection."[46] Emerson is the hinge figure in

Richardson's work, who connects the Puritans to the pragmatists because he models for Dewey and for James a rigorous method of distilling "from ordinary experience its extraordinary substrate of perception."[47]

James's and Dewey's twin gestures of pointing in lectures to the bare common passage, James in 1899 and Dewey in 1934, roughly bookend the development of pragmatism.[48] Before James has named the philosophical method, his talks to students uphold Emerson as a model of "living in the open air and on the ground" so that "over-sensibilities and insensibilities even themselves out" (*WI*, 857). As Emerson exemplifies for James, the ordinary activity of walking with one's eyes unblinkered cultivates a posture conducive to questioning unexamined beliefs and assumptions. This "recognizant" turn to the "novelty" of the world "present and alive" will become for James the posture of pragmatism (*WI*, 862, 875, 865). The foundational question that pragmatism directs at every experience – "What practical difference will it make?" – can only succeed in making a genuine difference when asked in an attitude of relaxed yet disciplined awareness (*WII*, 551). Emerson's essays make this supple brand of attention – open *and* directed, spontaneous *and* prepared – available to James and to Dewey.

I extend the work of New and Richardson by arguing that the perceptual practices Emerson enables for pragmatists also leave a lasting legacy in literary modernism. Dewey concludes *Art as Experience* by suggesting where pragmatist and modernist aesthetics intersect, using his final chapter to consider the changing status of art in the context of mechanical reproduction – concerns that Benjamin will famously echo two years later in "The Work of Art in the Age of Mechanical Reproduction" (1936). Dewey worries that advances in industrial and commercial production will further divide aesthetic and everyday experience: "Mass production by mechanical means has given the old separation between the useful and fine a decidedly new turn."[49] Acknowledging the irreversibility of urban and industrial change, Dewey resists declarations of crisis and warns against "preaching the need of returning to the past."[50] Proceeding on the premise that "psychological conditions" are always malleable, he foregrounds the formative force of art that reshapes perception.[51] "Modernistic" and pragmatic interests converge in aesthetic experiences that train new "habits of the eye."[52]

Deweyan habit – what he describes here as "internal functional adaptations" – helps one remain responsive to the relentless movement of life.[53] In a study that declares Dewey as its "unassuming philosophical hero," Lisi Schoenbach claims the term *habit* as an unlikely source of common ground between pragmatism and modernism.[54] As she demonstrates, the habits of pragmatism are irreducible to the habits of deadening routine that Viktor Shklovsky and other proponents of avant-garde innovation held up as the chief enemy of art. Schoenbach shows how Darwin provides Dewey with an evolutionary model of habit "in which continuity and adaptation to the environment are continually balanced with positive actions and constantly changing reactions."[55] Pragmatism and modernism overlap where they work to keep those habits supple.

This study similarly connects pragmatist and modernist methodologies by way of a mutual Emersonian influence. Whereas Schoenbach identifies Deweyan habit as the site where modernism and pragmatism converge, I focus on perceptual practices that Dewey and others derive from what Emerson calls his "method of nature."[56] Before mapping out this Emersonian methodology in detail, I will briefly outline several key "instructions" Dewey credits Emerson with imparting – practical insights which are likewise taken up by Emerson's modernist inheritors.[57] Dewey anticipates readers may be "repelled by any suggestions of teaching and learning in connection with art" but insists that the "idea of education" he has in mind lifts aesthetic encounters "far above what we are accustomed to think of as instructions."[58] The invaluable pedagogy Dewey attributes to Emerson does not arrive in the form of prescriptive directives but rather reveals itself in ongoing perceptual practices that extend into a "conduct of life" (*EL*, 943).[59]

In a talk delivered on the centenary of Emerson's birth, Dewey counters those who fault Emerson for his "lack of method."[60] Critics reduce him to "a writer of maxims . . . and abrupt aphorisms" because they are accustomed to the rubric of essayistic conventions and expect to find a philosophical "method separately propounded."[61] By contrast, Dewey argues that Emerson is a poet-philosopher whose methods cannot be extricated from the act of making or the "maker" himself: "A man is a method, a progressive arrangement, a selecting principle."[62] Dewey frames Emerson's teachings in terms that structure much longer debates, which I will elaborate in Chapter 2, around the role of surprise in processes of learning and discovery. "The surprise of reception," Emerson teaches, is "more potent than reasoning."[63] Dewey repeatedly privileges spontaneous perception over deliberative deduction in this talk; to learn is "to uncover rather than to analyze; to discern rather than to classify."[64] The Emersonian paradigm Dewey draws on directly inverts Descartes's influential account of surprise as a dangerous threat to rational judgment (see Chapter 2); yet, it is easy to overlook Emerson's own rebuttal of the

Cartesian model because he is so often denied the status of philosopher that Dewey affords him.[65] As I will ultimately contend, in overturning a prevailing philosophical model, Emerson reactivates surprise as a formative force in shaping theories of mind, philosophies of life, and acts of literature through the twentieth century.[66]

The Method of Nature

Near the end of his writing career, Emerson reflects in a journal entry on his ongoing process of "learning to read his own manuscript severely – becoming really a third person."[67] Crucially, the third-person perspective he seeks to cultivate is limited rather than omniscient; "the best part of each writer," Emerson argues, is that "which he does not know" (*EL*, 293). Here he suggests that the same is true of readers. If his severe discipline of reading achieves a vantage of impersonal unknowing, "then all the words will be spritely, & every sentence a surprise" (*EJ*, 556). His prose will only succeed in seizing his audience, Emerson determines, if the surprising force of his words and sentences does not depend on a first-time encounter. The paradoxical task, then, is to stage unexpected encounters with what is most familiar to him: his own writing.

Emerson's notebooks and journals formulate various compositional guidelines for fostering a renewable responsiveness to surprise. He asserts, for instance, the following "rhetorical rule": "The word should never suggest the word that is to follow it, but the hearer should have a perpetual surprise, together with the natural order."[68] While structure and spontaneity seem opposed, Emerson explains in another journal entry that "we have two needs": "Being & Organization." "Organization" requires us to "set in order," while "Being" demands that we "renew as oft as we can the pleasure of the eternal surprise."[69] According to Emerson's account of his own writerly formation, he discovers a compositional method that will reconcile these two needs in Georges Cuvier's cabinets of comparative anatomy at the Muséum d'Histoire Naturelle in Paris (commonly called the Jardin des Plantes), an exhibit that teaches him to read "the true order of nature" as a language of strange surprises (*EL*, 118).

On July 13, 1833, the day of his formative visit to the Jardin des Plantes, Emerson's journal reports the spontaneous emergence of his "method of nature." Wandering in rapt attention from the botanical garden through the gallery of birds to the mineral display, Emerson is struck by the sense that Cuvier's taxonomies distill nature's composition into a decipherable language. The cabinets' ordering principles present him with a model for composing into essays the various "specimens" he had collected in voluminous notebooks – impressions, quotations, reflections, and other miscellany – over the better part of a decade.[70] Just as Cuvier's taxonomic order enlivened otherwise dead displays of comparative anatomy, Emerson sought to reanimate past writings through their concerted arrangement and rearrangement. Emerson's strategies of revitalization appear at first antithetical to spontaneous renewal; new work emerges out of a painstaking process of mining earlier writings for arresting figures and formulations to be recast and recirculated.

"Composition," as Emerson defines it, is the construction of a "living chain," yet the method of nature he discovers at the exhibition does not confirm any great chain of being or predetermined design.[71] Instead, Emerson mimes nature's compositional order by weaving animating threads of his notebooks and journals into contingent noncausal patterns. "If you desire to arrest attention, to surprise," an entry advises, "do not give me facts in the order of cause & effect."[72] A contingent web of connection emerges out of Emerson's elaborate system of indexing his notebooks, journals, and essays. "The using & perusing of what was already written," whether days or years prior, initiates for Emerson the "art named composition" (*EJ*, 138–39). The vast organizational infrastructure he constructs draws unexpected links among key terms, figures, and phrases, while also keeping them close at hand. The result is a rigid system of classification that spurs impromptu invention: index topic headings become essay topics, while epigrammatic notes tagging individual entries frequently generate aphoristic formulations.[73]

Instead of establishing authoritative statements, Emerson continuously revises and recharges his assertions by keeping them in constant circulation. For instance, he reassembles his journalized impressions of the museum into a lyceum lecture delivered a month after returning to Boston (in November 1833), which in turn provides the germ for *Nature* and various essays that followed. The lecture titled "The Uses of Natural History" walks his audience through the exhibition's cabinets, casting an observant "eye" over "more surprising objects than were known to exist" (*EAL*, 10–11). Surprise and order converge in the relation of "the outward world to the inward world of thought and emotions" – a "radical correspondence" he aims to transmit to his listeners (*EAL*, 24; *EL*, 22).

The lecture describes "Nature's proof impressions" as a "grammar of botany," a "natural alphabet," a "green and yellow and crimson dictionary" (*EAL*, 7–8). When Emerson declares, "I will be a naturalist," he commits to

learning the "alphabet," "grammar," and "dictionary" of Nature (*EAL*, 10).
The lecture closes with a confirmation of this commitment in terms he will
reiterate in the "Language" chapter of *Nature* three years later: "Nature is
a language and every new fact one learns is a new word . . . I wish to learn
this language . . . that I may read the great book which is written in that
tongue" (*EAL*, 26). If, as Emerson asserts, words are "signs of natural facts,"
then reading the "great book" means grafting those signs onto "sensible
things" (*EL*, 20). "Language taken to pieces and dead" is reanimated when
words withered by rote usage are rooted in their referent (*EAL*, 26). Words
reunited with "natural facts" become "surprising objects," as Emerson
experienced at the Jardin des Plantes (*EL*, 20).

Emersonian Surprise

Emerson's compositional method stages unexpected encounters within his
own prose – writing that takes him "by surprise, and yet is not unknown"
(*EL*, 11). The question remains: how does Emerson extend the experience
of "perpetual surprise" to readers beyond himself? His guiding mantra –
"First we read, then we write" – suggests one answer (*EJ*, 298). According
to Emerson's definition, "creative reading" – the conversion of another's
words into an inventive impetus – must spark "creative writing" (*EL*, 59).
When Emerson writes that books "are for nothing but to inspire," he
means to be taken literally: reading, when properly practiced, should
breathe animating life into new sentences (*EL*, 57). As I will show in the
following chapters, some of Emerson's most creative readers found these
same forces of reanimation in his prose, a powerful means of reinspiring
sentences of their own that threatened to similarly stagnate under the
pressures that had plagued Emerson: belatedness and preconception.

By framing the act of writing as an extension of reading, Emerson was
himself returned to the unavoidable realities of belatedness and preconception. Too often, the process of reading only succeeds in confirming what
someone else has thought before (belatedness) or what we think we already
know (preconception). By contrast, genuinely creative acts of reading and
writing must proceed as processes of discovery that usher "an unlooked for
result" into the world and onto the page (*EL*, 484). As Emerson repeatedly
confirms, "In the thought of genius there is always a surprise" (*EL*, 483).
How then, does Emerson propose that readers and writers avoid seeking
out only old formulations that can confirm preexisting ideas?

Instead of giving direct recommendations, Emerson models how to incite
the creative impulse at the level of syntax. Perhaps no critic has attended as

closely to Emerson's sentences as Julie Ellison, whose careful parsing culminates in a central insight: "His style successfully gratifies his desire for both conscious power over his material and the feeling of being surprised by it."[74] Emerson's stylistic surprises are evidence of his authorial control, in Ellison's account. Making the case that his "oscillat[ion] between self-awareness and forgetfulness" is carefully calibrated, Ellison counters critics who condemn Emerson's apparent contradictions as a failure of style.[75] A nineteenth-century reviewer distills the tenor of critical complaint most frequently leveled at Emerson's writing: "His style is too fragmentary and sententious. It wants the requisite words or phrases of connection and transition ... His beautiful things are *slippery*, will not stay in the mind."[76] Rather than faulting the slipperiness and fragmentation of Emerson's prose, I frame his disjointed "lubricity," which lets his sentences "slip through our fingers when we clutch the hardest," as a deliberate and potent strategy (*EL*, 473). Offering his own rejoinder to critics who charge him with incoherence, Emerson retorts, "I know better than to claim any completeness for my picture. I am a fragment, and this is a fragment of me" (*EL*, 491).

The process of slippage, of forgetting, Ellison explains, frees us from "the inhibitions imposed by memory and 'usage.'"[77] Emerson's amnesiac prose supports, in his own words, "a spontaneity which forgets usages, and makes the moment great" (*EL*, 483). This line features in "Experience," an essay that begins and ends with Emerson's affirmation of "Surprise" as one of "the lords of life" – a guide to living, writing, and reading (*EL*, 469, 490–91). As quickly becomes clear, an essay written under the sign of surprise guides by deepening disorientation. The unsettling and emblematic opening query – "Where do we find ourselves?" – is met with a response that only exacerbates uncertainties: "In a series of which we do not know the extremes" (*EL*, 471). But this response also offers clues as to how we might proceed without any guarantees beyond a belief in "the middle region of our being" (*EL*, 480). Emerson's insistence that "the mid-world is best" points back to his opening invocation of seriality without extremity, and forward to the essay's hinge phrase, repeated several times: "Life is a series of surprises, and would not be worth taking or keeping, if it were not" (*EL*, 481, 483).

To live life as a series of surprises is to inhabit the middle regions of time and perception, between recollection of the past and projection into the future:

> God delights to isolate us every day, and hide from us the past and the future. We would look about us, but with grand politeness he draws down

before us an impenetrable screen of purest sky, and another behind us of
purest sky. "You will not remember," he seems to say, "and you will not
expect." (*EL*, 483)

Emerson echoes these divine decrees with sentences and paragraphs that
defy remembrance and expectation. Writing under the tutelage of nature
and its "organic movements," Emerson organizes "Experience" (1844)
according to "undulatory and alternate" rhythms which propel us
"Onward and onward!" but in unpredictable directions (*EL*, 483, 486).
This insistent yet erratic onwardness makes it easy to forget precisely where
the essay has been or to anticipate where it is going.

The fragmentary slipperiness for which Emerson is disparaged is intrinsic to his "method of nature," a compositional strategy strictly intended to
stall the mechanisms of memory and anticipation. As I have described,
Emerson incorporates the undulating "pulses" of nature into his prose with
an indexing system that emulates the natural order he first witnesses at the
Jardin des Plantes (*EL*, 483). As writing, what does this look like? Taking
major index topics as his starting point, Emerson composes essays by
grafting together phrases and passages that were "found separate," often
written years apart, under varied circumstances, in disparate registers.[78]
Following his revelation at the museum exhibition, Emerson frames this
process as a lifelong commitment to becoming fluent in nature's "surprising objects." He embraces what emerges in the spontaneous act of composition, declining to smooth or unify startling shifts in syntax, tone, and
organization, instead considering these shifts as his chief means of furthering a fluency that depends on forgetfulness. Emerson's lubricious sentences
are not intended to stick (*EL*, 473). Instead, readers grasping for the
handholds of logical, sequential argumentation and linear narrative will
find themselves clutching at gaps and absences – openings where Emerson
locates the potential for surprise.

Emerson suggests how to extend singular surprises into a self-renewing
series in "Circles" (1841), an essay that concludes by again reiterating the
central claim of "Experience": "Life is a series of surprises." Just as the
opening of "Experience" finds us "in a series of which we do not know the
extremes," "Circles" begins with a destabilizing invocation of seriality:
"Every ultimate fact is only the first of a new series. Every general law is
only a particular fact of some more general law presently to disclose itself"
(*EL*, 405). Emerson first makes this realization when confronted with the
"bewildering series of animated forms" on display at the museum of
natural history. The taxonomic principles so gloriously arrayed "must be

looked on as temporary" because classifications are always countered by phenomena that overwhelm totalizing schemas: "Nature ... resents generalizing, and insults the philosopher in every moment with a million of fresh particulars."[79] The poet-naturalist's attunement to "particular facts" demands the ongoing revision of natural laws which are ill-equipped to accommodate their specificity (*EL*, 68).

Emerson's spiraling formulations both describe and enact this endless oscillation between particularity and generality. "Circles" presents itself as an exercise in "reading the copious sense of this first of forms" as it dilates from "a ring imperceptibly small ... to immense and innumerable expansions" (*EL*, 403, 404–5). Anticipating the reader's disorientation, he asks, "Is this too sudden a rushing from the centre to the verge of our orbit?" (*EL*, 410). The relentless rush denies his audience any "principle of fixture or stability": "People wish to be settled; only as far as they are unsettled is there any hope for them" (*EL*, 412, 413). Emerson's sentences leap from discrete details to expansive orbits, yet just as often they contract back to intimate proximity: "I am a God in nature; I am a weed by the wall" (*EL*, 406). The dizzying shift in scale is counterbalanced by a parallel construction that gives equal weight to vast abstractions and "the near, the low, the common" (*EL*, 68).

Having put the reader's eye through its circular paces, "Circles" follows "Experience" in giving the final word to surprise:

> The one thing which we seek with insatiable desire is to forget ourselves, to be surprised out of our propriety, to lose our sempiternal memory, and to do something without knowing how or why; in short, to draw a new circle ... The way of life is wonderful: it is by abandonment. (*EL*, 414)

Surprise sloughs off social convention and linguistic conformity, but it also demands a more radical abandonment of propriety; the process of self-forgetting that Emerson describes dissolves the idea that essential properties belong to a stable subject. While he is often understood to celebrate unbounded individualism, Emerson underlines the limits of bounded subjectivity: "As I am, so I see; use what language we will, we can never say anything but what we are" (*EL*, 489). To shed the proper self is to access vision beyond the constraints of the individual "I" and to use language to discover what we *could be* instead of confirming "what we are." Abandoning the proper self, the "experimenter" makes "the moment great" by projecting a "new prospect" (*EL*, 412, 483, 405).[80]

Who is equipped to answer Emerson's call, to the relentless pursuit of oscillation, dissolution, and unsettlement? Surprising the self out of its propriety can sound like a solipsistic endeavor available only to a privileged few. However, Emerson insists that seeking such surprises is a necessity, not a luxury. "The results of life are uncalculated and uncalculable," he writes, and these unknown odds expose all living beings to contingency and risk (*EL*, 483). As William James first pointed out for teachers and students, Emerson can be seen to cultivate "habits of attention," which make it possible to confront the uncertainties intrinsic to an open-ended "world of chance" (*PP*, 286; *WI*, 576). Both Emerson and James ask their audiences to make an "ethical and practical" choice in the face of an unknown future: the choice between acting in conformity or acting out of surprise – between clinging to false certainties or doing "something without knowing how or why" (*EL*, 414). Indeed, both insist that "ethical reformation" is only possible in a universe without guarantees (*EL*, 256).[81] Subjecting ethics to the laws of nature, Emerson dispels the illusion of immutable principles: just as "there are no fixtures in nature," there is no such thing as a final ethical position (*EL*, 403).

The Ethics of Surprise

For Emerson surprise is an imperative force that "makes the moment great" – but should its function be considered essentially *good*? The ethical implications of surprise develop from the scenario described in the paragraph above, where the experience of human uncertainty requires choosing either the moral assurance of incumbent values or the adaptive precariousness of pledging oneself to the unknown. From the start, this ethical framework risks the simplification for which Emerson is frequently attacked, seeming to present, on the one hand, an overly abstract ethics of "ethereal principle" (typical of an Emerson "living preferentially in the mind") or, on the other hand, an overly improvisational ethics that is "entirely relativist" (typical of an Emerson "living passionately in the moment").[82] Crucially, it is the conditions of surprise that supply Emerson with a third path, an "emergent ethics" in which the orientation for a responsible life is responsively derived from the spontaneous experience of living itself.[83] In shifting away from religious notions of eternity – "There is no other world; here or nowhere is the whole fact," he says – Emerson turns with conviction to taking direction and seeking deliverance in the provisional revelations of the diurnal (*EJ*, 286). It is only after having "shed Christianity's aim beyond this life so that he could be continually astonished by the world itself" that Emerson ordains his new "lord of life" – surprise no longer uncertainty's erratic byproduct, but rather a key mechanism through which uncertainty can admit and propagate the self-possession of a secular grace.[84]

In a life lorded by surprise, the gaps, jogs, or irregularities in the surface of a text or the fabric of experience become vitally charged, presenting openings where conformity and linear determinism give way to truly emergent forms of response. One of surprise's chief merits – for Emerson, and later for Silvan Tomkins – in fact stems precisely from its unique capacity for creating such potent gaps. In his seminal catalog of affect, Tomkins situates surprise as a major category that broadly encompasses many related but subordinate affects (including both shock and interest). He also importantly notes that surprise itself remains affectively neutral, despite catalyzing further affects that can range widely from positive to negative (delight, fear, rage). Yet the main reason Tomkins bestows surprise with special status involves the special function it performs as a "circuit breaker" when it interrupts a prevailing feeling and clears space into which new responses can arrive.[85] When appraising surprise as the facilitative breach through which new relations manifest, or as the suddenly vacated form into which new content issues, its role for an emergent ethics clarifies, as the disorientation it provokes also provides "a reorienting affect" (per Adam Frank) toward newly current and urgent objects of attention, modes of feeling, and lines of action.[86]

While these emergent adjustments may be constructive or destructive, and will in turn remain provisionally subject to further interruption and reorientation, Emerson's larger claim is that ethical investments should not bolster preconceived certainties but should acknowledge the state of contingency that human life, like nature, inevitably asserts. As Brian Massumi claims, "Ethics is about how we inhabit uncertainty, together," a definition that replaces rigid and internally recursive habits with fluid and outwardly turned inhabitations.[87] This mode of responsiveness clearly echoes and collectivizes the methods of pragmatism – as James writes, "Each of us literally *chooses*, by his way of attending to things, what sort of universe he shall appear to himself to inhabit" – infilling surprising gaps with engaged adaptations and necessitating that practices of ethical action emerge without dogmatic prescription (*PP*, 401).

Yet despite this emphasis on neutrality and process, my argument here is strongly predicated on the dislodging function of surprise offering an intrinsic and positive value. *Practices of Surprise* shows how Emerson methodically interrupts and reorients his own entrenched habits of reading and writing as a model for likewise interrupting his entrenched habits of living. I extend this model primarily toward the

modernist writers whose practices Emerson informs, but also toward the
contemporary critics, teachers, and students whose senses of intellectual
and ethical entrenchment have likewise, in my personal experience and
often in my presence, been profitably unsettled by surprise. To this
point, I would suggest there is a specific salutary value in surprise's
capacity for activating and enriching states of uncertainty, ambivalence,
or repetition – states that have long borne negative affects for readers,
writers, and teachers. Across the surprising latticework of narrative gaps
this project explores, I hope to trace practices that supersede the
negative affects that often undermine literary response (intimidation,
paralysis, boredom, cliché) by instead enabling a correlative set of
positive affects (curiosity, discovery, spontaneity, renewal). While
I engage less directly with moral verdicts than with methodological
processes, my position will remain epistemologically reliant on and
ethically invested in valuing action above atrophy, attentiveness above
disinterest, pliancy above fixity, and emergence above conformity.

The Uses of Surprise

If Emerson's persistent interest in the praxis of thinking affirms his role as
a "proto-pragmatist," his exploration of "practical wisdom" is rooted in
literary methods (*EL*, 633). He initially signals the correlation between
"Use" and "Surprise" in the poem that serves as epigraph to "Experience,"
and in a passage of "Circles" these terms conjoin once more to suggest
a reading practice devoted to "the use of literature" (*EL*, 408). Literature is
useful, Emerson explains, because it provides "a point outside of our
hodiernal circle, through which a new one may be described" (*EL*, 408).
The act of reading affords perspectives beyond our own, "a platform
whence we may command a view of our present life, a purchase by
which we move it" (*EL*, 408). "We value the poet" because he allows us
to practice a kind of partial self-loss; when we read, we are surprised by
a consciousness not our own (*EL*, 409). For a time, the "concentric circles"
of these consciousnesses overlap so that our perspective is doubled (*EL*,
409). Standing within but also to the side of the circle drawn, one accesses
points of view from inside and outside the circumference of the self. From
this vantage, it is possible to inhabit the all-consuming experience of
surprise while simultaneously reflecting upon the moment when the self
was forgotten.

Emerson looks to literature to break "my whole chain of habits, and . . .
open my eye on my own possibilities" (*EL*, 409). Reading can induce

a process of self-forgetting, but the self is only half-forgotten when it cohabitates with another consciousness. In this sense, literary texts serve as practice grounds where one can experiment with self-loss while remaining partially present to the experience. In his journals, Emerson envisions a literary encounter that will enact a more complete obliteration of subjectivity: the book "invades me[,] displaces me; the law of it is that it should be first, that I should give way to it."[88] In this more radical literary encounter, "each new mind we approach seems to require abdication of all our past and present empire."[89] Surrendering to the invasion by another, the "I" is reduced to "nothing by ... an entire new mind."[90] "A new mind," Emerson affirms, "is a new method."[91]

Emerson's martial figures of aggression and surrender recall the original usage of surprise, the term's military origins designating an attack without warning.[92] Reading for surprise, according to this definition, depends on the extraordinary force of the text and the defenselessness – not to say defensiveness – of the reader. In one sense, readers are vulnerable to being overcome because they are unprepared. Yet in another sense, such readers must in fact become prepared and willing to drop all resistance in the face of overwhelming forces. Without proper training, we are often too ready to hold fixed positions when overpowered, instead of abandoning futile posts. What feels like total loss, Emerson assures, will yield immeasurable gains: "We thrive by casualties. Our chief experiences have been casual" (*EL*, 483). Yoking "casualties" to the "casual," Emerson recalls the etymological evolution of the word surprise: the life-and-death stakes of a military attack are caught up with quotidian events that might otherwise be dismissed as insignificant – an unplanned encounter, a fleeting glimpse, an unguarded moment.

As a study of how such states of preparation and responsiveness were cultivated by a post-Emerson tradition of writers and thinkers, this book works to displace long-standing models of modernist perception defined by shock defense, proposing alternate models of reception that proceed from paradoxical practices of surprise. Stein's fascination with the military tactic of *surprendre* offers one such example: denoting surprise's earliest etymological usage, the definition of this Old French verb – an unforeseen seizure of one force by another – in Stein's hands signifies a positive state of astonishment. The threat of sudden capture by strange forces is not to be guarded against but instead welcomed as the precise effect of a new compositional method; comparing herself to an army general, Stein treats her grammar experiments as training grounds where perceptual practices are tested and honed. The various tropes I track – military, spiritual, physical, and emotional exercises – all signal the potential for regimented disciplines of reading and writing to open startling new avenues of invention. In charting the development of these aesthetic practices across several major modernist practitioners, I hope the canonicity of my selected texts bolsters my claim: that Emersonian surprise is lodged at the heart of literary modernism.[93]

The model of literary exchange that Emerson outlines makes enormous demands on writers as well as readers. Authors are called to write overpowering prose that inundates a reader's consciousness, yet somehow leaves room for reflection. They must expose their audience to great risk, while making them feel safe enough to let down their defenses. Indelible sentences must simultaneously invite forgetting so that readers are released to realize their own "creative power" (*EL*, 466). Those who heed Emerson's call for fostering unexpected encounters in their writing must negotiate the same perceptual and temporal pitfalls he faced. Each of the following chapters will examine the work of a modernist writer who engages surprising perception, surprising temporalities, and surprising narration, drawing on Emerson's "method of nature" to transform the apparent impediments of preconception and belatedness into sources of spontaneous discovery.

Aesthetic innovations exemplified by Stein's experimental grammar (Chapter 4) or Larsen's atmospheric structure (Chapter 3) are guided by a shared imperative: to construct sentences, paragraphs, and scenes that take unexpected turns – in some cases unforeseen even by the person who wrote them. I especially distinguish these experimental formal turns from more familiar notions of literary surprise, such as the plot twist or the lyric epiphany. Instead, I focus on particularities of style – such as the famously labyrinthine sentences of James or Proust that in their slow unfolding may at first seem unsuited to the task of seizing readers suddenly. It's simple enough to seize attention for a moment, but in place of bombshell shocks or manipulated revelations, these writers hone their distinctive syntax as fields of protracted disorientation and reorientation, an ongoing practice of exceeding and upending previous frames of reference.

Yet while these syntactic surprises may operate differently than startling narrative events, they remain narratively structured in ways that are distinct from, say, Wordsworth's "spots of time" or Woolf's "moments of being." If epiphanies distill a full but fleeting experience of the present, narrative surprise is often experienced as that unsettling gap or absence that marks the suspension of time and cognition. In this ungrounded state of disorientation, all bearings are lost, yet "everything is still possible ... for nothing is yet decided."[94] The writers I study elaborate and extend

Emerson's formal strategies for prolonging the too-swift interval opened by surprise. The challenge in each case is to express an apprehension that exceeds full comprehension without domesticating it into syntactical or narrative convention.

In few cases can these formal sources of surprises be located in a specific word, predicate, or event, instead registering an elision that unmoors the surprised consciousness from its habitual patterns of perception. Where one might expect to find connective threads binding one sentence or moment to the next, Emerson and his modernist inheritors introduce strange folds into the fabric of their prose by way of syntax and logic that is continually overturning itself. Slipping digressive bursts into his rhetoric mid-proposition, Emerson models the potential for such turns against expectation to swell the text's surface with new dimensions of possibility.

For Baudelaire, Proust, James, Larsen, and Stein, preparing to be surprised merges with the experiencing of surprise at the point where reading spurs new writing. Extending Emerson's efforts to yoke spontaneity with discipline and reception with protection, these writers variously produce reinventions of the essay and novel form. I trace these formal renovations through four registers of representation: mimesis in Baudelaire and Proust (scenes of surprise), syntax in James (sentences of surprise), plot in Larsen (structures of surprise), and grammar in Stein (morphologies of surprise).

When understood through the terms of surprise, sites of aesthetic experimentation that are frequently taken to epitomize modernist difficulty or obscurity unexpectedly disclose their practical potential. I take up critical writings in which these authors explicitly assert the use-value of their aesthetic innovations: they stake their work on the wager that representations of surprise might prime their readers to live in ways that anticipate and invite surprise encounters. This desire to close the gap between art and life manifests in compositional methods that similarly aim to bridge scenes of reading and writing. For instance, James's prefaces to the New York Edition (1907–1909) and Stein's *Lectures in America* (1934–1935) both return to the authors' own oeuvres with the aim of cultivating a reading experience that is shaped by surprise in the same way they describe the process of writing having been; these recursive returns to past work revitalize the present moment of composition while projecting new horizons of possibility. Practices of surprise produce remarkable stylistic variation, but the process of recalibrating perception in each case unfolds according to a distinctive threefold temporal structure: (1) an unanticipated encounter disrupts a previous pattern of perception, prompting (2) a turn of attention, heightened and attuned to the present moment, as well as (3) a perceptual opening toward unforeseen, perhaps otherwise unforeseeable, possibilities of future engagement. The prospective turn projects a vantage from where one can reflect on the present moment as a recollected past that might be recast or better grasped.

* * *

Emerson's seldom-noted influence on two of Benjamin's touchstone writers, Baudelaire and Proust, provides the starting point for this project and for a transatlantic remapping of modernism that joins France to Massachusetts by way of ancient Greece. Chapter 1 uncovers how Benjamin's primary navigators of "shock experience" cultivated receptivity to sudden seizure by embracing an Emersonian model of reading. Guided by Emerson's practices of attention, Baudelaire and Proust developed modernist methods that fuse contingency and control into forms of structured spontaneity. In my reading, Baudelaire's *correspondances* and Proust's *mémoire involontaire* are not emblems of rupture and retrospection, but instead register the authors' future-oriented commitment to renewal. While Benjamin gives Baudelaire pride of place as the first modern poet, Baudelaire himself looks to Emerson's poet-walker for his model of the modern artist. In a foundational essay on modernist aesthetics, Baudelaire identifies Emerson as a quintessential figure of modernity whose transatlantic influence stretches beyond the confines of nineteenth-century New England into the cosmopolitan center of Paris. Like Baudelaire, Proust locates Emerson's modernism in daily disciplines of reading and writing that renew his attention to "an everlasting Now." Proust extends the perceptual practice he finds in Emerson's essays – perceptual exercises that I trace to Emerson's reading of Plotinus – into a narratology of surprise that entwines the narrator's and readers' processes of perceptual preparation over all six volumes of *A la recherche du temps perdu* (1913–1927).

My second chapter traces Henry James's trajectory from employing an economy of shock in his first expatriate novels to developing a more integrative model of surprise in the novels of his late phase. This later narrative model emerges in response to William James's insistence that his brother reread Emerson. An early work like *The American* (1877) stages a cultural collision between a New World sense of wonder and a shock-saturated Old World. By pitting America against Europe, and innocence against experience, James initially constructs his novels according to the oppositional logic that subtends a shock-centered narrative of modernism. By contrast, *The Ambassadors* (1903) and *The Golden Bowl* (1904), which epitomize James's dense and fully realized late style, are organized around surprise encounters between representatives of each continent. In these set-piece scenes of recognition, I chart the convolutions of his increasingly elaborate sentences around the pivot of surprising temporal reversals. Rather than marking the sudden shock of new knowledge, the logic of Jamesian recognition unfolds according to a distinctive syntax of surprise; his acrobatic shuttling between tenses carves out a shared ground of experience where the borders between the known and unknown become a commutable frontier of open potential. I conclude by elaborating the model of critical reading that James develops in his prefaces to the New York Edition, which work to reorient his relation to his own oeuvre for the purpose of comprehensively revising it.

"Our moods do not believe in each other," writes Emerson, and in Chapter 3 I examine how Larsen's novels bear out this sentiment (*EL*, 406). Since the publication of *Quicksand* (1928) at the height of the Harlem Renaissance, confounded critics have drawn on W. E. B. Du Bois's concept of double consciousness to make sense of the baffling mood swings that fuel the restless movements of Larsen's protagonist, Helga Crane. I instead recall Emerson's original usage of "double consciousness" (upon which Du Bois's theory also draws), arguing that his critical vocabulary illuminates key connections between Larsen's heroine's volatile humors and the weather changes that backdrop her movements. Whereas Du Bois's framework diagnoses the *antagonistic* relation between inner and outer life, Emerson's definition of double consciousness describes the mind's capacity to come into *atmospheric* relation – a nonoppositional coalescing – with its ambient surrounds. Helga is tellingly introduced as a protagonist who is "sensitive to atmosphere": her changeable moods converge with weather changes in a series of "atmospheric events" that are guided by a strange logic of pathetic fallacy.[95] In *Quicksand*, ever-present clouds provide an aptly fleeting model for a character, as well as for a narrative, that might at any moment lapse into formless flux. Yet rather than embracing contingency for its own sake, Larsen questions the political possibilities that are opened by such atmospheric unsettlement. Her incongruous final imposition of a formulaic frame on Helga's unpredictable wanderings underlines the difficulty of escaping the closed logic of race and reproduction. *Quicksand*'s stock ending registers as a surprise ending precisely because the novel has cued the reader to expect open-endedness in place of typical closure.

Chapter 4 focuses on the habits of attention Stein developed in response to a sudden onslaught of fame and notoriety in the early 1930s. Stein's new sense of public exposure jeopardized her career-long commitment to cultivating what she called "open feeling" – an undifferentiated responsiveness that precedes categories and concepts.[96] While it is well documented that Stein drew on her teacher William James's theories of perception, I demonstrate that it was in fact Henry James who provided her with a practical model of attention – at once permeable and protective – as she negotiated the expectations of a new audience. In anticipation of her American publicity tour, Stein wrote a meditative essay titled "Henry James" (1933–1934), which established his capacity to merge martial discipline with spontaneous reception as a touchstone for her own mode of composition. The rigors of reading James, she reports, prepared her to meet the unexpected without preconception or defense. Only with such a robust yet supple infrastructure of attention in place can Stein fully realize her improvisational practice of composing in "the continuous present."[97] Her declared goal is to register *in writing* the bodily experience *of writing* so that the process of composition becomes its own subject. Drawing a line from Emerson through James to herself, Stein asserts her place in a literary lineage devoted to training a structured openness that can accommodate unpredictability without being overwhelmed. As I argue, this American line offers a crucial counterpoint to what Jonathan Crary diagnoses as a modern crisis of distracted attention.

In the literary genealogy traced by this project, Stein's non-narrative writing tests the outer limits of paying attention to the nonreferential. My coda argues that the blank spots punctuating her prose inaugurate an unexpected compositional legacy in a new medium that bypasses language altogether – what John Cage describes as structured silence. As Cage would attest, the exacting process of learning to read Stein taught him to activate fresh angles of attunement to indeterminacy. Under the tutelage of Stein's prose, Cage became aware of how life's contingencies unpredictably inflect what he called "composition as process."[98] Exporting Stein's compositional experiments from the medium of language into sound, Cage's "silent piece[s]" – starting with his infamous *4'33"* – reduced the border between art and life, between attention and distraction, to the most permeable threshold possible (*S*, 98). As I argue, Stein's lessons were strongly reinforced by Cage's teaching experiences at Black Mountain College, a hub of cultural and educational innovation that was guided by the pragmatist understanding of art as experience. In erasing the distinction between aesthetic representation and lived encounter, Cage understands himself to be creating the conditions under which one might more readily send or receive what he calls a "message of surprise" (*S*, 161).

The weather tropes examined in Chapter 3 offer a more general figure for the permeating presence of surprise in the novels and essays featured in this study. As a facet of narrative time, surprise's presence can remain barely discernible, hovering between sentences and at the fringes of scenes. As a structure of attention, its floating openness can be quickly overtaken by more directive or demanding dimensions of experience. The designation of surprise as "Emersonian" only anchors this nebulousness in an equally amorphous figure. As Irving Howe has argued, "to confront American culture is to feel oneself encircled by a thin but strong presence: a mist, a cloud, a climate." For Howe, the term "Emersonian" evokes the "dominant spirit in the national experience."[99] In *Practices of Surprise*, Emerson's national importance is secondary to the broad transatlantic reach of his models of time and perception. His pervasive yet elusive idea of surprise moves atmospherically through the work of each writer in this study; it circulates as an ambient mood and feeling rather than as a readily locatable source of influence. If Emersonian surprise constitutes an indeterminate opening with indefinite effects, what might be the value of exploring its aesthetic representation? For writers who understand writing to be an extension of living, it is a matter of remaining vitally responsive to a universe that offers fewer guarantees than the weather.

Pragmatist Methods

How does a person methodically establish a readiness for surprise? I contend that this epistemological paradox elicits a pragmatist response from the modernist writers surveyed by this study, all of whom adopt artistic practices that generate states of spontaneity through forms of discipline. This is to claim that a pragmatist purpose is vested within the signature methods that each of these writers develops: I see Proust, Henry James, Stein, and Larsen each addressing a similar problem of practical aesthetics that probes how literature might sufficiently transmit the surprising nature of experience, while also (paradoxically) acclimating readers to the salutary effects of this surprise. However, while the challenge of recurrently transmitting and receiving surprise is this book's central concern, I also want to frame this challenge – within the texts I examine, via the critics I engage, and in the spirit of my own teaching commitments – in pragmatist terms that are not just methodological but also pedagogical.

I here return to the opening pages of this introduction, where I point to the precise genesis of this book: a classroom scene focused on Emerson and the bare common passage. This scene could be summoned from my own experience of regularly teaching a standard survey of American literature, a survey that presents me with the annual challenge of making familiar writers, texts, and passages new again, for students and for myself. Or this scene could equally be summoned from a pivotal moment in the history of education I earlier invoked, when in 1899 William James first delivered his "Talks to Students" to the graduating class of Boston Normal School of Gymnastics. This lecture series marked a period of transition in James's teaching career, from the psychology department (where he had taught for more than twenty-five years) to the philosophy department. At this crucial turning point, James uses his lecture platform to revisit Emerson's bare common passage in pointedly pedagogical terms, unmistakably signaling the conjoined roles that Emerson and teaching will play in the imminent development of his pragmatic method. One of my goals in the chapters that follow is to find ways of bridging the distance between these two classroom scenes – between the personal, quotidian discoveries of my vocation, and James's seminal declaration of pragmatism as pedagogy, moments separated by a century but equally invested in what still issues surprisingly from Emerson's bare common. This is to say that I aim to describe instructive experiences that might resonate with the teachers and students who are my intended audience, and to connect these experiences with the formative educational encounters of the writers, readers, teachers, and students who are this study's subjects. In this bridging endeavor, my own methodology owes much to the work of Richard Poirier, who describes and performs a practice of reading that can uniquely unify the methods of the critic with the methods of the classroom.

Poirier frames his foundational study, *Poetry and Pragmatism* (1992), with two emblematic classroom scenes of his own, likewise doubly centered on William James and on acts of reading. His introduction opens by establishing that the line of Emersonian pragmatism he wants to trace is first and foremost a pedagogical lineage. His first key classroom scene belongs to James, whose institutional purview Poirier identifies as the main "point of transmission" linking a through line from Emerson to Gertrude Stein, Wallace Stevens, and Robert Frost, all of whom studied at Harvard under James's "renowned and popular" influence.[100] As Emerson's godson, James receives direct mentoring in the Emersonian practice that Poirier describes as "a form of linguistic skepticism."[101] These early lessons inform for James a lifelong practice of reading that is "at once grateful to the cultural inheritance of language and suspicious of it, congenitally uncertain as to the meaning of words and correspondingly attentive to nuance."[102] In Poirier's portrayal, James's classroom in turn cultivates this actively skeptical quality in students, a voracious attentiveness that expresses both indebtedness and incredulity toward its objects of study, thereby equipping them to read, write, and act without illusion or intimidation, despite the congenital uncertainty endemic to human life.

In an essay that became the concluding chapter of *Poetry and Pragmatism,* Poirier asserts his own place in the story of pragmatist pedagogical inheritance, tracing a genealogy of mentorship from Emerson to himself: tutored by Emerson, James in turn taught Frost, who then taught Poirier's most formative mentors at Amherst College and Harvard. The process of pedagogical training can typically call to mind didactic instruction or rote repetition, yet Poirier introduces his study by attributing to his Emersonian education a learned capacity for unorthodox and unresolved investigation, an endlessly enlivening "inspiration for the kind of criticism" he undertakes in his chapters and which he hopes "will come to be practiced beyond them with some frequency."[103] It is most notable that despite employing and encouraging an Emersonian approach to criticism, Poirier resists programmatically outlining or explaining the structure of his methods, preferring instead to model these methods surreptitiously in the shape of his prose.

By emulating Poirier's methodology while also working to make this methodology less elusive, I aim to enter my book into a post-Poirier tradition of pragmatist literary criticism, while also distinguishing this project from scholarship by other critics working in Poirier's wake. This section on methodology is divided into three parts, each of which offers a new tack for drawing out the pragmatist critical methods that remain implicit in Poirier's writing. I first analyze Poirier's essay on teaching, which comes closest to outlining in schematic terms what it means to read pragmatically. I then link Poirier's ideal model of the pragmatist literary critic back to the precursor figure he finds in Emerson's "The American Scholar." Finally, I take up Poirier's pragmatist critical genealogy and extend it forward to the present, following his line of influence through the work of several scholars whom he mentored (and who in turn mentored me).

Fundamentally, it is from Poirier that I take my method of reading major modernist texts pragmatically. Modernism might best be identified, Poirier suggests, as "a special kind of reading habit."[104] This modernist habit of reading prizes difficulty as "necessary and virtuous" insofar as this difficulty is attributed to "an unprecedented break in cultural continuity" around the turn of the twentieth century.[105] Defined by "difficulty-as-virtue," modernist literature becomes a site of anxious dislocation, but also "a privileged and exclusive form of discourse," accessible only to a select few.[106] What difference would it make, Poirier asks, if canonical works of modernism were alternately read with pragmatist habits of mind – that is, not anxiously but with a more peaceable uncertainty?

Poirier's oeuvre considers many extended responses to this question, but an essay on "Modernism and its Difficulties" offers a concise guiding insight: "Modernism 'happened,' when reading got to be intimidated."[107] In exploring the readerly value of inviting surprise, I find this to be a profound observation, the intimidation of a readership aptly distilling a familiar epochal story of modernist duress. The problem with intimidation is that it feeds defensiveness, which is the enemy of discovery. As my investigation into Poirier's methods reveals, reading pragmatically is most often a matter of shifting one's orientation. For instance, in a pragmatist frame of mind, a reader may be capable of recasting the intimidating "difficulty" of modernist prose as an approachable and immersive "density" (the term Poirier prefers).[108] Pragmatist techniques for approaching dense prose may still require "stamina, persistence, discipline," Poirier admits, but such efforts liberate and proliferate "spontaneous acts of reading" rather than bowing the reader under cowering expectations, defensive postures that only reinforce a closed and wary set of preconceptions about literature and about the world.[109] In this methods section, I extract from Poirier's critical pragmatism the tools that most effectively minimize intimidation and maximize spontaneity in acts of reading, teaching, and writing about modernist literature. When approached pragmatically, potential sources of modernist intimidation – unsolvable paradoxes, effaced subjectivities, allusive enactments – can be disarmed and reimagined as productive sites of pedagogical exchange.

1.   Reading and Teaching Pragmatically

Poirier opens the essay that concludes *Poetry and Pragmatism* by recalling its origins in a 1988 MLA panel discussion with J. Hillis Miller devoted to "some problems of reading and their relation to criticism and pedagogy," which he developed into a piece first printed in *Raritan* in 1990, titled "Hum 6, or Reading before Theory," and then retitled and republished two years later in its final form as "Reading Pragmatically: The Example of Hum 6."[110] The essay recounts Poirier's formative experience as a teaching assistant in the 1950s for a General Education course, "The Interpretation of Literature" (or "Hum 6"), that Reuben A. Brower established at Harvard after founding an equivalent class at Amherst, which Poirier had previously taken as an undergraduate. Poirier credits the Hum 6 course with teaching him to read in "slow motion," a phrase Brower coined to describe the distinctive variety of close reading that students practiced in his class.[111] For Brower and his students, Poirier explains, this practice stood in stark contrast to the era's most prominent critical techniques: "Reading ideally remained *in* motion, not choosing to encapsulate itself, as New Critical readings nearly always aspire to do."[112]

The essay's pointedly evolving title and the divergence Poirier emphasizes between Brower and the New Critics both mark the significant historical, pedagogical, and political stakes of the critical practice Poirier alternately describes as *reading before theory* and *reading pragmatically*. When Poirier's work is invoked in contemporary critical conversations, he is most often cast as a contributor to the general "revival" of pragmatism across the fields of philosophy, law, and literature in the 1980s and 1990s. However, Poirier's insistence on Emersonian pragmatism as a durable strain in American criticism fundamentally resists this recovery narrative, presenting instead an American method so inexhaustibly rooted in self-renewal that it could never need "reviving."

So for Poirier, what does "reading pragmatically" evoke that "reading after theory" does not? What's the use of calling his reading method a pragmatist act? With this instrumentalist query, I deliberately echo the confrontational question Stanley Cavell posed in "What's the Use of Calling Emerson a Pragmatist?," a talk delivered at a 1995 conference called "The Revival of Pragmatism."[113] Poirier's title change might best be understood in the context of these wider debates around the relationship between Emerson, pragmatism, and literary criticism. As Paul Grimstad has argued, Cavell declines to name Emerson a pragmatist for precisely the same reason that Poirier claims Emerson as one: the singularity of his prose style. As Grimstad notes, Cavell's well-known account of Emerson's stylistic "distinctiveness" and linguistic skepticism are directly indebted to Poirier's less widely circulated ideas about Emerson's literary pragmatism – though Cavell distinctly refuses to employ the label "pragmatism" and does not engage with Poirier at all.[114] Joan Richardson goes further, devoting a full chapter of her recent introduction to pragmatism to making the case for Cavell's own pragmatist leanings.[115] While Richardson persuasively argues for Cavell's inclusion in discussions of literary pragmatism, Poirier is largely excluded from her overview. His lone mention comes in her brief summary of pragmatism's supposed "revival" narrative. I will quote

Richardson's short but dense account to highlight the difficulty of pinning down Poirier's role in the narrative. Richardson begins by admonishing Cavell for failing to engage with such pragmatists as William James and Charles Peirce more deeply. Had he done so, Richardson contends, Cavell

> would clearly have understood the "use of calling Emerson a pragmatist," a use and claiming articulated by Richard Poirier, among others, that, following Richard Rorty's publication of *Philosophy and the Mirror of Nature* in 1979, led to the revival of pragmatism as a field of inquiry and as a culture-critical tool during the last decades of the twentieth century.[116]

Richardson can so efficiently condense this story of pragmatist revival because the two premises she outlines are largely uncontested: first, that pragmatism retreated into a kind of critical eclipse for the majority of the twentieth century, and second, that its cross-disciplinary reemergence coincides with the publication of Rorty's study. However, it's worth pausing to unpack Richardson's précis because even her syntactical construction consigns Poirier to an ambiguous role in the story. Poirier here seems to be "following" Rorty in claiming Emerson as a pragmatist. In fact, Poirier and Rorty part ways decisively on precisely this claim: Poirier lays out a lineage of pragmatism that "doesn't have much to do with Rorty" because the philosopher refuses to grant Emerson "any founding role."[117] Reading Richardson in another sense, Poirier could be understood to be "following" Rorty purely chronologically, in that his contribution to the pragmatist revival emerges after and is made possible by *Philosophy and the Mirror of Nature*. Yet Poirier is emphatic that the revival of pragmatism should not be dated to Rorty's 1979 publication because Emersonian pragmatism does not need reviving; in Poirier's view, this version of pragmatism remains in persistent circulation and renewal within the work of Emerson's closest readers.

In discussions of pragmatist literary criticism, Poirier is often hailed for bringing the "culture-critical tool" to literary studies for the first time. Morris Dickstein argues this point in his introduction to the published proceedings of the 1995 conference on "The Revival of Pragmatism," where he credits Poirier with "undermining the once-dominant way of reading American literature."[118] Dickstein is of course referring to "New Critical formalism," the mid-century's most recognizable literary instrument.[119] In Dickstein's account, Poirier defangs a "toothless lion," since the New Criticism was "already a tired movement," even by the 1960s.[120] Given that the New Critics scarcely seem to require further undermining, Poirier's interest in invoking and dismantling their earlier primacy would appear to intervene in a longer history of literary criticism. Indeed, scholars seeking to explain why pragmatism failed to take meaningful hold as a method with literary applications in English departments during the period of its broader ascendency often blame the New Criticism.[121] At the moment that pragmatism was being declared "almost the official philosophy of America," one can readily imagine why New Critics would prefer to restrict its influence on literary study, for the pragmatist method of measuring practical use and considering experiential effects is wholly anathema to the strictly systematic and impersonal interpretive project of asserting the autonomy of aesthetic objects.[122] In the narrative of pragmatist revival that Dickstein describes, Poirier is working to correct an earlier mischaracterization, and can be elevated as the actual originator of "the pragmatist-poetic line" because the New Critics had ensured that at least in the field of literary studies there would be nothing to revive.[123]

Poirier resists this nearsighted origin story for literary pragmatism as emphatically as he rejects the larger revival narrative. As the Hum 6 essay suggests, the stakes in recalling the relationship between New Criticism and pragmatism are rooted for Poirier in the context of the classroom. Poirier contrasts the kind of close reading that was the signature practice in Brower's courses with the New Critical directives codified and disseminated by another of his teachers, Cleanth Brooks, in the influential textbook, *Understanding Poetry* (published with Robert Penn Warren in 1938). Instead of "undermining" New Criticism, Poirier insists on localizing and specifying the "exasperatingly inexact" use of the theoretical label.[124] "Any kind of close reading in the fifties and sixties came to be called New Criticism," he observes, because literary critical histories of the period only account for "what got into publication almost to the exclusion of what went on in the classrooms with teachers who published little."[125] Whereas published polemics tend to arrive at decisive conclusions, Brower teaches close reading as a practice in "the art of *not* arriving" – never achieving the closure of final statements or general theories.[126] I would emphasize that the brand of pragmatism Poirier is interested in was being practiced and disseminated by teachers while not necessarily being published: its privileging of moving, changing, and provisional practices fits it better to the fluid scene of the classroom than to the fixing scene of publication. Pragmatism as a "theory" rather than as a "practice" is already inimical to pragmatism's tenets; hence its susceptibility to faddish devaluation and subsequent revival is only explicable in terms of "theory." In the terms of "practice," something that did not cease never needs to be revived.

The contrast Poirier draws between his two teachers, Brower and Brooks, suggests two paths for literary criticism. These paths fork, I contend, at precisely the point that the New Critic installs the concept of paradox as a core tenet of close reading. In "The Language of Paradox" (1947), Brooks makes a tautological case: since paradox is "the language appropriate and inevitable to poetry," the job of the critic is to identify the tensions and hypocrisies produced by a poem's paradoxical language.[127] As a New Critical method, reading for paradox becomes an end unto itself, reinforcing its own inevitability as every new example of paradoxical language is uncovered in the closed critical system. Here Brooks exemplifies a broader tendency for literary critics to put theory before reading, the prioritizing of conceptual rigidity above contingent experience that Poirier would work to reverse. When codified into a preformulated program and a prescribed procedure, a potentially useful pedagogical tool comes only to confirm what the theorist already purports to know.

With the title "Reading before Theory," Poirier registers his recovery of a second path for criticism, one that does not disavow theory but rather draws attention to the theoretical insights enacted in literary texts. Critical narratives that put theory before reading too often occlude classroom efforts to unearth "theories of language already deployed *within* literary works themselves."[128] The only theory worth engaging, Poirier suggests, is one that is cued by the process of reading. But by what means does one derive a framework for reading from the thing being read? Pedagogical practices like Brower's are not easily summarized, much less easily generalized into exportable methods. Resisting encapsulation, such practices remain flexibly responsive but in their experiential singularity are left unmarked by literary critical history.

It is perhaps this realization that prompts Poirier to anchor the literary critical approach he advocates within the field of pragmatism. With the final title assigned to the Hum 6 essay – "Reading Pragmatically" – Poirier designates "pragmatism" as the only "'theoretical' label" he is comfortable with.[129] In aligning his reading practice with pragmatism, Poirier affiliates with a long-standing philosophical tradition, but one which is a "method only" (*WII*, 509). Yet even as literary pragmatism resists cohering into theoretical doctrine, Poirier remains invested in establishing the continuity of this methodology by noting its critical lineage. Tracking the "pedagogical career" of pragmatism from Emerson to Brower, Poirier unites authors and critics, theorists and practitioners.[130] For any readerly disposition, a pedagogically minded practice of reading is pragmatist in the sense that it "appears less as a solution," to recall William James's definition, "than as a program for more work."[131] This description of pragmatism raises the question of how a "program for more work" resists becoming programmatic. Poirier offers a clue when he affirms that Emerson serves as the "nourishing source" of literary pragmatism because he teaches readers how he wants to be read: "with the discipline, with the expectation of difficulty and surprise."[132] While Poirier does not directly probe the tensions between these terms, with the chapters that follow I want to suggest that it is precisely the paradoxical relation between discipline and surprise that fuels the pedagogic potential of pragmatism.

2. American Scholars

So how is pragmatist pedagogy transmitted? Toward naming an ideal agent for this task – the pragmatist who can model, profess, and mentor others in such methods – the closest prototype Poirier offers is found in his introduction to *Poetry and Pragmatism*. Here he hails the "heroic mind" that is "perforce devoted to action," as described by Emerson in "The American Scholar." Poirier cites Emerson's definition of action as it is articulated in what he considers to be one of Emerson's "most crucial, overlooked, and naggingly suggestive sentences": "The preamble of thought, the transition through which it passes from the unconscious to the conscious, is action." While acknowledging this as "very cryptic indeed," Poirier wants to emphasize how this sentence "helps us better understand the enormous investment [in action] in Emerson and in pragmatism generally, despite the easy recruitment of the term, by James and others, in the service of blustering athleticism and worldly enterprise."[133] In some conventional sense, action manufactures interpersonal interventions and visible consequences; Poirier is showing how Emerson and pragmatism instead address the raw states of experience that give rise to thinking and inform the composition of what follows, like the action of mining and refining upon which the action of manufacturing depends. This "preamble," the space of transition where the conscious emerges from the unconscious, has clear pedagogical connotations: it names the exploratory action of the student and the preparatory action of the teacher, plus all the other loosely investigative actions of the classroom that anticipate the wider world and guide one's graduation into it. (Of course, pragmatism also functionally insists on the wider world remaining a classroom; on all future moments remaining equivalently teachable.)

This Emersonian definition of action becomes less cryptic when combined with the other guiding educational principles (the lessons of nature, the conditions of reading) that shape and prepare Emerson's ideal scholar in "The American Scholar." Encompassing artist and critic, teacher and student, this figure is defined by a capacity for surprising thinking – thinking that emerges from unruly experience, thinking that surprises itself. As such, this Emersonian model of pedagogy (which I will sketch in brief detail over the next pages) offers, I would argue, a rough map for Poirier's own pragmatist methodology, and by extension, for the methodology of this book.

"The American Scholar" opens by drawing a distinction between two kinds of scholars: the scholar-theorist Emerson calls "a mere thinker" or "the parrot of other men's thinking," and the scholar-practitioner he calls "*Man Thinking*" (*EL*, 54). The theory-driven scholar who parrots the thought of others can only repeat and reinforce "accepted dogmas" (*EL*, 57). For this passive figure, paradoxes are sites of contemplative study that serve as ends unto themselves – the tautological end of lending warrant to theory by merely rehearsing its application. By contrast, for the practice-driven scholar, a paradox is not abstract or inert but a tangible and salutary predicament that one can learn to live with and through. As I argue in Chapter 1, Emerson inherits a paradox of preparation from his Puritan forefathers, for whom the discipline of spiritual exercises – the challenge of reconciling a rigorously disciplined faith with unconditional and spontaneous salvation – posed an unsolvable problem. In "The American Scholar," Emerson reassures his reader that this paradox is not in fact a problem that can be theorized into submission or finally solved and set aside. Instead of seeking dubiously definitive solutions or relaxing into the stasis of the double bind itself, Emerson embraces and exacerbates the pedagogical power of paradox to keep thinking rigorous and on the move.

Emerson confirms that "Man Thinking" may emerge from college classrooms "when they aim not to drill, but to create," yet his sources of instruction also expand beyond institutional walls (*EL*, 59). As indicated above, "The American Scholar" next names three "main influences" on scholars who privilege live practices over dead theories – influences that each in turn inform pragmatic method: nature, books, and action (*EL*, 54). Emerson begins by distilling the lessons learned from nature into a concise motto: to study nature is to "Know thyself" (*EL*, 56). Excerpted as a free-standing aphorism, this "ancient precept" confirms the primacy of knowledge and the stability of the self that attains it (*EL*, 56). Further, when encountered on its own, the adage seems the opposite of surprising, instead confirming the commonsense importance of finding value in self-reflection. However, when encountered in the essay, an age-old "abstraction" about self-knowledge becomes rooted in a complex web of lived experience described in detail (*EL*, 55).

By studying the natural world, the scholar learns that knowledge and the self are subject to the same "principle of Undulation" as "the ebb and flow of the sea" or "the inspiring and expiring of the breath" (*EL*, 62). Emerson compares the experience of undulation to an experience of sublimity, a dizzying oscillation between "the farthest pinnacle" and "the lowest trench." As he affirms, students of nature will discover "a sublime presence" in the regular rhythms of ordinary life as readily as they will in "the extremities of nature": "Man is surprised to find that things near are not less beautiful and wondrous than things remote." Surprise reveals that everyday "trifles" – "the meal in the firkin; the milk in the pan; the ballad of the street" – refer "to the like cause by which light undulates and poets sing" (*EL*, 69). These undulating movements between the near and the remote unsettle the potential "polarity" of thought, those viewpoints of inflexibly contrarian extremes, and instead reveal nature to be "one thing and the other thing, in the same moment," living demonstrations of paradox, vivid and pulsing (*EL*, 62). A seemingly stable self undulates into an impersonal "*other me*," allowing knowing and not-knowing to flow into each other (*EL*, 60). Subjected to these forces of fluctuation, the double bind of paradox gives way to a methodological capacity Emerson calls "double consciousness." I track the complex trajectory of this phrase in Chapter 3 but here will simply recall Emerson's account of the "use of literature": to double one's perspective by traversing other minds, including the other minds within oneself, which the undulations of nature can reveal.

Having received the teachings of nature, the scholar observes the free circulation of personal and impersonal forces; as the scholar's second source of instruction, books offer the conditions for a firsthand experience of one's own consciousness commingling with another. When read creatively, books catalyze ideas "springing spontaneous from the mind's *own sense*" at the same time that sense becomes startlingly permeable with minds that are not one's own: "There is some awe mixed with the joy of our surprise, when this poet, who lived in some past world, two or three hundred years ago, says that which lies close to my own soul, that which I also had wellnigh thought and said" (*EL*, 58). These moments of unexpected resonance "teach us to abide by our spontaneous impression," but as Emerson makes clear, the surprise of recognition marks the beginning of the scholar's education, not the end (*EL*, 259). If such surprises are to retain their spontaneity, the book-as-teacher has the double duty of both conveying content and disciplining attention, of bracing the scholar's mind with new capacities for "labor and invention" so that it becomes a fertile site of "transmission and reflection" (*EL*, 59, 62). The scholar's reflective turn potentially spurs a second surprise: the belated realization that seemingly spontaneous insights are in fact the product of "some preparation" (*EL*, 59). Books transmit their teachings through the developmental repetitions of reading that prepare and efface the very process of preparation, allowing the surprises contained in their pages to spring forth with ever-sharper spontaneity.

Finally, the scholar encounters the instructive force of action, as Poirier singles out in his introduction to pragmatism. Emerson's third source of instruction here applies earlier lessons in perceptive undulation and literate spontaneity to the experience of marking oneself as a human actor in the world (*EL*, 60). The principle of undulation teaches that thinking and doing are contiguous processes, thus closing the gap between "speculative men" and "practical men": "The mind now thinks, now acts; and each fit reproduces the other" (*EL*, 62, 60). In place of a stereotypical causality where action follows thought, Emerson defines action as the "strange process" through which "experience is converted into thought" (*EL*, 60). The "world of actions" is thus the incubator of a creative mind, capable of nurturing formless floods of experience into the "new arrangement" of thinkable forms (*EL*, 64, 56). While oriented toward those clarifying actions that feed the mind, Emerson does not expand upon the possible wider social and interpersonal impact of these new arrangements of thought. However, in a final section of the essay devoted to the American Scholar's "duties" Emerson suggests that thinking becomes an action in the world when the student-scholar becomes a teacher (*EL*, 63).

Emerson aligns the sensitive scholar who has undergone "the long period of preparation" by nature, books, and action with the imaginative poet whose "spontaneous thoughts" succeed in surprising readers with their immediate resonance (*EL*, 64). The scholar's task is to bring art's sources of poetic surprise into contact with "the topics of the time": "The literature of the poor, the feelings of the child, the philosophy of the street, the meaning of household life" (*EL*, 68). As Emerson concludes, the scholar who is capable of bridging the socially concerned "mind of this country" with the raw impactfulness of the poet's mind will serve a mighty function as "a university of knowledges" (*EL*, 70). In other words, scholars who have undergone the kind of training Emerson describes will themselves become invaluable founts of learned vitality, transmission points of surprising inflow and outflow that charge educational contexts with conductive spontaneity. It is in this way that pragmatist critics, myself included, through our own preparation and investigation try to learn and convey an actionable purpose similar to the pragmatist artists we study.

Emerson's capacious category of "scholar" thus encompasses both the authors who are my subject and the critics among whom I situate myself, authorial and critical genealogies that converge in *Practices of Surprise* through each of the three sites of scholarly "education" he outlines (*EL*, 63). Focusing on the literary lineage, my chapters argue that writers who practice Emerson's undulating "method of nature" learn to navigate fixed polarities as flexible paradoxes. Under the sway of Emersonian nature, Proust balances receptivity with protectiveness, James glimpses immediacy in belatedness, Larsen finds openness in closure, and Stein focuses attention in states of distraction. While nature-as-method propels the undulating movements of the mind, books provide an arena where such movements can be registered, examined, and exchanged. Each chapter is organized around a series of Emerson-inflected reading relations that stage the unsettling experience of effacing one's own consciousness before another. And action, for these writers, is located in the transition from reading to the process of composition; it yields creative insights in the moments when conscious knowing is suspended. This is to say that Emersonian action imparts its lessons in moments when authors manage to suspend advance knowledge of what they are going to write so that they might be surprised by what they finally find themselves writing.

In what remains of this section on how the methodologies of Emerson, Poirier, and pragmatism inform the methodology of this book, I outline and append myself to a lineage of pragmatist critics who likewise look to Emerson's American Scholar as a model for their pedagogical practices. Having internalized the lessons of Emersonian nature, Poirier and those mentored by him employ the logic of undulation in their supple navigation of epistemological paradoxes. These pragmatist critics register what they have learned from Emerson's distinctive approach to books and action in what I will elaborate as their styles of *effacement* and *enactment*. As I hope to demonstrate, Poirier proceeds with a pedagogical purpose when he effaces himself from his prose, enacting his argument in sentences that internalize the syntax of his literary subject. In staging a reading encounter and then immediately working to remove himself from it, Poirier prepares his audience for the primary "use of literature," as Emerson sees it: the practice of inhabiting other minds and other ways of moving through the world. I want finally to make the case that effacement and enactment constitute "actions" according to "Emerson's most punctilious use of the term";

actions in the sense that they facilitate pedagogical transmissions from
teacher-scholars to student-scholars, who might in turn themselves become
teachers.[134] As we shall see, this process of transmission has generated
a post-Poirier tradition of pragmatist critics who extend their mentor's
stylistic strategies in their own work.

Before turning to those critics, I want briefly to reflect on Poirier's
account of "the political consequences" of Emersonian action, which he
glosses as "an attempt to make oneself conscious of things before they go
public, as it were, before they can be known publicly by virtue of having
passed into language."[135] As Poirier anticipates, Emerson's counterintuitive
understanding of action will dissatisfy critics seeking to claim literary
scholarship as an instrument of "social changes" and "worldly
enterprise."[136] To those who would call him "politically naïve," Poirier
counters by calling out the naïveté of critics who assume that the shifting
ground of Emerson's literary pragmatism is stable enough to support
a fixed political platform – whether it stands for exceptionalist ideology
or "redemptive values."[137] Where scholars "might possibly *begin* to help
change existing realities" is in their capacity as teachers and mentors.[138]
If there's any "social or communal efficacy" in scholarly work, it's modestly
limited to making room, in class and on the page, for the quiet forms of
reflection Emerson calls action.[139] The Emersonian pragmatists I study in
the pages that follow are united in their efforts to open intervals for the
spontaneous infilling that is the "preamble" of meaningful thought and
that therefore provides crucial preparation for public pronouncement and
political affiliation.

3. *Pedagogical Pragmatism After Poirier*

The pedagogical legacy of Poirier's pragmatist method is perhaps most
evident in the work of critics who credit Poirier with teaching them how to
read. Intriguingly, scholars who avow deepest gratitude for Poirier's
"inspired mentoring" pervasively express this debt in the auxiliary spaces
of their monograph acknowledgments, prefatory remarks, and footnotes –
while often not citing Poirier explicitly in the main body of their
criticism.[140] This curious combination of crediting influence both fer-
vently and ambiguously – where the singularity of Poirier's stature is
both spotlighted and effaced – is exemplified by two works of twenty-
first century pragmatist literary criticism that take Poirier's Emersonian
line as the backbone of their studies and open by situating Poirier as
a formative influence.

Joan Richardson's introduction to *A Natural History of Pragmatism* (2007) affirms that without Poirier she "would not have learned to write, as well as to read, 'in slow motion.'"[141] In this verbatim propagation of a critical method, Richardson thanks Poirier for a readerly approach identical to what Brower modeled for him. Richardson extends the line of influence by invoking a fellow Poirier pupil, Steven Meyer; she notes that the acknowledgment of Poirier in Meyer's preface to *Irresistible Dictation* (2001) "could, with the substitution of 'Stevens' for 'Stein,'" have served as her own, then thanks Meyer for comments on her manuscript which are likewise "attendant on reading in slow motion."[142] As Brower first defined it, this method is a practice in "slowing down the process of reading to observe what is happening, in order to attend very closely to the words, their uses, and their meanings."[143] Having forcefully affirmed the formative reading practice in her introduction, Richardson defers actually defining what it means to read "in slow motion" until the final chapter of the book.[144] The long-deferred definition is multiply mediated: describing Stein's reading practice, Richardson cites a footnote by Meyer, who in turn quotes the above definition from Brower's introduction to *In Defense of Reading*, the 1962 volume of essays compiled by teachers of Hum 6 (coedited by Poirier).[145]

I trace the circuitous path of Poirier's influence through Richardson and Meyer to demonstrate how Poirier's strategic emphasis on self-effacement can have the effect of obscuring his presence in works where he is acknowledged most emphatically. To point to Poirier as a mentor is in a sense to point to a self-absenting critical function or to point past him toward his own mentors, behind whom Poirier always seems happy to stand. Yet having learned and internalized Poirier's model of effacement, these critics have also internalized what Ross Posnock has described as Poirier's key pragmatist method: "enactment." In his review of *Poetry and Pragmatism*, Posnock observes that Poirier's criticism affords "a rare opportunity to witness a critic going beyond exposition and analysis, criticism's usual domain, and entering the realm of enactment, that pragmatist poetic space where action, not entity, is all."[146]

Posnock's praise of Poirier echoes Poirier's praise of the way Emerson "*enacts* the struggles" to give "present life" to his ideas in words, which "are always *past*" once spoken or written.[147] Taking Emerson as both his subject and his methodological inspiration, Poirier analyzes Emerson's technique of "troping" – the continuous turning of words away from past or predetermined meanings – at the same time that he enacts this turning in his own writing. Like Emerson, Poirier repeats key terms, including "action," "power," and "work," without arriving at "a precise or static definition" for any of them.[148] The task of the pragmatist critic is not to pin down these terms but rather to continue Emerson's work with "sentences that insist that readers, too, must involve themselves in the salutary activity of troping." The activity is "salutary," Poirier contends, because it can make readers "less easily intimidated" by words "inherited from the historical past or currently employed in the directives of public policy."[149] Freed from intimidation, these readers might be better equipped to confront the kinds of authority that structure sentences and paragraphs around "ideological or gendered assumptions."[150]

Scholars mentored by Poirier, including Posnock, consciously extend a genealogy of criticism that relies on enactive Emersonian methods. If Poirier models what it means to go "beyond exposition," it follows that his most devoted students likewise limit their reliance on explicit explanation or attribution, to likewise dwell in "the pragmatist poetic space of enactment."[151] In this sense, Richardson's and Meyer's methodologically oblique invocations of their mentor can be taken as a tribute to his pragmatist pedagogy. Both critics uphold his practices by stylistically enacting their subject, by merging and even at times subordinating their critical voices within the voices of their subjects. Anchoring their writing in extended quotations, they usher readers through swaths of lengthy excerpting, with sentences that mime the syntax, cadence, and diction of the passages they introduce. These carefully framed passages invite a reading experience of deep immersion, guided by commentary that does not retreat to a differentiating critical remove but instead uses its enmeshed timbre to compel readerly engagement of unusual immediacy.

Like Richardson and Meyer, Posnock has cited Poirier only rarely outside of acknowledgments and footnotes (his review of *Poetry and Pragmatism* excepted).[152] While Posnock's most recent work, *Renunciation* (2016), makes just a single parenthetical mention of his mentor, from the outset the book announces its methods in terms that strongly resonate with Poirier's account of "reading pragmatically": "I fashion a critical approach in the spirit of my subject."[153] Posnock exemplifies Poirier's ideal pragmatist reader when he rejects any theoretical apparatus that is imported and applied. In the case of *Renunciation*, deriving his methods from the specificity of his subject means resisting "the rules of context and of boundaries, temporal and disciplinary, the better to let the material, the specificity of the object, take the lead and impart something of the resonant, if ineffable presence that surrounds acts of renunciation."[154]

Posnock portrays his decades-long process of unwittingly preparing to write *Renunciation* as "a professorial enactment of what Emerson called 'abandonment.'"[155] Citing the final paragraph of "Circles" (which I earlier quoted), Posnock links this preparatory process with Emerson's expressed desire to forget himself, to be surprised out of his propriety, "to do something without knowing how or why."[156] Posnock describes this passage as "a pedagogical touchstone" of his own lectures but belatedly realizes that he has also, even more surprisingly, been structurally enacting what it describes in his unconventional approach to composing *Renunciation* as an extended experimental essay in an "Emersonian" mode.[157] Inspired by a "trust in attunement," the book's "zigzagging form" weaves in and out of "American and European periods, contexts, genres, and disciplines," proceeding without chapter breaks or signposting.[158] Where many works of literary criticism argue and explain, Posnock's essay "'coordinates' in the sense that it displays specific examples, moments, intersections rather than embedding them in a linear, progressive, historical narrative."[159] The purpose of these formal arrangements is "to produce for writer and reader 'an open intellectual experience,'" wherein Posnock's own method of "receptive reading" will ideally serve to "quicken receptivity" in his audience.[160] Given his decades-long process of "attunement," Posnock's expressed hope that his "reader will grow attuned" to the "rhythm" of renunciation over the course of reading the book may seem optimistic.[161] Poirier likewise expresses "hope" that he can transmit something of his Emersonian methods to readers, yet he recognizes the degree to which his critical approach has been guided by a sense of "deep personal obligation": "Reading is nothing if it is not personal," he reminds us.[162] In surveying the work of critics under Poirier's tutelage, I mean to suggest that this deep sense of personally obligated reading can be taught.

I have repeatedly insisted in this methodology section that if reading pragmatically is personal, it is also pedagogic. As a student of Poirier's students, I have been the beneficiary of pragmatist pedagogy in class and conversation, as well as on the page. In the self-effacing Poirier style, each of these teacher-critics has brought an unintrusive but unmistakable pedagogical touch to my training in pragmatist reading, pulling the right book off the shelf at the right time, invoking an illuminating anecdote, or pointing to precisely the passage that would unlock my thinking. In these ways, they have primed me for discoveries in reading that felt like my own. More than once my experience of reading their books was punctuated by a "belated revelation" (to borrow Posnock's phrase): the startling realization that an idea I assumed was my own had in fact been cultivated by an earlier pedagogical exchange.[163]

In a recent graduate course I taught as an introduction to pragmatism and American aesthetics, I paired Posnock with James, Richardson with Stevens, and Meyer with Stein on the syllabus, imagining that these critics would augment and guide students' reading, just as these mentors continue to guide my own reading of these texts. I began by explaining that the critical pairings might be read first, as preparation for the primary text, or might be read afterwards, offering an opportunity for reflection. Yet students expecting glosses or directives often reported feeling disoriented by these secondary readings rather than stabilized by them; this disoriented state elicited defensiveness more readily than receptivity.[164]

While the class dwelled for most of the semester in "the pragmatist poetic space of enactment," our eventual turn to John Dewey underlined the pedagogic power of explanation. Poirier distinguishes Dewey's use of language from the other members of the "Tribe of Waldo" on the grounds that Dewey explains but does not enact Emersonian-pragmatist ideas about language.[165] For this ostensible reason, Poirier rarely engages with Dewey's work. Indeed, Posnock points to Poirier's "evasions of Dewey" as the most striking "gap" in Poirier's "lifetime of remarkable work with language."[166] This gap seems particularly striking in the context of the classroom, where Dewey's and Poirier's shared investment in pedagogy suggests the potential compatibility of their pragmatist methods.[167]

Dewey's writings on education emphasize the crucial importance of merging explanation and enactment in the classroom; as a champion of experiential learning, Dewey prizes enactment as a teaching tool. His renowned devotion to progressive educational reform is guided by the fundamental recognition that knowledge cannot be "externally imposed" and needs instead to be internalized through experiences that are "enacted and undergone."[168] Yet Dewey resists all false dichotomizing of theory and action, refusing to put "experience in opposition to rational knowledge and explanation."[169] Earlier in this introduction I suggested how Dewey derived from his lifelong process of reading Emerson a model of "aesthetic education" that accentuates processes of "preparation" and "reflection." Anticipating pushback against the notion that encounters with art should be framed with preparatory "instructions," Dewey clarifies that his Emersonian paradigm of instruction is not opposed to spontaneity but rather works in spontaneity's service. The pedagogical challenge of harnessing the "power of explanation" rests in ensuring that it does not become "an affair of 'telling' and being told" but remains "an active and constructive process."[170]

As a reminder that putting "enactment into practice" is not "self-explanatory," Dewey recalls for me how my own reading of enactive writing has been supported by mentors who have continually confirmed the essential "connection between education and personal experience."[171] I have witnessed and benefited from their collective penchant for providing classroom explanations that proffer and guide while remaining actively processual. Cued by these experiences, I now experiment with framing my own classes in a Deweyan mode. Most often, this means laying out a paradoxical problem presented by the text and then establishing the terms and techniques that our reading has itself provided for beginning to approach that problem. The majority of our class time is then spent in something closer to enactive processes of reading in slow motion. As this process frequently reveals, paradoxes that seem to pose unsolvable problems contain within them not exactly the seeds of a solution but perhaps invite some kind of salutary critical callisthenic that allows the problem to be more fully considered, recognized, and accepted.

The potential pitfall in structuring a class like this is that too much preparatory framing risks overdetermining our reading and shutting down openings for unexpected discoveries. Yet a concertedly minimal amount of explanation seems to go a long way toward fostering "an open intellectual experience." Equipped with rough frameworks for grounding and focusing their own thinking, students frequently seem primed to inhabit our readings in new ways. In this sense, the purposes and methods of this book are informed by and directed back toward my teaching; here, as in my classrooms, I have sought to strike a generative balance between a Deweyan mode of explanation and a Poirierian mode of enactment. As a preliminary and preparatory burst of explanation, this introduction aims to establish the scaffolding of the project, drawing aesthetic and critical lineages, defining key terms, and situating my argument within a wider field of ongoing pragmatist conversation. Similarly, each chapter opens by briefly sketching the stakes and contours of the largely enactive readings that follow.

Embracing the explicit and explanatory alongside the implicit and enacted, my goal is to draw attention to the pedagogical work of literary pragmatism, which has only obliquely been registered in a post-Poirier critical tradition. In this endeavor, I hope to amplify self-effacing critical voices, which are too easily drowned out by the "loud mouth of contemporary criticism."[172] As I have suggested, enactment and explanation come together in all the classrooms that have instigated, tested, and substantiated the framing ideas of this book. As such, my coda leaves off by considering Dewey at Black Mountain College, in classes that were roughly contemporary with Poirier's enrollment in Hum 6. As I conclude by demonstrating, the methods absorbed by Poirier in Brower's course and the methods activated at Black Mountain through Dewey's reforming principles share striking affinities, each similarly furthering the critical and pedagogical legacy of pragmatism through the fertile, influential, and paradoxical institutionalization of surprise.

The Message of Surprise

In turning to the pragmatist readings in modernism of the chapters that follow, I pose my orienting and disorienting question once more: what is to be made of surprise, as an experience that creates gaps and courts strangeness in ways that can compromise narrative coherence or even basic intelligibility? Why should such blips register to readers, and why do they matter? As a last inaugural note, I want to suggest that in training our attention to notice and engage with the lacunae of surprise, we also confront the most fundamental conditions of reading. As defined by this book, surprise is broadly experienced as an unsettling suspension of time and cognition; the surprised consciousness is temporarily unmoored from its conventional and well-trod patterns of perception. Such a generally ungrounded state of attention may seem to bear little resemblance to the condition of a mind undertaking the focused act of reading. However, literature's proficiency and methodology for aesthetically representing the workings of consciousness share many operational congruencies with the affective workings of surprise. Both a reader's experience of consciousness in narrative and the generic experience of surprise require traversing an uncertain border between *me* and *not me*. Both reading and surprise are explicitly predicated on a constitutive gap between discrepant orders of consciousness: when we read we encounter another's consciousness as if it were our own, and when we are surprised we encounter our own consciousness as if it belonged to another. Such encounters baffle all efforts to demarcate the boundaries of a discrete self who apprehends another. Instead of a separate subject and object of apprehension, there emerges a simultaneous sense of apprehending and being apprehended by a consciousness that both is and is not one's own.

As I will argue, this sense defines the effect of novels like Proust's *Recherche* and James's *The Ambassadors*, which invite readers to open themselves to the thoughts and feelings of their protagonists. Yet instead of facilitating a seamless merging of reader and character, such an invitation opens space for a more disjunctive jostling between consciousnesses, a space where the reader can experience the character's thoughts as both *mine* and *not mine*. Even the most powerfully intimate and immediate encounter between reader and text is marked by the slight hiatus between what characters like Marcel or Strether feel, the reader's intake of that feeling, and their necessarily belated response of co- or counter-feeling. This feeling gap, this blip of unconsciously wondering what in the next second the self will become, can register in antithetical directions: as a disconcerting delay that highlights the alienation between the self and its surroundings, and conflates uncertainty with risk; or as a momentary chance for breaking form, for richly alienating the self from itself and for embracing the irruption of uncertainty as the only channel to meaningful renewal. Instead of papering over such gaps with the assurances of continuity, the writers examined in this study each use their work to heighten and train their reader's appetite and capacity for reckoning with schism, exposing and exaggerating the revelatory methods that give modernist literary consciousness not less but more structural affinity with the willingly exposed and undefensive posture of surprise. Displacing a commitment to certainty and security with a readiness for the vulnerabilities of unknowing, these writers establish unique means that can in John Cage's later phrasing "send a / message of surprise," a transmission whereby message startles method in a continuously interruptive line of pragmatist endeavor characterized by surprising transfigurations all the way along (*S*, 161).

CHAPTER I

Marcel Proust's Perceptual Training

No surprise in the writer, no surprise in the reader.

Robert Frost

In a 1905 essay titled "Sur la lecture" ("On Reading"), Marcel Proust describes a reading practice that originated in the childhood room where he would retire with a book after mealtimes.[1] Even for this fledgling Proust, reading presents forms of perception and encounter unavailable through other sources; immersed in a book, his transported consciousness mingles with "lives profoundly different" from his own, plunging him "into the depths of the non-ego."[2] "Full to the brim with the soul of others," the young Marcel is surprised at discovering "the impetus of another mind" becoming lodged in his own consciousness (*OR*, 19, 41). Yet the older Proust who writes reflectively in "Sur la lecture" refuses to idealize this youthful immersion in books as truly transformational; walled within his bedroom, this thrall is ultimately naïve for bearing "no connection with life" (*OR*, 25).

As a theory of reading, "Sur la lecture" describes the hermetic tendencies of Proust's own childhood bookishness in order to map the maturation that follows, once the true "utility of reading" can be realized later in life for its capacity to permanently "awaken" the "life of the spirit" (*OR*, 69). Crucially, the "spiritual life" that reading enables and invigorates is not conducted on some ethereal plane of transcendence; rather, it assumes a thoroughly practical form through the training of perception – the activation of life through the act of reading (*OR*, 43). Proust's essay traces the process of development that transforms his youthful reading posture into a fully realized practice of reading and writing – a transformative process given narrative form in *A la recherche du temps perdu*, a novel which likewise begins in a childhood bedroom and ends with the realization of the narrator's readerly and writerly vocation. To realize this vocation, Proust's growth as a writer and Marcel's progress as a character mutually require a disciplining of their literary sensibilities, a daily discipline that can bind reading practices and life practices together. The search for this program of discipline steers toward an unacknowledged American influence: as this chapter argues, Proust discovers his ideal guide in Ralph Waldo Emerson.

In recovering an Emersonian lineage for the reading practices that Proust embraced and demonstrated, this chapter's stakes are threefold. First, this recovery corrects the persistent and reductive forms of idealism so readily associated with both Emerson and Proust. When critics link these writers to Platonic idealism, reading is understood as an abstract means of transcending the limits of the mundane material world. I instead demonstrate that these authors share a long-standing commitment to Neoplatonic practices of attention that root them in the immediate, tangible conditions of daily life. Second, I contend that Walter Benjamin's shock-centered narrative of modernism has overshadowed Emerson's surprise-oriented influence on Proustian perception. In Benjamin's influential interpretation, Proust's *mémoire involontaire* is an emblem of historical and psychological rupture, as well as an index of his readers' increasing unreceptivity. I question Benjamin's diagnosis of a shock-fueled crisis of defensiveness by uncovering how Proust countered rupture and unreceptivity with Emersonian methods of perceptual renewal. Recognizing in Emerson and Proust a perceptual affinity, I elaborate a discipline of structured spontaneity, a practice of "perpetual surprise" by which both reorient their relation to reading and writing, seeing and living.[3] In asserting Emerson's role in shaping modernist methodologies, I follow Baudelaire, who asserts Emerson's status as a modern "stoic" whose meditations on cosmopolitan modernity bely his perceived provincialism.[4] I conclude by offering a new perceptual prescription for the Emersonian eye, suggesting that Emerson's enlivening methodological effect on Proust contests an Americanist scholarly tradition that too rigidly equates vision in Emerson with exceptionalist and expansionist interests.

This chapter is roughly divided into two parts, each navigating a critical impasse that has prevented scholars from identifying Emerson's full import for Proust, and for a transatlantic story of modernism. I begin by disputing critics who unite Emerson and Proust by way of a shared Platonizing impulse that privileges ideal essences over physical existence. I recover Plotinus as a conceptual forerunner for their mutual model of perceptual practice, a powerful method of entwining the spiritual and the sensory world.[5] Emerson, I argue, transforms Plotinus's spiritual exercises into the perceptual exercises upon which Proust's reading practice is based, an idiosyncratic trajectory I trace from Plotinus's *Enneads* through Emerson's *Nature* to Proust's "Sur la lecture" and the *Recherche*. The second half of the chapter then reframes methodologies of reading commonly linked to modernism, displacing models of defensive reading oriented by Benjaminian shock and locating alternative models of receptive reading oriented by Emersonian surprise. I show that Proust as well as Baudelaire – Benjamin's central writers of urban modernity – followed the transatlantic influence of Emerson in framing their approach to reading as a paradoxical process of preparing to encounter the unexpected. Emerson's techniques for opening himself up to the experience of being suddenly seized as such similarly enabled writers across the Atlantic to reconcile preparation with surprise. Finally, I assert that Proust's portrayal of Emersonian perception as a practice of exposure and reception serves to recast Emerson's controversial role in the influential and agonistic narrative by which America envisions itself into being.

Practicing Surprise

"Sur la lecture" warns against an ever-present danger: all-consuming absorption in the world of literature can too easily displace the exigencies of everyday life with "a beautiful Platonic myth" (*OR*, 41). This mythic idealism engulfs but also enervates readers by alienating them from the vitality of the world and their own bodies. Continuing autobiographically, Proust describes a reader in whom this life-sapping, idealizing impulse was left unchecked, resulting in a neurasthenic "impossibility of willing [une sorte d'impossibilité de vouloir]" as well as the "organic decay" of the body (*OR*, 41). In Emerson, Proust finds a model of reading that provokes an opposite effect, restoring his intellectual spirit and physical health rather than sacrificing this vitality.

Proust's essay introduces Emerson by comparing him to an archetypal literary guide. Just as Virgil led Dante "to the threshold of paradise," Emerson models reading that acts as an "initiator whose magic keys open to our innermost selves the doors into which we would not have known how to penetrate" (*OR*, 43). Following the tutelary figure he finds in Emerson, Proust descends "spontaneously into the deep regions of the self where the true life of the mind begins" (*OR*, 41). Yet to adhere to Emerson's reading model is ultimately to reject any structure of literary tutelage that asserts a guide to be followed. From Emerson, Proust learns to live by what he describes as a law of spiritual and intellectual optics ("un loi singulière . . . de l'optique des esprits"), which dictates the following: "Our wisdom begins where that of the author ends" (*OR*, 34, 35). As this law mandates, it is reading itself, rather than any individual author, that must serve as an "initiator," a perceptual "stimulus" that enlivens the mind to its own creative capacities (*OR*, 41, 43).

While Proust's Virgil analogy frames the journey into reading as a descent into the subterranean caverns of private psychology, Emerson navigates the potential pitfalls of such terrain with "leaps" and "flights" (ubiquitous terms in his essays), hurdling any obstacles and spanning all divides. The first gulf to be bridged is the chasm between inner and outer life. An Emersonian approach to reading, Proust holds, is the "sole discipline that can exert a favorable influence" because it is not externally imposed (*OR*, 41). Emerson's guidance instigates a "discipline" of attention that shuttles between the "innermost self" and "another mind [un autre esprit]" (*OR*, 40). This "contact between minds" is only transformational insofar as it feels like a "foreign intervention [intervention étrangère]" (*OR*, 41). Following Emerson, Proust's definition of reading is recast as "an intervention which, while coming from another, takes place in our . . . selves" (*OR*, 40). To avoid solipsistic self-imposition or unreflective communion, readers must attune themselves to disjunctions as well as congruencies between their consciousness and the book. Proust stresses the strangeness of an encounter that is as much an invasion as it is a reciprocal exchange.

A book worth reading "penetrates" psychological depths only to propel readers' resurfacing. According to the Emersonian definition Proust inherits, reading should "awaken" vision to the world beyond its pages: "that mist which our eager eyes would like to pierce is the last word of the painter's art . . . Then he tells us: . . . Look! Learn how to see!" (*OR*, 37–39). With a double gesture of pointing inward and outward, Proust's guide directs him beyond a second pitfall that divides literature from life. In childhood, the young Proust's world within books substitutes itself for the world outside them. Emerson's model of "creative reading" offers a powerful corrective to this displacement (*EL*, 59). When reading is creative, in the Emersonian sense, the real world does not disappear; it is remade.

Reading remakes the world by refreshing one's eyes in their alternation between inward and outward looking, an ongoing process of reorientation which sets "creative activity in motion" (*OR*, 43). Having emphasized the dangers of Platonic idealism, Proust identifies a counterintuitive function for Plato as a primary source of creative "stimulus" for Emerson (*OR*, 41).

Proust clarifies that Emerson's reading of Plato serves practical rather than idealist ends because Emerson's engagement is "at once essential and limited": he takes what he reads as a provocation for active and immediate response (*OR*, 35, 43). "Creative reading" reframes an author's "Conclusions" as "Incitements" to further thought and expression (*OR*, 35). Only when books are taken as creative instigators, not static idols, can the latent possibility inherent in readerly receptivity become animated in the realm of worldly action.

Emerson's guiding mantra – "First we read, then we write" – demands that "creative reading" generate "creative writing" (*EJ*, 298; *EL*, 59). The "exaltation" Proust feels when he reads essays like Emerson's makes it easy for him to respond to that demand by unleashing his own inventive impetus (*OR*, 43). "Sur la lecture" is one such act of creative response – one in which Proust explicitly announces that his primary motive is to incite likewise in his readers a set of similarly productive responses. His stated aim is to describe and enact this model of reading "with enough force" that his audience might be able "to follow now, as if within" themselves, the process Proust himself has undertaken (*OR*, 27).[6]

Scholars who have noted Proust's formative engagement with Emerson's essays have largely limited the scope of his influence to juvenilia predating the *Recherche*. "Optimism versus disenchantment, moralism versus art for art's sake, transcendentalism versus impressionism": when critics take these entrenched binaries as starting points, Proust is somewhat lazily characterized as an apparently disenchanted aesthete who must over-turn everything that the moralizing transcendentalist stands for in order to write his modernist magnum opus.[7] I challenge a critical trajectory that would frame Proust's progress from unworldly idealism to fully realized modernism as one that would require inverting all he learned from Emerson.[8]

Emerson and Proust

Critics weigh the multiple invocations of Emerson in Proust's early writ-ings and correspondence against a single mention in the *Recherche* and consider this imbalance as evidence of an early mentorship that Proust outgrows.[9] I will demonstrate that this narrow focus on Proust's direct references to Emerson misses continuing structural and conceptual con-gruities between their writings. The few studies that move beyond cursory enumerations of Proust's Emerson citations remain restricted by their reliance on a reductive concept of Platonic idealism. An article written in

1952 by Reino Virtanen first draws suggestive parallels between passages in Emerson's essays and the *Recherche* but skews the comparison by insisting on their common "allegiance to Platonic philosophy": "Emerson's thought curve[s] up into the empyrean, while Proust's weaves closer to earth, still tangled, because more faithful to fact, in the web of sensual life. Emerson's Platonism was optimistic and could look forward. That of Proust was precisely the 'mystique' of looking backward."[10] Conversely, I would say that Emerson's and Proust's orientations toward time and earthly existence in fact intersect at the very point where Virtanen locates their divergence.

It was four decades before a second article conceding Emerson's long-term importance for Proust was published. Everett Carter brings the writers together on the common ground of "transcendental idealism" – a form of idealism that sounds distinctly Platonic when he claims that Emerson and Proust share a desire to reveal "a real world" concealed behind "the world of appearances."[11] I build on the insights of a third scholar, Michael Murphy – the lone critic to note striking similarities between the authors' compositional methods – to suggest that these similarities stem from a very particular source: the writers' shared commitment to transposing Plotinus's perceptual practice into reading and writing practices.[12]

When Plato is taken as the starting point for establishing a link between Proust and Emerson, Plato's readers are understood to share an idealist outlook that opposes inner and outer life. Very different models of perception emerge if we take Plotinus in place of Plato as a point of departure for considering Proust and Emerson's relation.[13] Proust's reading of Emerson is easy to overlook in part because Emerson's reading of Plotinus has so long been subsumed within oversimplified accounts of his Platonism. My claim, then, is that Proust's Neoplatonism is distinctly Emersonian.[14]

Emerson and Plotinus

Many of Emerson's best critics have worked to combat a remarkably resilient portrait of Emerson as a naïve prophet of idealism; perhaps unsurprisingly, such critics seldom look to Plotinus in their efforts to shed new light on a figure whose complexity has been concealed by the long shadow of Platonism. Branka Arsić's incisive critique of "a long-standing tradition" of reading *Nature* as "an exercise in Platonizing" cites Emerson's reference to Plotinus's shame in his body as evidence that Plotinus represents the tradition of "ancients" who make misguided attempts to get "out of their bodies to think."[15] Arsić then makes only one more passing

connection between Emerson and Plotinus, raising Emerson's use of a key
Plotinian term that suggests where he might distinguish Plotinus from the
"Platonists-Idealists" who are "ungrateful" for "the reality of the external
world."[16] She notes that Emerson regularly invokes Plotinus's image of
thought as "flight" to describe a mode of thinking that is nimble and
impulsive enough to reconcile "contraries."[17] For example, when Emerson
declares, "Thin or solid, everything is in flight," he describes aspects of
thinking that demonstrate "oscillatory movement," mixing ephemeral and
material registers of experience together in a restless dynamism.[18] Thought's
capacity for flight is experienced as "ecstasy" when it "is characterized by the
absence of all duality."[19] Yet so long as Plotinus's thinking is constrained by
bodily shame, "this beatitude comes in terror, and with shocks to the mind
of the receiver" (EL, 663). For Emerson, flights of ecstasy are only prevented
from tipping into terror when they are rooted in tangible, terrestrial life.
Ecstatic unions that merge spirit and substance make way for illuminating
surprises rather than fearful "shocks."

Emersonian surprise is distinguished from Plotinian shocks in several
important ways. Whereas Emerson locates shock's point of impact in "the
mind," the sudden seizure of surprise is first physically felt. Emerson
concedes that shocks can stimulate an "unquestionable increase in mental
power" (EL, 663). But insofar as this disembodied intellection is divorced
from "practical power" (another key term for Emerson), flight gives way
to a "trance" that "drives the man mad; or, gives a certain violent basis,
which taints his judgment." He describes shock-induced illumination as
"somewhat morbid" because it often has "the accompaniment of dis-
ease" – the mental illness of a mind floating free of its body.
By contrast, Emerson claims that the experience of surprise rejuvenates
mind and body by returning "the receiver" to the "pith and marrow" of
the here and now (EL, 663). Plotinus may have disavowed his body, but
he nevertheless wrote a "spermatic book," Emerson asserts (EJ, 252). He
credits Plotinus's viscerally generative force with making him "bold"; its
"provocation" rouses him to "draw out of the past genuine life for the
present hour" (EL, 98). Elsewhere he affirms that Plotinus is "good to
read" because he "sets the reader in a working mood."[20] In other words,
Plotinus has the power to move Emerson from "creative reading" to
"creative writing."

The experience of reading Plotinus opens for Emerson an order of time
he describes in terms that map onto the contours of Proust's formulation
of mémoire involontaire. In "Contre Sainte-Beuve," Proust outlines the
object relation and temporal schema that will take narrative form in the

Recherche. His primary concern is to correct a critical misconception tipped by the misleading word "memory." Proust rightly anticipates that his readers will too easily equate his account of remembrance with the act of recollecting time past. What is "restore[d] to us under the name of the past," he insists, "is not the past":

> In reality, as soon as each hour of one's life has died, it embodies itself in some material object, as do the souls of the dead ... There it remains captive, captive forever unless we happen on the object, and recognize what lies within, call it by its name, and so set it free.[21]

Robert Richardson identifies this passage as a rearticulation of Emerson's view of "the relationship between mind and world," only stripped of its spirituality.[22] But to read these lines simply as a secularization of Emerson's claim that "the Universe is the externisation of the soul" is to miss how Proust's conception of the involuntary incorporates Emerson's revision of Neoplatonism (*EL*, 453).[23]

Proust brings together vital facets of Emersonian and Plotinian thought when he envisions each hour of lived experience lodged in the world of objects. From Plotinus, Proust learns to awaken "true vision" by activating an "inward eye" that discerns congruency between "the perceiver and the thing perceived."[24] As Plotinus writes, "every soul is and becomes, that which she contemplates."[25] Emerson's insistence on the physical immediacy of perceptual transformation emphasizes for Proust the palpability of this process. By the end of the *Recherche*, as we will see, Proust's narrator is not speaking figuratively when he explains that "every impression comes in two parts, half of it contained within the object and the other half ... extending into us."[26] He will, in other words, make literal Plotinus's directive to "become the object" by "enter[ing] deep into ourselves."[27]

What does it mean to "become" an object by entering the self? Plotinus's answer to this question is rooted in his model of perception – a model that Emerson renovates in ways that make it available to Proust. Before taking up Proust's *Recherche*, I will briefly turn to Emerson's *Nature* to highlight three points where Emerson both adheres to and departs from Plotinian principles of perception training: first, the equation of spiritual exercises with perceptual exercises; second, the premise that any process of becoming depends on a "conversion of attention"; and third, defining the "self" as "a center of perspective."[28] These points of adherence and departure instructively suggest how Proust's own Plotinian program owes its inflection to Emerson.

Emersonian Flight

Like Plotinus's *Enneads*, Emerson's *Nature* is staked on the transformative potential of perceptual attention. Emerson published *Nature* with an epigraph from Plotinus that reads: "Nature is but an image or imitation of wisdom, the last thing of the soul; nature being a thing which doth only do, but not know" (*EL*, 1139).[29] The chapters that follow think with and against this statement. In Plotinus's hierarchy, "wisdom is the first thing," while "nature is the last" because the natural world is servile to dictates that are imposed from above. *Nature* replaces Plotinus's hierarchies with equivalences. Rather than locating nature behind, beyond, or below wisdom, he places them on an equal plane by asserting that nature's pragmatics of "doing" is a primary source of "knowing."

Emerson's equation of nature and wisdom (or "intellect") redirects the path of Plotinian flight: instead of a vertical ascent that leaves the physical world and body behind, Emerson's journeying remains rooted in terra firma. Even when he is famously "uplifted into infinite space" to "become a transparent eye-ball," Emerson remains "standing on the bare ground" (*EL*, 10). Despite having traded hierarchy for equality and a vertical trajectory for the horizontal, Emerson identifies in Plotinus's writings effective means of moving from "superficial seeing" to an "attentive eye" (*EL*, 10, 15). From Plotinus, Emerson learns that metamorphosis comes not in an epiphanic moment of transcendence but rather through a lifelong training regimen. Tellingly, Emerson takes another key Plotinian term – "discipline" – as the title of a pivotal chapter in *Nature* where he locates the "practicable meaning of the world" in the juncture between "use" and "Universal Spirit" (*EL*, 32, 34, 30).

Emerson's exposure to Neoplatonism is framed by *The Life of Plotinus* (301 CE), written by the disciple Porphyry, which details the demanding spiritual exercises that organized the philosopher's everyday existence. Porphyry's spiritual biography of his teacher would have foregrounded for Emerson his methodological affinities with Plotinus. As Porphyry describes, Plotinus drew from a voluminous collection of notes and fragmented writings, compiled over decades, for his lectures and debate. Porphyry then himself assembled, edited, and revised those notes into the final arrangement of the *Enneads*, which he divided into six books of nine treatises each and prefaced with *The Life of Plotinus*. As I described in the introduction, Emerson similarly gathered many years' worth of notes, drafts, observations, and other miscellany within a series of journals and notebooks. Emerson likewise drew on that compendium of writings for his lectures, which he then revised, arranged, and published as essay collections. In Plotinus, then, Emerson finds a teacher and writer whose compositional methods are likewise motivated and shaped by his pedagogy.

Porphyry's portrait of his mentor makes abstractions like "divine union" inseparable from Plotinus's daily program of perceptual exercises. As Emerson would have read in his well-worn translation of Plotinus's *An Essay On the Beautiful*, the work of his preparatory practice is to "stir up and assume a purer eye within, which all men possess, but which is alone used by a few."[30] This capacity for spiritual seeing remains unrealized, Plotinus observes, because so few people are committed to cultivating the concentrated attention required to align the faculty of sensation with the "faculty of the soul" (a Plotinian phrase Emerson imports into *Nature* and "The Method of Nature").[31] Emerson's first major publication is hence a testament to his commitment to aligning the sensible and spiritual in the way Plotinus advises. He frames *Nature* as an unlikely instruction manual for "unlock[ing] a new faculty" in himself and in others (*EL*, 25). Yet both philosophers recognize that even the strictest adherence to the "tedious training" of vision – a process of perceptual readjustment that continues "day after day, year after year, never ending" – offers no guarantee that we "shall we come to look at the world with new eyes" (*EL*, 26, 48). Each day is devoted to creating the conditions under which an object might be "rightly seen," but ultimately illumination arrives unbidden (*EL*, 25). When all at once, "the universe becomes transparent" in the opening scene of *Nature*, Emerson's fleeting sense of "perfect exhilaration" seizes him out of nowhere (*EL*, 25, 10). The experience of ecstatic union is untethered from causal logic, yet every page that follows provides a record of the "constant exercise" that rendered him receptive to this unexpected exaltation (*EL*, 26).

Emerson follows Plotinus in his disciplined efforts to bring "a state of potentiality . . . into actuality," but he radically reconceives of what constitutes "the actual."[32] Their respective accounts of exaltation indicate where Emerson forks from the Plotinian path: at the point that vision leaves the body and the self departs the world of things. The lone explicitly autobiographical passage in Plotinus's writings describes his "'flight from the world,' that constant theme of Plotinian preaching," like this:[33]

> Often when by an intellectual energy I am roused from body, and converted to myself, and being separated from externals . . . I then . . . become the same with a nature truly divine: . . . I arrive at that transcendent energy by which I am elevated . . . in a divinely ineffable harbour of repose. But after this blessed abiding in a divine nature . . . I am led to doubt how formerly and at present my soul became intimately connected with a corporeal nature.[34]

Plotinus's preparation of perception accounts for the physicality of vision to a point, but at the moment that perceptual potential becomes actual, the faculty of vision breaks free of the body. To be inside the newly awakened "self" is to be "separated from externals," and the body is counted among those external objects. Having fallen from his state of transcendence, Plotinus is surprised to find his self lodged once more within the body he hoped he had left behind for good.

Plotinus "becomes vision" (a repeated refrain in the *Enneads*) by leaving his body, whereas Emerson "sees all" by becoming an eyeball. Rather than dissolving the physical world, the eyeball's transparency puts it in visceral contact with its immediate surroundings. Transparency, a "radical" permeability with the world, is available when the "axis of vision" is coincident with the "axis of things" (*EL*, 22, 47). In the moment that the "I" sees all, it is reduced to "nothing": "all mean egotism vanishes" (*EL*, 10). The "self" becomes the point where these axes intercept one another and open onto an unlimited angle of view.[35] Here Emerson echoes Plotinus's definition of the self as "that point from which a perspective is opened up for us."[36]

Yet, notably, their perspectives open in opposite directions.[37] In his capacity as spiritual guide, Plotinus advises that "the soul must be trained, first of all to look at beautiful ways of life: then at beautiful works . . . then at the souls of the people who produce the beautiful works."[38] Addressing the soul converted by this aesthetic training, he announces, "You have become sight," and commands: "Concentrate your gaze and see."[39] Plotinian conversion constitutes an interior turn – a return to a "self" that surpasses itself when "corporeal life" is reunified with "universal life."[40] Whereas Plotinus points the ecstatic eye inward, away from the distractions of the corporeal, Emerson's deictic pointing initiates an outward turn. His primary concern is to repair "the ruin . . . that we see when we look at nature." The ruinous "blank" is not in the natural world, he insists, but rather "in our own eye" (*EL*, 47). Therefore, to restore nature is "to purge the eyes" of their blinding preconceptions (*EL*, 25). Thus purged, the Emersonian eye discovers sources of reinvigorating surprise in, for example, the prosaic ordinariness of the town commons and the nearby fields and woods.[41]

"Barren contemplation" gives way to "new creation" when vision animates both the perceiving subject and perceived object (*EL*, 18). As Emerson writes, "a new interest surprises us, whilst . . . we contemplate the fearful extent and multitude of objects; since, 'every object rightly seen, unlocks a new faculty of the soul'" (*EL*, 25). These objects are surprising because they manifest an agency external to human will. Contemplating this unruly "multitude" rather than the abstraction of divine "Oneness," Emerson realizes a "radical correspondence between visible things and human thoughts" (*EL*, 22). Plotinus's "mystical" or "divine union" is recast as an "occult relation" between, for example, "man and vegetable" (*EL*, 10). Such a relation is founded on a practice of perception that heals the split between people and things – in this case, between human and herbaceous life. Emerson's investment in the "occult" only hinges on a belief in the supernatural to the extent that ordinary things disclose the extraordinary.[42]

Object Relations

Such key differences between Plotinus's and Emerson's concept of what it means to "become an object and potentially ourselves" help to explain the strange mix of Neoplatonism and Emersonianism in Proust's writing. One might hear an echo of Plotinus's exhortation to "concentrate your gaze and see" in Proust's command – "Look! Learn how to see!" – from "Sur la lecture." Like Plotinus, Proust cultivates a "transporting vision," seeking to "become one with this supreme beauty."[43] As Eve Kosofsky Sedgwick has observed, Proust's narrator regularly makes overtly Neoplatonic claims, such as "there exists but a single intelligence of which everyone is co-tenant."[44] But for Proust, as for Emerson, this "intelligence" capaciously enfolds animate and inanimate life. The *Recherche* moves toward what Emerson calls "the beauty of health," where "our health" is defined as "our sound relation to external objects" (*EAL*, 368; *EJ*, 199). The healing process is protracted over three thousand pages – an entire lifetime – but the novel is punctuated by episodes (such as the one to which I will soon turn) that glimpse the beauty of health beyond bipolar thinking.

The narrator's healthy relation with objects is contingent on his capacity to feel alone in their company. For much of the novel, Marcel is constantly retreating from companionship, perceiving his contemplative energies to be drastically depleted by the negotiation of worldly relations. In this retreat, he upholds Plotinus's definition of "contemplation" as "the flight of the alone to the alone."[45] Plotinus compares the practice of preparing the soul for reunion with "the Solitary One" to sculpting: "Imitate the statuary; who when he desires a beautiful statue cuts away what is superfluous, smooths and polishes what is rough, and never desists until he has given it all the beauty his art is able to effect . . . Become thus purified residing in yourself . . . perceiving your whole self to be a true light, and light alone."[46] For Plotinus, art acts as an "heuristic" for contemplating the "Beauty and Good, by which the soul is enabled to behold and become united with her divinely solitary original."[47] Art's usefulness for contemplation breaks down when it enmeshes contemplation with the world of the senses. The apex of Plotinian "flight" is a solitude that has chiseled away all material attachments to "sensible forms."[48]

Art serves a contrasting heuristic function for Emerson, and in turn, for Proust. Instead of urging a flight from the world, art provides a practice ground for inhabiting the world more fully. Likewise, both writers' experiences of art alter for them what it means to be alone. Plotinus's touchstone phrase – "The flight of the alone to the alone" – evidently resonated for Emerson.[49] But in his repeated returns to the quotation over the course of his career, Emerson not only reroutes the Plotinian flight path; he also explores various dimensions of solitude. In *Nature*, he affirms, "I am not solitary whilst I read and write, though nobody is with me" (*EL*, 9). Proust reports making the same discovery in the essay where he names Emerson as his guide in reading. There, Proust explains that when we read, we receive "the communication of another thought, while we remain alone, that is to say, while continuing to enjoy the intellectual power we have in solitude, which conversation dissipates immediately; while continuing to be inspired, to maintain the mind's full, fruitful work on itself" (*OR*, 31). "Sur la lecture" and the *Recherche* reveal that Proust internalized Emerson's amended model of solitary contemplation – a model which demands that the mind's work in contemplating itself also extend into contemplating the world around it.

"Sur la lecture" narrates the progressive extension of Proust's reading practice into a practice of "simply being there" in the solitary company of an "enchanted" object world.[50] Reading in the bedroom of his youth, Proust's immersive plunge into the world of books threatens to subsume all life outside their pages. As his reading practice progresses, he learns to strike a better balance between immersion and cohabitation. Proust draws mutually animating lines of continuity between enlivening encounters with books and objects in a variety of rooms where he has spent time reading and thinking since childhood. In one instance, he evocatively recounts his stay at "one of those provincial hotels" in a room that is "full to the brim with the souls of others" (*OR*, 17). During his visit, Proust learns to live alone but also alongside those lives lodged in various bedroom objects. In the solitary company of carpets, curtains, and corridors, his "imagination is excited by feeling itself plunged into the depths of the non-ego" (*OR*, 17). The essay's elaborate rendering of this room anticipates a pivotal episode in a provincial hotel featured in the third volume of the *Recherche*.

Bedrooms are charged places in Proust's novel. They are sites of creative contemplation, but they also return the narrator to childhood scenes of upheaval. For that reason, Marcel dreads his hotel stay in the garrison town of Doncières, where he has traveled to visit a friend stationed there. In the strange room he expects "to face the world with that 'self' which ... had never grown up since Combray" – in other words, to be stifled by "the unbreathable aroma, which every unfamiliar bedroom ... exhaled" (*G*, 78). Upon arrival he wonderingly observes that he "had no time to be miserable" because he was "never alone" (*G*, 79). Up to this point, unknown persons or objects have always interrupted the contemplative solitude he seeks, foreclosing aesthetic receptivity with an "anaesthetic" response (*G*, 82). But in the Doncières hotel, the objects "acquired a sort of life," which made them impossible to categorize either as "stranger[s] [étrangères]" or as "neighbours [voisins]" (*G*, 79). Hovering between familiarity and unfamiliarity, the narrator learns to feel alone in their company.

Imprinted by multiple histories of use and residence, the furnishings are irreducible to the narrator's relation with them. He describes the room as an "enchanted domain [féerique domaine]" where the difference between solitude and communal cohabitation is somehow suspended (*G*, 81). The hotel objects have independent existences, even as Marcel describes himself partaking of their experience. In contingent contact with lives that are not his own, the narrator experiments with "prospective" forms of relation for which he has no prior paradigms. Instead of being paralyzed by the shock of the new or unknown, Marcel is galvanized by object encounters that he frames in the terms of surprise. "No longer shut in," the narrator opens himself to reciprocal exchanges where his own surprise merges with a sense that the room's inhabitants are equally startled by him (*G*, 80). His explorations uncover new hotel corners that receive him in "amazement [étonnées]"; at the same time, lively objects are "discovered [je surpris]" that heighten his "attention beyond its usual pitch" (*G*, 79, 81).

Proust's narrator finds his perceptual habits reoriented as opposed to ruptured at Doncières. He sidesteps all-or-nothing models of change to explore the mutual "modification" that is possible in middle ranges of experience (*G*, 81). For example, Marcel describes the hotel wallpaper as "a violent red dotted with black and white flowers which suggested they would take some getting used to" (*G*, 86). Where he anticipates coming "into conflict," he instead comes "into contact with them": "They affected me as something novel," he observes (*G*, 86). In past bedrooms, Marcel has aimed to efface such novelty; here he embraces the subtle changes that his environment institutes in him. Rather than attempting to overwrite the strange wallpaper, the narrator dwells in "the heart" of the flowers. As Marcel declares, this new perspective dramatically transforms the way he "viewed the world" (*G*, 86).

Remembering to Forget

The Doncières bedroom is so often overlooked in readings of the *Recherche* because it does not neatly echo the novel's best-known bedroom in Combray. The surprise encountering of animate objects that the narrator comes to welcome in the garrison town hotel was previously feared as a source of threat and suffering in the bedroom of his youth. In the novel's famous opening scene, the young Marcel's drama of going to bed alternates between two poles of experience: the shock of the unfamiliar and the analgesic of habit. This alternation is initiated by a "magic lantern," which destroys the room's familiarity without providing pleasurable diversions as his parents intended. Bathed in the lamp's "multicoloured apparitions," a doorknob whose handling was so unconscious "it seemed to open of its own accord" suddenly becomes an intruder.[51] The reconsidered room wrenches the narrator from the intimacy that "the anaesthetizing influence of habit" had wrought between his consciousness and its surroundings.[52] When his mind is aligned with its lodgings, Marcel is free to pay "no more attention to the room than to the self"; only then can he can reflect on other things.[53] But any intrusive disturbance restarts the cycle and habit's work must begin again.

Benjamin's seminal reading of the *Recherche* in "On Some Motifs in Baudelaire" provides a formative framework for extending the Combray pattern of unrelenting oscillation between newness and numbness into a broader paradigm of modern experience. As discussed in the introduction, Benjamin frames "Motifs" as a provisional investigation into the applicability of Freud's shock "hypothesis" beyond the purview of his model of wartime trauma (*M*, 160). Despite Benjamin's proviso that his diagnosis of a wider "crisis in perception" remains unconfirmed, it's hard to overestimate the lasting influence his narrative of shock modernity has had in shaping the critical reception of his two literary case studies: Baudelaire, and Baudelaire's "incomparable reader," Proust (*M*, 180). Benjamin privileges these writers as the primary navigators of "the modern age," which he characterizes as a "series of shocks and collisions" (*M*, 194, 175). According to Benjamin's experimental framework, sensory assaults of every order – whether issuing forth from the magic lantern, from "the amorphous crowd of passers-by," or from shellfire at the fighting front – all contribute to the defining dynamic of modernity: as in the Combray bedroom, experience swings warily between the poles of shock and "shock defense" (*M*, 165, 163).

Proust's *mémoire involontaire* records psychic as well as temporal breaks between his own time and a premodern period that enjoyed unhindered access to immediate presence. At points, the premodern past being broken with seems to float "outside history," but Benjamin ultimately anchors the definitive historical moment of "breakdown" in the nineteenth century, where Baudelaire could bear firsthand witness to it (*M*, 181). For Benjamin, Baudelaire's "*correspondances*" stand closest to a fullness of authentic experience, which has been "irretrievably lost" (*M*, 190). Half a century later, Proust's *mémoire involontaire* can only access such authenticity through accidental encounters: it has thus become "a matter of chance whether an individual ... can take hold of his experience" (*M*, 158). Proust's dependence on chance confirms for Benjamin the "atrophy" of sensorial richness and perceptual responsiveness in the modern era (*M*, 159).

The model of vision I've traced from Plotinus through Emerson to Proust makes various shifts in orientation – from inner to outer, from mental to material – but what remains constant is a fundamental belief in the eye's trainability. By contrast, Benjamin points to Proust's *mémoire involontaire* as evidence that "eyes have lost their ability to look" (*M*, 189). The traumatic shocks of war, urbanization, and technological change have "overburdened" the city-dweller's eye to such an extent that the protective function of perception had permanently overtaken its receptive function by the turn of the twentieth century (*M*, 191, 161–62). Benjamin's timeline locates a writer such as Emerson in the premodern moment when perceptual experience was not yet permanently compromised. His sensorium might therefore have remained responsive to training, but for those writing in Emerson's wake, the practice of perceptual receptivity had become increasingly futile; an "unarmed eye" was too vulnerable to the shocks of modernity to remain open (*M*, 223).

The association of Emerson with a premodern plenitude has occluded his vital importance for Proust – and, as I will elaborate shortly, for Baudelaire. I conclude by reading a climactic scene in the final volume of the *Recherche*, which suggests that the perceptual training Emerson provided for both writers allowed them to stay open-eyed in the face of rapid modern change. While Benjamin gives Baudelaire pride of place as the first modern poet, Baudelaire himself looks to Emerson's poet-walker for his model of the modern artist. Likewise, Proust's narrator can only embrace his vocation at the end of the *Recherche* because an extended Emersonian program of perception training has prepared him for it.

Benjamin's investigation into Proust, Baudelaire, and shock contributes to a broader line of inquiry that asks: how do practices of reading and writing index social and historical change? Benjamin turns to Proust to answer this question because Proust exemplifies the modern writer who documents shock, but also the modern reader who must reckon with a depleted capacity for reception. Benjamin cites a passage from *Le temps retrouvé* (the last volume of the *Recherche*) as evidence that even Baudelaire's best reader suffers diminished access to the "data of prehistory" on account of a fundamental "change in the structure" of modern experience (*M*, 182, 156):

> There is no one else who pursues the interconnected *correspondances* with such leisurely care, fastidiously and yet nonchalantly – in a woman's scent for instance, in the fragrance of her hair or her breasts – *correspondances* which then inspire him with lines like 'the azure of the vast, vaulted sky, or 'a harbor full of flames and masts.' (quoted in *M*, 183)

In Benjamin's interpretation, Proust reads Baudelaire with nostalgic long-ing for a time when *correspondances* were "not occasioned by chance," when the writer could voluntarily "take hold of his experience" in all its authentic fullness (*M*, 183, 158). But when Benjamin roots *correspondances* in the "realm of the ritual," where they are imbued with "the data of remem-brance" and traditions past, he misses an equally vital facet of Baudelaire's emblem of modernity: its future-oriented capacity to surprise the writer and his audience (*M*, 182). In *Le temps retrouvé*, Proust recovers this prospective dimension of *correspondances* and of *mémoire involontaire*. Rather than merely representing forms of retrospection, these hallmarks of modernism fuse "fugitive" impressions with "eternity" in what Emerson calls an "everlasting Now."[54]

The passage from the *Recherche* that for Benjamin signals an irreparable break with the aesthetic and experiential richness of the past in fact introduces the narrator's extended meditation on the unbounded (though equally uncertain) potential of a future devoted to writing. Marcel's reflections on Baudelaire's *correspondances* affirm his dedication to a literary "vocation" that will similarly transpose sensations – beginning with "the taste of the madeleine" – into "aesthetic impressions" (*FT*, 228). Far from dispiriting Marcel, Baudelaire's example motivates him to "estab-lish a place for [him]self in such a noble tradition" and assures him that "the work which [he] no longer had the slightest hesitation in undertaking was worth the effort [he] was going to devote to it" (*FT*, 229).

In this context, the gap between the narrator's accidental "reminiscences" and Baudelaire's deliberate pursuit of *correspondances* is one Marcel aims to shrink by applying himself with the same "leisurely care," a kind of relaxed precision, to his newly declared occupation (*M*, 180). For Proust, chance is as integral to *correspondances* as it is to *mémoire involontaire*: Baudelaire can no more predict what wafting aroma might inspire his connection with the arc of azure sky than Proust can foretell what taste will bring forth the full sweep of the way by Swann's. Yet if writing is to be a process of discovery rather than a confirmation of preexisting ideas, this uncertainty remains a source of potential rather than a liability. Though the particulars of the encounter must remain undetermined, with proper training the receptive state that gives occasion to such surprising events can be carefully calibrated to increase their frequency and their expressive impetus.

Emerson and Baudelaire

Proust narrows the gap between *mémoire involontaire* and Baudelairean *correspondances* so they meet on shared Emersonian ground. Both these aesthetic signatures are founded on Emerson's central insight regarding the nature of creative activity: "The thought of genius is spontaneous; but the power of picture or expression, in the most enriched and flowing nature, implies a mixture of will, a certain control over the spontaneous states, without which no production is possible" (*EL*, 413). Following Emerson, both Baudelaire and Proust develop modernist methods that fuse contingency and control into forms of structured spontaneity. Baudelaire defines *correspondance* as the unexpected convergence of two disparate elements: the "eternal and invariable" (an enduring aesthetic quality unaltered by shifts in fashion and taste) with an unpredictable "circumstantial element."[55] Art that yokes these heterogeneous experiences of time is "always surprising [toujours étonnant]," writes Baudelaire.[56]

Proust's readings of Baudelaire and Emerson resonate with one another for good reason. Baudelaire's study of his exemplary modern artist, "L'Oeuvre et la vie d'Eugène Delacroix" (1863), identifies Emerson as a fellow figure of modernity whose "transatlantic" influence extends from Concord to Paris.[57] Baudelaire declares his intention to free Emerson from his "reputation as the leader of that wearisome Bostonian school." Dismissing the popular understanding of Emerson as a transcendental "moralist," Baudelaire confers on him the status of a modern "stoic" who "effectively stimulates meditation" on contemporary life.[58] Beyond claiming Emerson's cosmopolitan modernity, Baudelaire upholds his definition of artistic "genius" as one where "perceptiveness" pairs spontaneous investigation with a "passion for method" and "firm maxims."[59] The challenge, for Baudelaire's "painter of modern life" as for Emerson's poet-walker, is to "digest and transform" the "heap of raw materials" without deadening them into "inanimate nature."[60] Emerson offers a model of the kind of radical openness coupled with exacting structure to which Baudelaire had long aspired in his own life and writing.

Baudelaire reports a "surprising reawakening of interest in Emerson" a decade after he read the first series of essays, at a time when he was beginning to draft his major statements on the methods of modernism.[61] Baudelaire first records his newly intensified engagement in the journals he began to keep in 1857, shortly after Emerson's second series of essays were translated. Whereas Emerson's journals were a lifelong project, Baudelaire's idiosyncratic assemblage marked a transitional moment in his life and career. Though they differ in scope and tone, both journals represent their authors' efforts to respond with immediacy to experiences of reading, writing, and daily life. As did Emerson, Baudelaire gathered (in his translator Christopher Isherwood's words) "an assortment of wonderful fragments, cryptic memoranda, literary notes, quotations, rough drafts of prose poems, explosions of political anger and personal spleen."[62] For Emerson, repositories of impression fueled the majority of his published writings; for Baudelaire, such journaling became the site of ferment for his most influential essays on the modern artist.

Critics have generally read the material posthumously collected in a volume titled *Journaux intimes* as Baudelaire's response to personal breakdown.[63] The journals are scattered with aphorisms from Emerson on autonomy, genius, and heroism, mostly paraphrased from *The Conduct of Life* (1860). In these citations, Baudelaire formulates a dogmatic version of self-reliance that is pitched toward consolidating "a well thought-out individualism [l'individualisme bien entendu]."[64] To this end, Emerson's shifty locutions are recast as moral maxims that promote productive work habits he felt himself to be lacking. For example, Baudelaire echoes the strident assertions of Emerson's "Power" on the importance of focused attention and disciplined will in a section of the notebooks headed "Hygiene. Morality. Conduct [Hygiène. Conduite. Méthode]."[65] Baudelaire sounds similarly dogmatic when he quotes Emerson directly to describe a "conduct of life" that is also a method of composition in the case of his exemplar, Delacroix: "The one prudence in life is concentration; the one evil is dissipation."[66]

Yet while Baudelaire initially works against the dispersal of attention and subjectivity, in both his journals and his essay on Delacroix he goes on to emulate the signature Emersonian move of conjoining terms he at first opposed: "Of the vaporization and centralization of the Ego. Everything depends on that [De la vaporisation et de la centralisation du Moi. Tout est là]."[67] Any perceived solidity of "le Moi" is portrayed as a temporary state that could at any moment be dissolved and decentered. Alternately vaporous and concentrated, Baudelaire's self-conception aligns with the Emersonian self of "Illusions," for whom "dissipation" is not "evil" but simply a condition of living. Emerson's essay opens with an epigraphic poem that reframes "power" as the enduring capacity to ride out the "wild dissipation" of existence:

> To change and to flow,
> The gas become solid, [...]
> And endless imbroglio
> Is the law and the world,—
> Then first shalt thou know,
> That in the wild turmoil,
> Horsed on the Proteus,
> Thou ridest to power [...]   (*EL*, 1113–14)

When the law of the world is continual change and flow between material and psychic states, the protean self must weather "endless imbroglio." The essay proceeds to establish "incessant flowing" as the only constant (*EL*, 1121).

For Emerson as for Baudelaire, "Life is an ecstasy" when the "everlasting" and "fugitive" converge (*EL*, 1113). In "The Method of Nature," Emerson spatializes the temporality of ecstatic experience: the "work of ecstasy [is] to be represented by a circular movement, as intention might be signified by a straight line of definite length" (*EL*, 120). Baudelaire follows Emerson in countering "straight" time with spiraling correspondences that connect a fleeting experience of the "now" with an enduring law of contingency. The myths of the heroic individual and the original genius have a clear appeal for Baudelaire, but his journals' fragmentary form ultimately performs a self in process. As Jean-Paul Sartre argues in his seminal study, *Baudelaire* (1947), the unresolved tension between these impulses to organize and disperse the self is the principal drama of Baudelaire's work.[68]

Sartre portrays Baudelaire as a writer so entrenched in his own consciousness that he yearns to escape self-scrutiny: "Baudelaire was the man who never forgot himself. He watched himself see; he watched in order to see himself watch."[69] This doubled perception of perception can yield illuminating insights, but Baudelaire describes and bemoans a claustrophobic closed loop of "auto-idolâtrie."[70] According to Sartre's reading, Baudelaire's writing unfolds as a series of failed attempts to "take himself by surprise": "He simulated a disconcerting spontaneity, pretended to surrender to the most gratuitous impulses so that he could suddenly appear in his own eyes as an opaque, unpredictable object, appear in fact as though he were Another Person."[71] Yet the opacity and unpredictability Baudelaire sought remained elusive.

Baudelaire's efforts to surprise himself were doomed to fail, Sartre concludes, because "abandonment was as unknown to him as spontaneity."[72] Contriving "his own plan" to simulate spontaneity and pretend to surrender, Baudelaire always "foresaw and measured his own astonishment" and therefore remained "identical with the person he wished to surprise."[73] While Sartre concludes that Baudelaire has no access to "the way of life . . . by abandonment," I want to suggest that Baudelaire's best-known essays on the modern artist, composed alongside his *Journaux intimes*, elaborate practices of self-forgetting – of being surprised out of one's propriety – which owe a debt to Emerson (*EL*, 414).

Methods of Nature, Methods of Modernism

In the essay that claims Emerson's cosmopolitan modernity, Baudelaire advocates a compositional method that closely resembles the "method of nature" first articulated at the Jardin des Plantes. "Nature is but a dictionary," Baudelaire writes, echoing Emerson, and the "universe is but a store-house of images and signs."[74] Baudelaire's modern artist follows Emerson's naturalist-poet in the project of reviving and deciphering these natural signs. Delacroix is declared an exemplary "man of genius" according to Emerson's criteria that "there is always a surprise" in his creative activity (*EL*, 483). The primary pitfalls that for Delacroix deaden creativity – "copying and forget[ting] feeling" – follow likewise from Emerson.[75] The surprise of creation springs forth, in Baudelaire's account, from the similar stoicism he attributes to both Emerson and Delacroix. The poet and painter each pair childlike "perceptiveness" and "tyrannical whims" with "strong nerves"; "open to every sort of idea and impression," they are "armed in advance" with techniques for bringing "classified, ordered, harmonized" form to the chaotic influx.[76] Baudelaire portrays an artist who is as great a reader of literature as he is of nature's dictionary. Delacroix's process of composition is catalyzed by a practice of creative reading; his rapidly responsive brushstrokes are spurred by gestural sentences like those crafted by Emerson; prose that "seems to imitate the swift movements of thought" leaves the artist "full of sublime, swiftly-defined images."[77] Emerson's role in this essay and in the *Journaux intimes* suggests that his model of reading as a catalyst for creative activity helped Baudelaire navigate a new relationship with his "hypocrite lecteur." The unpredictable path of transmission from writer to reader was a long-standing source of anxiety for Baudelaire, but Emerson reframed this volatility as a site of creative potential. Bernard Howells argues that the reader's power to alienate Baudelaire's work from its original intentions "contaminated the writer's spontaneity," yet he relaxed his need for inter-pretive control, I contend, at a time when his work was most strongly marked by the influence of Emerson.[78]

Baudelaire's journals assert a "universal misunderstanding" between reader and writer: "The unbridgeable gulf [le gouffre infrachissable] – the cause of their failure in communication remains – unbridged [reste infranchi]."[79] By the time he writes "Le Peintre de la vie moderne" (1863), however, Baudelaire had developed two key figures who present alternate approaches to navigating this gulf between consciousnesses. The figures of the dandy and artist are sometimes conflated, but Baudelaire's painter of modern life "parts company trenchantly from dandyism [se détache violemment du dandysme]."[80] As his essay sug-gests, they are differentiated specifically in their respective attitudes toward surprise.

The dandy maintains his "cult of the ego" by "causing surprise in others and . . . never showing any oneself."[81] Surprise, then, marks his desire to assert the difference between a controlling self and a susceptible other. Tellingly, Baudelaire compares the dandy to an impassive military man: "Accustomed as he is to surprises, the soldier does not easily lose his composure."[82] For the dandy, as for the soldier, commanding self-control must be maintained at all costs. While "the dandy is blasé," aspiring to "self-containment," the painter of modern life "hates blasé people" and keeps the self permeable.[83] Moved by an "insatiable passion" for "seeing and feeling," Baudelaire's artist invites the unexpected to "flood chaotically into him."[84] Ideally, this susceptibility will spread: "Next to feeling surprise oneself, there is no greater pleasure than giving someone else a surprise."[85] The artist neither laments nor reinforces the divide between maker and audience, but instead seeks modes of expression that invite an unpredictable commingling of "le moi" and "le non-moi." As "an ego athirst for the non-ego," the painter of modern life seeks dissolution in "the ebb and flow [dans l'ondoyant, dans le mouvement] of the fleeting and the infinite."[86]

Though they pursue *correspondances* by different means, Baudelaire's dandy and modern artist are united in their efforts to access moments of modernity where "the transient" coincides with "the eternal."[87] Though Benjamin groups these figures with the flâneur as navigators of modernity, Baudelaire's definition of "the modern" is distinctive. While Benjamin's flâneur witnesses a singular moment of modern rupture at the turn of the twentieth century, Baudelaire's dandy and artist find "a form of modernity" at transitional moments in every era.[88] Fusing the "contingent" with something "immovable," Baudelaire's figures of modernity share a common silhouette with Emerson's poet-walker.[89] The distinctive temporality of *correspondances* characterizes the immersive experience of the crowd, but it also distinguishes Emerson's solitary experience of "crossing a bare common ... under a clouded sky" and, as we will see, Marcel's experience of tripping over a courtyard paving stone (*EL*, 10). The Baudelairean artist's desire "to see the world, to be at the very centre of the world, and yet to be unseen of the world" is precisely the achievement of Emerson's "transparent eye-ball."[90] It is also the achievement of Proust's narrator-turned-writer and the defining achievement of the *Recherche*.

Time Regained

By definition, moments of *mémoire involontaire* cannot be willfully controlled, yet Marcel's reflections on Baudelairean *correspondances* mark his realization that his ready receptivity to them need not be left to chance. With this recognition he devotes himself to creating conditions under which he might be spontaneously seized; the narrator prepares himself to be a writer by preparing himself to be surprised. Accordingly, Marcel begins to experience *mémoire involontaire* with far greater frequency. Where involuntary encounters previously revealed the invisible potential stored in objects, his own obscured potential now comes into view. Stumbling over an uneven paving stone, the narrator dislodges the apprehensions impeding the "'famous' work" that he had "so long hoped each day to begin the next" (*FT*, 162, 164):

> Just as at the moment when I tasted the madeleine, all the uneasiness about the future and all the intellectual doubt were gone. Those that had assailed

me a moment earlier about the reality of my intellectual talent, even the reality of literature, were lifted as if by enchantment. (*FT*, 175)

What differentiates the paving stone from the madeleine is the investigative purpose that the narrator brings to the moment. On this occasion he refuses to "resign [him]self to not knowing" how this transformative force might be tapped (*FT*, 179).

Marcel's deliberate turning of contemplative attention makes way for further involuntary encounters triggered in rapid succession by the sound of a spoon against a plate, the touch of a napkin against his mouth, the resonance of the title of George Sand's *François le Champi* (1894), pulled at random from a bookshelf: "The signs which were, on this day, to bring me out of my despondency and renew my faith in literature were intent on multiplying themselves" (*FT*, 176). The narrator swiftly quadruples his experiences of *mémoire involontaire* by attuning himself to aspects of his immediate environment that might otherwise pass unnoticed. In each instance, a fleeting but palpable sensation expands his perceptual and temporal consciousness; every expansion further frees him from paralyzing anxieties around "the vicissitudes of the future" (*FT*, 179). The liberating power of this involuntary series of events stems from Marcel's understanding that preparing to be struck by attuned observation indeed amounts to the embodiment of his chosen vocation.[91] The feeling of attention blooming into new words – of attention felt as writing even before it has been physically inscribed – instantiates the narrator's sense of inevitable correlation between preparatory perception and the act of writing itself.

Time is regained in the final volume of the *Recherche* by shedding prior paradigms of perception. As preconceptions fall away, the Proustian self begins to have the "impression that it is losing itself" (to draw once more on a Plotinian formulation).[92] Marcel has been practicing a solitary process of self-forgetting in objects and books; his acceptance of the Princesse de Guermantes's invitation to a party – his "return to society" after a long retreat from Paris – marks a resolution to learn to lose himself in the company of other people (*FT*, 227). Reading in solitude, time seemed easily suspended. Reentering the social world, the narrator confronts time's passage in the startling realities of "old age" (*FT*, 240). Upon arrival at the party, he is initially convinced that his friends have all donned powdered wigs, makeup, and costumes to masquerade as elderly versions of themselves. When the narrator finally grasps that they have grown old, as indeed has he, time comes unhinged.

Rather than going into defensive or nostalgic retreat, the narrator perceives "we are living in a new world": "Time had not only brought about the ruin of the creatures of a former epoch, it had made possible, had indeed created, new associations" (*FT*, 257). Significantly, he compares the "revelation of Time" in the wizened figures to the "magic lantern show" that transformed his "bedroom doorknob in Combray" (*FT*, 233). Far from mourning the "lost time" of childhood, this return to the paradigmatic bedroom facilitates his "astonished [on s'étonnait]" appreciation of how "one could read the tally of years" in faces that offer "something much more valuable than an image of the past" (*FT*, 233, 234). Aesthetic revelation turns out to be a gradual accumulation: "having lived one day to the next since [his] childhood" Marcel has amassed the "raw material" for his prospective book. "Now," he writes, "I understood the meaning of death, loves, the pleasures of the mind, the use of suffering" (*FT*, 240).

Freed from a limited perceptual framework, Marcel discovers what Emerson describes as "a spontaneity which forgets usages and makes the moment great" (*EL*, 483). Only by forgetting former certainties about friends and foes can the narrator "transition from a past to a new state," which is "not present, so much as prospective," in Emerson's phrasing (*EL*, 261, 486). To forget, Emerson observes, is not to erase but to awaken "the present, which is infinite" (*EL*, 394). Understood in this sense, the extraordinary closing passage of Emerson's essay "Circles" comes closest to capturing the full significance of Marcel's process of self-forgetting: "The one thing which we seek with insatiable desire is to forget ourselves, to be surprised out of our propriety, to lose our sempiternal memory, and to do something without knowing how or why; in short, to draw a new circle" (*EL*, 414). Recast in this way, Proustian memory is as much a matter of forgetting as of remembrance.[93]

Training in Transparency

The *Recherche* and "Circles" offer the same concluding insight regarding the "use of literature": it allows us to practice seeing with a kind of double vision (*EL*, 408). Our vision is doubled when we are afforded perspective from points of view situated both inside and outside the new circle drawn. Books provide a "platform" from where "we may command a view of our present life," writes Emerson, and, adds Proust, "a point of departure for a new life" (*EL*, 408; *FT*, 240). In the all-consuming moment of *mémoire involontaire*, "there is no outside" (*EL*, 405). Yet a writer like Proust allows readers fully to inhabit that moment while standing slightly to the side of it, from where they can reflect on the immersive experience. "Literature," Emerson writes, "is a point outside of our hodiernal circle, through which a new one may be described" (*EL*, 408). Proust puts it this way: literature allows readers "to possess other eyes, to behold the universe through the eyes of another, of a hundred others, to behold the hundred universes that each of them beholds, that each of them is."[94] It's no accident that the novel Marcel will write – the one Proust's readers hold in their hands – provides the same endless expansion of vision as Emerson's transparent eyeball.

By contending that Proust's and Baudelaire's modern artists extend the sightlines of Emerson's eye, I have suggested that these writers' readings of the sage of Concord serve to reframe a Benjaminian narrative of modernist shock. Having focused on future-oriented angles of Emersonian vision, I will conclude by demonstrating how Proust's attention to the Plotinian dimensions of Emerson's perceptual paradigm also reorients an influential Americanist account of the eyeball's vantage on the past. Few episodes in American literature have generated more contesting scholarly interpretations than Emerson's experience of transparency on the common; I perforce confine my reference to Emerson's "endless expansion of vision" as calling to mind a particularly well-established critical calculus that equates the Emersonian eye with acquisitive cultural desire.

As I have suggested in my introduction, this equation is most forcefully instantiated by Sacvan Bercovitch, who argues that Emerson's vision "serves to reaffirm that of the Puritans" by propagating the American ideology of "elect nationhood."[95] Bercovitch points to the many "cultural continuities" that draw Puritan New England and "classics of the American Renaissance" into ideological affiliation; hence, for his advocacy of nationalist individualism, Emerson is identified by Bercovitch as exemplary among nineteenth-century writers.[96] Tracing the Puritan rhetoric of exceptionalism through Emerson's "exaltation of the individual," Bercovitch argues that Emerson's writings "facilitated the movement from . . . sacred errand to manifest destiny, colony to republic to imperial power."[97] When framed by this dominant critical narrative, Emerson's bare common appears as fertile ground for expansionist "self-interest," his eyeball becomes an emblem of empire, and "the inspired perceiver" is cast as an "imperial self."[98]

Conversely, by casting Emersonian perception in the light of Plotinus's model of transparency, Proust rediscovers how Emersonian vision might be enacted, not as a gaze that imposes or appropriates but as a yielding mode of receptive surrender.[99] This is to say that Proust's reading of

Emerson suggests where the legacy of Puritan perception – a literary line-age that critics working under Bercovitch's influence have continued to route through the trope of transparent vision – may veer and fork in unexpected directions. The Plotinian perceptual paradigm that Proust finds in Emerson is anathema to a rapacious "eye" or a tyrannical "I." Transparency, as Plotinus describes it, is only available when vision has relaxed its vigilance into a state of open responsiveness. In such a state of receptivity, the eye relinquishes its capacity to seize objects of view so that it might itself be seized by something unforeseen. When "all things are transparent," Plotinus posits, "there is nothing dark or opaque": "All things are clear to the inmost part to everything; for light is transparent to light. Each there has everything in itself, and sees all things in every other, so that all are everywhere."[100] Transparency is achieved when the inner sight of an enlightened eye merges with the light of a world infused with divine radiance. In these fleeting moments, perceiver and perceived are coexten-sive and the self disappears into the process of vision.

Reading in a Plotinian register, Proust understands Emerson to be describing something resembling such a moment of disappearance on the common: the self must become "nothing" in order to achieve a transparency that "sees all." When Emerson insists, "All I know is reception," he is attesting to the dissolution of the first-person "I" into a wholly receptive "eye" (*EL*, 491). As Proust frames it, there is no imperial self on the bare common, and transparency is antithetical to appropriation. Instead of holding the visual field captive to a mastering gaze, Emerson's lines of sight entwine the perceiving mind and perceived world into a thick weave of unmasterable experience. Crucially, both Emerson and Plotinus define this transparent register of experience – an immersive perceptual plenitude – in direct opposition to an experience that each describes as "privation": a state of separation from the goodness of God felt as isolation and loss. The oppositional relation between transparency and privation in Emerson's work points to the place where his Neoplatonism inflects his Puritanism – but a strain of Puritanism that itself stands opposed to the tradition with which he is frequently identified.

Plotinus compares someone living in a state of privation to a "blind man": deprived of divine light, the perceiver "beholds nothing but obscurity ... surveying absolute darkness."[101] Whereas transparency is equated with the fullness of "Being," the darkness of "non-being" is equated with "evil." Emerson follows Plotinus in defining "evil" as priva-tion in "The Divinity School Address" (1838): "Good is positive. Evil is merely privative, not absolute: it is like cold, which is the privation of heat"

(*EL*, 77). Emerson's language of heat and cold serves the same purpose as Plotinus's language of light and dark: both sensorial analogies invoke a conception of evil as an absence rather than an entity. By the time he writes "Experience," the Plotinian echo has only grown more forceful and direct: "Sin . . . is a diminution or less . . . shade, absence of light, and no essence. The conscience must feel it as essence, essential evil. This it is not" (*EL*, 489).

In the treatises of the *Enneads* on art and beauty that Emerson reads with the greatest attention, Plotinus develops techniques for overcoming privation that are then employed in *Nature* and other major essays by Emerson. Plotinus issues a challenge to his students and listeners that Emerson reformulates in his bare common passage. The challenge involves training sustained attention on an image of transparency that pushes the imaginative capacity to its outer limits: "So far as possible, try to conceive of the world as one unified whole, with each of its parts remaining self-identical and distinct. So that . . . all sentient beings are seen, as if upon a transparent sphere."[102] In the opening of *Nature*, Emerson, like Plotinus, sets up a thought experiment; in effect he asks whether his readers can imagine a transparent sphere that encompasses "all" yet maintains the distinction and specificity of each sentient part of the unified whole.[103] Refusing to divide the world into the oppositional "essences" of good and evil, Emerson instead projects the unity of essential goodness – a unity that is comprised of multiplicity. To envision this "manyness in oneness" (to borrow William James's phrase), Emerson wagers, will take a lifetime of practice. Having found a practice ground in Plotinus's meditations, Emerson devotes himself to extending this perceptual training throughout his body of writing, as Proust will so propitiously and forcefully discover.

I draw attention to Plotinus's and Emerson's shared understanding of evil as privation – a form of blindness or insensibility to the light and warmth of the Good – to suggest its affinity with a model of sin that Andrew Delbanco recovers in *The Puritan Ordeal* (1989). Privation needs recovery, he explains, because this strain of Puritan belief was quickly eclipsed by a competing model of "positive sin," rooted in the belief that evil is an active, palpable presence with the potential to contaminate and corrupt the unwary. As Delbanco notes, Emerson's father preached from the same pulpit as John Cotton, one of the most powerful Puritan articulators of privation in the early years of the New England colony.[104] Yet Cotton's own preachings index the dramatic shift from privative to positive views of sin over the first decade of colonial life. Thus, when Emerson addresses his New England audience nearly two hundred years after his ancestors' first arrival, his invocation of the privative resurrects an earlier belief in the "transcendent realm of plenitude" that is promised on the other side of privation.[105]

Positive and privative sin correspond with two models of perception. When evil is understood as a pervasive, threatening presence, Delbanco demonstrates, a new premium is placed on methods of perceptual and political control.[106] To draw on Elisa New's phrase once more, positive sin fuels "vision with a vengeance": perception is tasked with vigilantly patrolling the borders between inside and outside, me and not-me, ready to root out and exorcise corrupting forces that could lurk in anything or anyone. As Bercovitch has shown, this regulatory gaze supports exceptionalist claims by separating the Elect from the contaminated. While Emerson is often held responsible for extending exceptionalist vision into a literary legacy, Proust provides crucial evidence that Emerson offered and practiced a wholly different approach to perception. Whereas Puritan privation gave way to positive sin rather than promised plenitude, Proust suggests that via Plotinus, Emerson supplies alternative methods of training transparent vision. As I've tried to show, recognizing the Neoplatonic nature of Proust's Emersonian inheritance also requires revising well-established critical views on Emerson's model of perception. In claiming that the influence of Plotinus on Emerson is illuminated by Proust, I am underlining how a lineage united by literary practices promotes a counterintuitive (even anachronistic) logic of methodological transmission. In the Neoplatonic perceptual practices that Emerson finds in Plotinus, and that Proust finds in both the ancients and the New Englander, a straightforward story of influence becomes displaced. Indeed, the linearity implied by the word "lineage" fails to capture the strangely recursive reading relations I have been tracing through this chapter.

Privation, and the Plenitude of Pragmatism

I want to conclude by making explicit the connection between these reading relations and an equally recursive approach to teaching exemplified by Emerson, but also by his critics. In my introductory discussion of "The Method of Nature" I recalled that Emerson's essays were delivered at public lecture halls before they were ever read. Specifically, many of his lectures were sponsored, hosted, and later published by the Society for the Diffusion of Useful Knowledge, a national organization established with the goal of providing alternatives and supplements to the formal education

system in the United States. Emerson's involvement in the lyceum movement in the US followed his resignation from the Second Church of
Boston in 1832. Countering the deadening effects of "corpse-cold
Unitarianism" by trading the pulpit for the lectern, Emerson parlayed
the forms of the homiletic tradition into a new kind of teaching.[107]
However, Emerson did not consider himself to be breaking with the
religion of his father and forefathers; instead he was asserting his "lifelong
commitment" to a foundational belief that long preceded Unitarian
rationalism – to "the always endangered conviction that evil is
a privation."[108] As Delbanco argues, this conviction is in fact consistent
with the "pedagogic purposes" of John Cotton, his disciple Anne
Hutchinson, and American antinomians whose teachings were intended
to offset a "sense of chronic numbness" observed among brethren.[109]

While this condition of numbness may be chronic, Emerson concludes
"The Divinity School Address" by suggesting that it is not without
"remedy" (*EL*, 88). He closes with a call for "the new Teacher" who will
guide students forward by coming "full circle," that is, by reviving "forms
already existing" (*EL*, 92, 91). Again, the extant spiritual forms he affirms
are rooted in a model of sin that is "privative" not "absolute." "Men have
come to speak of the revelation as somewhat long ago given and done,"
Emerson acknowledges, yet he finds the potential for revelatory renewal in
practices that the Puritans shared with Plotinus, through which plenitude
prevails over privation (*EL*, 83). In this lecture, bygone spiritual and
intellectual teachers become new teachers whose time-worn "doctrine of
inspiration" might "rekindle the smouldering" so that benumbed
Americans "become plastic and new" (*EL*, 79, 91). Emerson concludes
the talk with a reminder addressed to his audience with urgency: "You are
open to the influx of the all-knowing Spirit" (*EL*, 90). This is precisely the
kind of influx that floods Emerson's vision on the common; further, as
Delbanco observes, this is precisely the kind of "transcendent vision that
contemporary ideological critics of American culture have tended to deva-
lue as escapist or apolitical."[110]

Delbanco frames *The Puritan Ordeal* as a contribution to "the history of
what the Puritans called affections," a facet of felt experience, which
remains in his reading "at least partly free from ideological coercion."[111]
A decade later, his student Elisa New identifies pragmatism as a powerful
resource for scholarly work that would resist unilateral condemnations of
"visionary Emersonianism" and that build on Delbanco's concern with
"the 'feel' of being in America, and of being an American."[112] New
celebrates "rising esteem" for the pragmatist criticism Richard Poirier

exemplifies, yet as I previously noted, Poirier's resistance to reducing his methods to a teachable template has prevented such esteem for his pragmatic teachings from mobilizing a "school" of followers.[113] By contrast, Bercovitch's ideological critique of the "exceptionalist self-regard" exemplified by "Emersonian 'originality'" continues to exercise widespread influence over Americanist scholarship.[114] Recent symposia commemorating the reissuing of *The Puritan Origins of the American Self* (1975/2011) and *The American Jeremiad* (1978/2013) confirm "the extravagant scholarly reach of [Bercovitch's] work."[115] Notably, both of these retrospective roundtable discussions were organized by devoted students of Bercovitch who testify to the transformative force of his teaching. As Christopher Looby has attested in an earlier tribute, "while there have been mechanically Bercovitchean essays and books published in the wake of his own, Bercovitch's students have learned precisely not to mimic his work but to reproduce, as well as they can, his independence of mind."[116]

In 2012 Looby and Cindy Weinstein coedited *American Literature's Aesthetic Dimensions*, a volume intended to exemplify the diverse legacy of Bercovitch's ideological criticism. Their introduction frames the collection of essays as a "companionate piece to Sacvan Bercovitch and Myra Jehlen's seminal *Ideology and Classic American Literature*," in the sense that the new volume seeks to examine "the aesthetic dimension of art and experience, but without abandoning the materialist and historicist approaches" exemplified by Bercovitch's work.[117] As the editors suggest, the "resistance to the resistance to aesthetics" they are advocating in fact finds unexpected inspiration in Bercovitch's own writing; they identify an easily overlooked "defense of the aesthetic" in his work, running alongside the form of "ideological analysis that has now, perhaps, started to run out of steam."[118] Their volume provides ample evidence that scholars working loyally after Bercovitch are developing powerful alternatives to "ideology critique."[119]

In Bercovitch's ideologically oriented reading of Emerson, I have found little room for "alternate forms of aesthetic engagement."[120] However, as Looby and Weinstein observe in an intriguing aside, American pragmatism "might very well provide valuable theoretical resources for a rematerialized aesthetic criticism," while noting that these resources remain underutilized.[121] They name Poirier as one of the "few Americanist critics to derive explicit guidance from pragmatism," and then seem to confirm Poirier's dearth of successors when the four hundred pages that follow feature only a single reference to pragmatism (in an essay by Elisa New on Susan Howe's *Peirce's-Arrow*).[122] In working against this neglect, I aim to affirm the utility of pragmatist literary criticism for scholars seeking alternatives to ideology critique. While my pragmatist methods are more explicitly invoked in the chapters that follow, Poirier's self-effacing influence is operative here in my emphasis on praxis and pedagogy, as well as in my own receptivity to idiosyncratic cues that push against canonical critical readings of canonical texts. For Poirier, the pragmatist method can never be abstracted from its object of study. Instead of positioning Poirier against Benjamin or Bercovitch, I look to literary pragmatism to resist the common critical move, often executed in their names, of in turn imposing preconceived frameworks on Emerson and Proust.

CHAPTER 2

Henry James's Syntax of Surprise

> There are two kinds of taste in the appreciation of imaginative literature: the taste for emotions of surprise and the taste for emotions of recognition.
>
> Henry James

When Henry James first identifies the critical duality outlined in the epigraph above, he is describing surprise and recognition as mutually exclusive. This cited line appears at the end of his tribute to the work of the recently deceased Anthony Trollope, published in *The Century Magazine* in 1883. The essay praises Trollope for writing "for the day, the moment" and for helping "the heart of man to know itself."[1] In this context, the reader's "emotions of recognition" are triggered by Trollope's capacity to make his protagonist's motives transparent and familiar. By implication, "emotions of surprise" are only elicited when a character's mind and heart remain opaque, his motivations unclear and strange. James's notice of Trollope's accessibility, it turns out, is double-edged. It is only owing to an artlessly uncomplex form, James suggests, that Trollope is so successful at provoking readerly recognition. This consideration of how narrative transparency either flatters or challenges readerly expectations proved instructive for James; as his own career as a novelist develops, his conceptions of surprise and recognition – as modes of critical appreciation, but also as structures of narrative creativity – will undergo significant adjustment.

In James's early treatments of his abiding expatriate theme, the possibilities of surprise are usurped by shock. *Roderick Hudson* (1875), *The American* (1877), and *The Portrait of a Lady* (1881) each hinge on a sudden moment of recognition where new knowledge arrives all at once. These novels each follow a pattern of similar emplotment, as a confrontational stalemate between awestruck Americans and stultified Europeans forecloses the potential for reciprocity between the continents' representatives. In both cases, the New World innocent's wide-eyed impressionability is overwhelmed, undermined, and finally neutralized by the shocking blows dealt by a representative of the Old World, whose apparently beneficent motives turn out to be a cover for malicious intent and a nefarious past.[2] Until the moment of shocking revelation, James withholds transparent access to this antagonist's heart and mind from both his protagonist and his reader. The reader's narrative perspective is focalized through the naïve American so that the shock of recognition strikes protagonist and reader simultaneously (though such simultaneity depends on the reader suspending his or her recollection of previous James novels that share similar story arcs and character types).

In the novels of his late phase, James relinquishes this organizing paradigm of stark shocks to mount more complex scenes of confrontation modeled on the structural intricacies of surprise. Instead of staging cultural collisions between a New World sense of wonder and a wearily guarded Old World, *The Wings of the Dove* (1902), *The Ambassadors* (1903), and *The Golden Bowl* (1904) feature scenes of mutually ambiguous recognition between transatlantic foils. Whereas the shock of recognition arrives all at once in the early novels, James distinguishes his late style with an idiosyncratic grammar of time. His key scenes of revelation feature labyrinthine sentences that pivot disorientingly between retrospection and anticipation. In place of a singular moment of full disclosure, the surprise of recognition unfolds gradually, drawn out for both character and reader by the sensation of shuttling unpredictably between past and future tenses. As I will demonstrate, this disorienting dynamic is exemplified by the central set piece of *The Ambassadors*, where a potentially violent confrontation is averted by an "overflow of surprise."[3] Just as "the situation was made elastic" thematically for the protagonist, James's sentences formally stretch to accommodate a psychologically and grammatically complex web of anticipatory projections and retroactive reflections (*AM*, 310). In this chapter, I trace a structural trajectory in James, from the narrow and transparent manipulation of shock to an elastic and elaborate syntax of surprise that opens a new horizon of narrative affect, a fluctuating pace and pattern of unfolding that will draw his late readers into unprecedented postures of appreciation.

Newman's Old World

The American epitomizes James's early oppositional approach to representing Old and New World relations. The first half of the novel is narrated from the ingenuously optimistic but also keenly acquisitive perspective of Christopher Newman. A fellow expatriate brashly characterizes the artless hero's project in Europe: "'You're the great Western Barbarian, stepping forth in his innocence and might, gazing a while at this poor effete Old World, and then swooping down on it.'"[4] Indeed, after successfully making his fortune as a manufacturing magnate in New York, the "superlative American" has come to Paris to seek, "in a word, the best article in the market," namely, a wife (A, 37). Newman's own droll embrace of this hyperbolic typecasting initially suggests that the culturally defined stereotypes of innocent barbarism and Old World corruption can be playfully inhabited and negotiated. From this vantage, Europe presents a bottomless source of excitement and pleasure. Propelled on his European tour by the transitory "charm of novelty" in his somewhat haphazard search for a never-ending supply of "new impressions," Newman is the very embodiment of wide-eyed wonder (A, 160).

Upon his introduction to Claire de Cintré, the beguiling daughter of the ancient House of Bellegarde, Newman's distracted impressionability becomes intensely focused. His knack for "piling up consistent wonders" through his "general hospitality to the chances of life" confronts a continental antipathy to any feeling or event that the aristocratic clan is "not perfectly prepared for" (A, 7, 98). As Claire's uncle dryly observes, "there have been no novelties in our house for a great many years" (A, 150). What Richard Poirier describes as The American's confrontation between "'free' and 'fixed' characters" entrenches itself through increasingly insistent and seemingly inevitable images of expansion versus contraction, hospitality versus seclusion, and freedom versus confinement.[5] However, while Madame de Bellegarde and her brother are irretrievably incarcerated by their obscure past, Newman's energetic force of will initially appears capable of liberating Claire from her bondage to the Old World. Viewing himself as "an antidote to oppressive secrets" that paralyze the rest of Claire's family, "what he offered her was, in fact, above all things a vast, sunny immunity" from traumatically repeating the familial history (A, 161).

Newman insistently associates Claire with metaphors of illumination and openness, suggesting she need only claim her rightful place beside him to exchange fixity for freedom: "She was a woman for the light, not for the shade; and her natural line was not picturesque reserve and mysterious melancholy, but frank, joyous, brilliant action" (A, 161). Indeed, he figures both Claire and her brother Valentin as "imprisoned Americans" who find themselves on the wrong side of the continental divide.[6] Claire's "clear bright eyes" gaze out of a face that speaks of New World promise with its "range of expression as delightfully vast as the wind-streaked, cloud-flecked distance on a Western prairie" (*A*, 125). Unlike the previous generation, Claire need only step "across the frontier of friendship" to "find the region vast" with Newman in the New World (*A*, 119).

The American turns on a sudden reversal that stamps out Newman's sanguinity and with it, the novel's lighthearted tone. The Bellegardes' retraction of their consent for Claire's hand in marriage is the first in a series of incidents that leave Newman "profoundly shocked" (*A*, 235). His complacent confidence in the capacity for sheer force of will to steer his future is shattered all at once by inexorable forces that operate with "the strength and insolence of Destiny herself" (*A*, 161, 251). The same impressionability that made Newman receptive to wonder is now recoded as a vulnerability to the ceaseless bombardment of bad fortune that overtakes the remainder of the novel. While these shocks violently impinge upon Newman's experience of the present and his prospects for the future, the source of their gravitational force is located in the Bellegardes' harrowing past, which pulls him irresistibly into its all-deadening orbit. Recognizing it is his own "tranquil unsuspectingness" that has left him so exposed, Newman abruptly armors himself, trading in openness for guardedness (*A*, 162).

Up to the point of the Bellegardes' betrayal, *The American* has primarily been focalized through Newman's previously good-humored attention to the spontaneous here-and-now. In the latter half of the novel, the culturally defined roles with which Newman had lightheartedly flirted begin to congeal into the immovable fixtures of timeless and tragic melodrama, complete with a fatal duel, a gothic convent, and patricide revealed. These hyperbolic plot twists are treated with humorless solemnity; if any comedic narrative vestiges remain, they are at Newman's expense. The narrator now holds him at a distance, even pointedly observing that "there was something lugubriously comical in the way Newman's thoroughly contemporaneous optimism was confronted with this dusky old-world expedient" (*A*, 273). Here, the narrator ironizes Newman's stalwart hope that his unflagging determination to claim his intended prize will eventually outstrip both the Bellegardes' vigilance and the inevitability of tragic fate. When Claire finally cloisters herself away in a Carmelite nunnery beyond both Newman and her family's possessive reach, any meaningful connections across continental borders are definitively denied.

Newman's swift and disillusioning passage from innocence to experience is matched by the novel's equally abrupt shift in tone.

The disconcerting switch from mannered levity to melodramatic gravity suggests James's difficulty in bridging an apparently insurmountable gulf between American and European categories of experience at the level of plot and form. Leon Edel summarizes a number of critical perspectives on how the novel derails itself: "What happened to *The American* was that it set off in one direction – a direction that gave great pleasure to its reader – and then it sharply veered into pathos and disaster."[7] Peter Brooks understands James to be attempting to choose between different novelistic models without yet mastering their integration.[8] The novel's apparent lack of formal coherence manifests a continental divide in its generic split between comic and tragic modes: there is no shared geographical or formal ground on which the representatives of the Old World and New World can meet.

If the novel had remained in the comedic mode, Newman may have achieved communion with Claire and Valentin through love and friendship; however, such an outcome depended on their predisposition for "frank, joyous, brilliant action" (*A*, 218). In the novel's economy, these attributes are aligned with an intrinsically American capacity for freedom. With the onset of melodrama, however, Claire is reclaimed by a gothic model of Old World femininity, living entombed in "monastic rigidity," while Valentin dies at the height of tragic masculinity in a duel of honor (*A*, 263). Unable to loosen stultifying social and novelistic constraints, Claire and Valentin are condemned to mortification, while Newman's capacity for wonder and humor is subsumed by the deadening shocks of their tragic world. Unlike a bildungsroman that tracks the progressive development from innocence to experience, this novel simply exchanges one category for the other. Dealt a decisive blow, Newman himself becomes a vengeful dealer of blows, perpetuating the repetitive cycle of repression and eruption that consumes the latter half of *The American*.

Comparisons can be drawn with *Roderick Hudson* and *The Portrait of a Lady*, which are marked by similarly dramatic turns. The sense of future potential that stretches out in the first half of both of those novels suddenly retracts as the Americans abroad are overcome by oppressive Old World pasts and an inexorable fate – literal death in the case of Roderick Hudson and the death of the vital world of the present for Isabel Archer, who permanently retreats into paralyzing misery. Unlike these protagonists, Newman recrosses the Atlantic, but his return to America finds him as numbed as the Bellegardes he tried to leave behind: "He was himself surprised at the extent of his indifference . . . He tried to interest himself and to take up his old occupations. But they appeared unreal to him . . .

The end of his strong activities had come" (*A*, 343). The only surprise he can muster is directed toward his own disinterest. Finding nothing of his formerly vigorous self in America, Newman ultimately returns to Europe, seeking a solitary existence as empty of shocks as it is of wonder.

The same dichotomies that divide American and European experience in James's early novels – new versus old, innocence versus experience, freedom versus fixity – also map onto the schism that Walter Benjamin establishes between urban modernity and the authentic traditions of an irrecoverable past. For Benjamin, the capacity for a wonder-filled fullness of experience is projected back into a nostalgically longed-for past, a sense James's early novels project back onto America. Whether the receptive capacity for wonder is located "back there" or "back then," shock is the source of geographic and temporal rupture. *The American* demonstrates how the experience of shock divides along geographical as well as temporal lines. These continental rifts and historical breaks are established by an antagonistic logic that dictates violent force will ultimately overpower vulnerability. This, then, is the closed, oppositional narrative structure that James will ultimately overturn, as I want to suggest, by developing an open-ended framework of surprise.

Scene and Non-scene

Since Percy Lubbock's *The Craft of Fiction* (1921) privileged the Jamesian moment of revelation – where complete relations are comprehended in a flash and the "great hidden facts [pass] into the possession of the reader whole" – the dynamics of sudden recognition have remained a linchpin in critical discussions of James's novels.[9] Lubbock idealizes a mode of reading that amalgamates narrative details and events into an immediately apprehended unity; new knowledge "spring[s] up complete and solid in the reader's attention" in the same way it congeals all at once for James's protagonist.[10] As Nicholas Dames argues, the job of Lubbock's ideal reader is not in fact to read but rather "to extract data from the novel that make up mental wholes, to avoid everywhere the temporal flow and affective identifications that infect novel-reading."[11] While the process of reading and the fullness of a novel's form necessarily unfold over time, Lubbock privileges the Jamesian scene as a kind of mnemonic device that momentarily brings the "shadowy and fantasmal form of a book" into sharp focus.[12] The scene counters the dispersal he associates with duration by compressing ranging temporalities into a comprehensive totality.

James's prefaces to the New York Edition of his work (1907–1909) place the narrative representation of what he calls "felt life" at the heart of his novelistic project.[13] Yet Lubbock's influential account of the sudden arrival of full knowledge has occluded the crucial role of feeling in defining the Jamesian scene. Consequently, scarce attention has been devoted to the relationship between feeling and his "scenic" conception of the novel. For James, the term "feeling" encompasses both instantaneity and duration: it describes an immediate visceral response to an event and a protracted process of interpreting the influx of sensory information. By contrast, critics who attend to the place of "felt life" in James's work often separate these entwined temporal orders of experience by privileging either the term "affect" to describe the dynamics of repression and eruption, or "emotion" to refer to allies or enemies of cognitive processing.[14]

When immediacy is opposed to duration, discussions of affects and emotions in James tend to be restricted by an either/or logic.[15] Martha Nussbaum, for instance, influentially argues that James's later work underlines "the cognitive role" that emotions play in making judgments that are responsible to the complexity of moral life.[16] For Nussbaum, emotions either support or inhibit the protagonists' slow progress toward rationally articulable forms of knowledge. In contrast with this cognitive approach to emotion, psychoanalytic discussions of Jamesian desire often subsume any plurality of affective experience into the unidirectional dynamics of repression and sudden exposure. As Kaja Silverman contends, James's "extraordinary obsession with the scenic principle" is evidence that his whole "corpus is bound up in some very fundamental way with the primal scene."[17] Affect is pushed beyond the bounds of conscious knowledge into the unconscious realm of originary trauma.

This equation of the Jamesian scene with either cognitive understanding or primal shock obscures James's own account of how feeling variously inflects his "scenic system" of representation. The scene, for James, is the narrative unit best suited to representing an integrated temporal and experiential structure of feeling, one that his brother William James first theorized in the field of psychology. William's revolutionary proposition is that "emotion . . . is nothing but the feeling of a bodily state" (*PP*, 459). He inverts the prevailing view that emotions are purely psychological states, which in turn catalyze (and thus precede) their bodily manifestations: "An emotion [is] *indicative* of physical changes, not a *cause* of such changes" (*PP*, 131). A stimulating event or object effects a set of "bodily commotions" that might include "quick breathing, palpitating heart, flushed face," which are in turn felt.[18] While there are no clear divisions in one's experience of this structure of feeling, for the purpose of explanation, William breaks it down into sequential parts:

perception of event → bodily response → feeling of bodily response.[19]

Henry James's late novels have internalized this structure, but unlike for the psychologist, explanatory clarity is not his primary aim. As Richard P. Blackmur observes of Henry, "his style grew elaborate to the degree that he rendered shades and refinements of meaning and feeling not usually rendered at all."[20] The famously intricate sentences of Henry's late novels evince an effort to express the imbrications of sensation and feeling that William worked to explicate. For both brothers, lived experience is constituted by the commotions catalyzed by an event coupled with the *feeling* of those fluctuations. As Henry's phrase "felt life" signals, life is fully lived to the extent that it is registered in feeling. The set piece scenes of his late novels suggest that he focuses in particular on scenes of surprise because the corporeal immediacy of encountering the unexpected can give rise to such varied feelings – can be so variously felt and thus so emphatically lived.

Henry James develops two approaches to representing processes of feeling, which eventually interpenetrate: the first, his "scenic system" of representing processes of feeling increasingly incorporates the second, what he calls "non-scenic" elements into his late novels of consciousness (*AN*, 157). A "scenic" treatment of the subject, as James clarifies in his preface to *The Ambassadors*, is synonymous with its dramatic treatment in the theatrical sense of the word; a scene does not portray anything beyond what would be visible to an audience member watching the action unfold on a stage. Conversation and action are depicted with minimal narratorial intervention and few reported thoughts or feelings. While the scene "closely and completely" describes an exterior view of "what 'passes' on a given occasion," the non-scenic elements shift the focus inward, from the event itself to a character's internal, perhaps imperceptible feelings in response (*AN*, 325). By James's own admission, only *The Awkward Age* (1899) and *The Tragic Muse* (1890) – his most direct efforts to "dramatise, dramatise!" – come close to conforming to purely "scenic conditions" (*AN*, 267, 90).

As James explains, *The Ambassadors* achieves dramatic intensity not through strict adherence to "scenic consistency" but through the interiorized perspective of a central consciousness, which determines the course of narrative representation from "beginning to end without intermission or deviation" (*AN*, 322, 317). The theatrically dramatic scene's "direct presentability [is] diminished and compromised" in order to reveal "true inwardness" (*AN*, 325). James's "alternations" between dramatic action and an internalized drama of consciousness move toward "fusion and synthesis" (*AN*, 323). Describing this narrative technique in terms of "opposition and renewal," James claims the "representational virtue" of its "repaired losses" and "insidious recoveries" (*AN*, 326). My goal in tracking his fluctuations between scenic and non-scenic modes in the pivotal episode of *The Ambassadors* is precisely to recover and repair losses of critical insight that are suffered in their conflation with dramatic or traumatic action. Rather than turning on the typical critical terms of sudden recognition and shocking new knowledge, this central encounter suspends familiar forms of knowing with unpredictable floods of feeling.[21]

Strether's Situation

James's exemplary "intensive perceiver" protagonist, Lewis Lambert Strether, overturns a New England mode of "fine cold thought" that "doesn't admit surprises" with experiences of Paris that have "taken all his categories by surprise" (*AN*, 71; *AM*, 297, 161). Sent to Paris from Woollett, Massachusetts, Strether is tasked with retrieving Chad Newsome from the ignoble influence of a married French woman and returning him to the family fold and business. As the name Newsome signals, *The Ambassadors* subjects the modernist category of "the new" to a kind of trial by surprise, testing whether it can continue to evolve. By contrast, the "newness" of Newman proves unrenewable, and *The American* stages a reversion back to entrenched social and novelistic tendencies. Instead of corrupted New World innocence, Strether finds "a case of transformation unsurpassed" has taken place in Chad Newsome under Marie de Vionnet's tutelage (*AM*, 90). This "phenomenon of change" unsettles the categorical thinking imparted to him by the Woollett-based Newsome clan, which leaves "no room . . . no margin, as it were, for any alteration" (*AM*, 90, 298). While the New England contingent of the Newsomes remains coldly immoveable, Europe's representative unexpectedly inspires in Strether a supple responsiveness. At the novel's crux, when Strether is confronted with the illicit intimacy he has long denied, Marie's capacity to surprise combines with Strether's capacity to be taken by surprise; in this chance encounter recognition and misrecognition find a strange coincidence with one another.

Initially, however, Strether replaces Woollett's "fine cold thought" with a "formula" that is equally impervious to surprises (*AM*, 71, 97). Imposing artificially ennobled interpretations of Chad as an archetypal "man of the world" and Marie as a paragon of feminine virtue, Strether stakes himself on a gilded vision of their "virtuous attachment" (*AM*, 97, 112). Even when critics have not explicitly designated the novel's climax as a primal scene, Strether's realization that "they knew how to do it" and "this wouldn't at all events be the first time" is generally read through the lens of shock (*AM*, 307). From this perspective, the scene of revelation, which I will read more closely in a moment, cements Strether's impotent position as an observer who is traumatized equally by what he has seen and by having been caught in the act of looking.[22] His final return to Woollett is taken to confirm Strether's failure to fulfill the injunction to "live all you can" as an actor rather than a bystander to one's own life (*AM*, 132). Ross Posnock conjectures that William James would have deemed Strether "a hopeless case of 'ontological wonder-sickness'" on the basis that he "renounces an active life for idealist, nostalgic contemplation."[23] In my view, something new emerges between Strether and Marie at the climactic convergence of James's "scenic" and "non-scenic" systems – something which is not reducible to originary trauma, nostalgic regret, or even paralyzing inaction.

On the pivotal day in question, Strether sets forth into the countryside outside of Paris, spurred by an "artless" urge toward picturesque "French ruralism," though his claim of artlessness is immediately belied by his description of the landscape as "the background of fiction, the medium of art, the nursery of letters" (*AM*, 301). The imaginative border Strether places around the pastoral setting further underscores his pictorial impulse as its "enclosing lines" align with the "oblong gilt frame" of a Lambinet canvas he was too poor to purchase as a young man (*AM*, 302). Strether now imagines he is viewing the countryside through the same window that stood between his youthful self and the unattainable canvas. At the same time that Strether seeks tight conformity between the landscape before him and his internal terrain of consciousness, the temporal and spatial barrier asserted by the phantasmic pane of glass denies any reciprocal exchange between himself and his environment. Strether "sufficiently command[s]" the elements of the scene before him into a fixed "composition" that achieves "a finer harmony" by conforming with Lambinet's "plan" (*AM*, 302, 303).

When two figures insert themselves into the frame, Strether at first succeeds in assimilating them into his idyllic order. The charming couple, he declares, is "exactly the right thing" to complete the desired compositional harmony: "It was suddenly as if these figures, or something like them, had been wanted in the picture" (*AM*, 307). However, at the same moment that polished aesthetic perfection seems within his grasp, the smooth calm that "the spell of the picture" had cast is disturbed by a "sharp start" (*AM*, 306, 308). Strether's heightened attention converges on the lady's parasol, "which made so fine a pink point in the shining scene," as it twirls to reveal the identity of the couple as none other than Chad Newsome and Marie de Vionnet (*AM*, 308). Observing that the two are "expert, familiar, frequent," Strether realizes he is intruding on a private tryst (*AM*, 307).

To allay the potential for the situation to spiral into a "sharp fantastic crisis," Strether extends his initial startle into a "performance" that they can all partake in: "He had but one thing to do – to settle their common question by some sign of surprise" (*AM*, 308, 311, 308). By exteriorizing his surprise into a show of signs that can be recognized from the water, Strether gesturally conveys a feeling that has not yet cohered into thought. In this way, the feeling of surprise becomes readable in embodied actions and expressions, though it momentarily remains an unreadably interior state, illegible even to the one experiencing it. Strether alternates between internalizing the encounter and externalizing the stance of detached observer who watches from a distance. As he moves between these two perspectives, the "scenic" and "non-scenic" become increasingly implicated.

When Marie's reciprocal "overflow of surprise" merges with Strether's own, "the situation was made elastic" (*AM*, 310). The eruption of "violence [is] averted . . . by the mere miracle of the encounter" (*AM*, 309). Though "their wonderful accident" is charged by the potential for eruptive conflict, one side doesn't overtake the other; all are seized by a surprise event that none anticipated. Strether and Marie pass through fluidly indeterminate states of mutual responsiveness where the "sudden and rapid" sense of shock and crisis bleeds into "blankness and wonder" (*AM*, 308). Through their shared effort to float in "vagueness," they together find "something to put a face upon," so that they can face one another – however shamefaced they may be – on the common ground of "their friendship, their connexion" (*AM*, 313, 310, 313).

The Temporality of Feeling

The critics who have been most attentive to the distinctive temporality structuring James's late style have tended to draw on psychoanalytic frameworks. Kent Puckett furthers Silverman's reading of James's "primal scene" by connecting Freudian trauma with his concept of *Nachträglichkeit*, translated as "afterwardsness," to nuance the dynamics of "retroactive understanding."[24] As Puckett explains, afterwardsness depends on a projection into the future, which in turn "*makes* the past."[25] Puckett contrasts Freud's insistence on the incommensurability of these positions, "forward or back," with James's insistence that one "cannot finally decide between reading forward or backwards, from trauma to symptom or from symptom to trauma."[26] I want to suggest that "James's particular investment in the middle" is meaningful in an even more general way than Puckett intends, specifically useful for considering the closed loop between "past traumas and present symptoms" but also broadly useful in figuring James's relationship to time.[27]

While Leo Bersani likewise looks to psychoanalysis to make sense of James's repeated invocations of a time "afterwards," his account of "retrospective reflection" similarly extends beyond traumatic events.[28] Bersani describes "the Jamesian tendency to extract *all* events, as well as all perspectives on them, from any specified time, and to transfer them to a before or an after in which they are de-realized in the form of anticipations or retrospections."[29] In extracting his protagonists from a "locatable time," James also refuses "all embodiment," transforming those characters into what Bersani calls "pure potentiality" or "pure virtuality."[30] Bersani concludes by aligning this potentiality at the heart of James's fiction with the therapeutic potential of analytic exchanges that entertain "any possibility of behavior or thought as only possibility."[31] Suspended in the virtuality of conversation, freed from physical or temporal constraints, "desiring fantasies" can proliferate and range widely.[32]

Following Brian Massumi, I aim to connect the idea of a suspended "middle" to the idea of "pure potentiality" by way of William James. In Puckett's and Bersani's usage, the terms refer to traumatic and therapeutic scenes, both of which are "sequestered" from ordinary existence.[33] By contrast, Massumi draws on James to define concepts of the middle and potentiality as "immediately embodied" experiences of everyday life.[34] To live in "the middle," Massumi asserts, is to live "life at no remove;" that is, to live "in the middling immediacy of its always 'going on.'"[35] Massumi then equates life's "messy middling goings-on" with its "pure potentiality."[36] From James, Massumi learns that "pure" in fact means mixed, referring to middle ranges of experience where subject and object, past, present, and future become entangled and indiscriminate.[37] This is the same messy, middling commixture that William James describes in his chapter on "The Emotions" in *The Principles of Psychology* and that Henry James represents in the French countryside scene above.

Both Jameses realize the impossibility of recovering some "raw" experience, prior to cognitive processing; instead they emphasize the way that processes of cognition come "back through the middle," which for William is embodied feeling and which Henry calls "felt life."[38] William explains how this works by correcting the following "commonsense" encapsulation of an unexpected encounter: "We meet a bear, are frightened and run" (*PPII*, 449–50). According to James, this sequence misses the bodily response that comes between the initial perception and the subsequent reaction. The sight of the bear excites changes in one's muscles, glands, heart, and skin, which are only recursively felt as fear; we may already be running by the time our emotional response catches up with the more immediate visceral reaction (*PPII*, 450). Emotions are for James always retrospective interpretations – the recursive action of feeling gets looped "back through the middle" of bodily states, and those physical excitations become *felt* as emotions. Crucially, there is for James no structural distinction to be drawn between a chance encounter with a bear or an old friend; both events trigger a set of sensations and reverberations in the body, which might variously be felt as fear or delight, as violent shock or pleasurable astonishment.

Massumi distills a pithy takeaway from James's bear example – "Participation precedes recognition" – which underlines deep resonances between William's psychological model of emotion and Henry's narrative models of scene and non-scene.[39] The countryside episode in *The Ambassadors* is remarkable precisely for the way it extends and enacts this participation as a protracted relational process that defers recognition and finally renders it beside the point. Strether externalizes the "sharp start" he feels at the prick of Madame de Vionnet's parasol as an outward show of an inward state. His enacted "sign of surprise" then allows its retrospective interpretation to unfold as a shared act, carried out on the "common ground" – what Massumi might call the "middle ground" – of his "connexion" with Marie. Mutually embodied feeling makes the situation "elastic" such that all interpretive frameworks remain suspended and supple.

Citing William James, Massumi likewise describes the participation that precedes recognition as a "lived relation" of surprise, declaring "relational surprises" to be "the norm" in a pragmatic universe where "belief is 'lived.'"[40] Yet we fail to tap this "inexhaustible reserve of surprise," Massumi cautions, when we preemptively convert "the surprise coming-to-consciousness" into "an anticipation of recognition."[41] The "preconversion of surprise into cognitive confidence" that Massumi warns against is the equivalent of patrician Woollett's "fine cold thought," which proudly "doesn't admit surprises."[42] The function of the virtual or "pure potential" – the detemporalized and despatialized concept around which Massumi orients his oeuvre – is to counter anticipatory certainties "and make *surprise* a universal, constitutive force."[43] He frames his experimental meditations on potentiality as his primary means of practicing the following pragmatism-ready injunction: "See it, be surprised, live it."[44]

Via William James's model of time, Massumi articulates some of the difficulties encountered in following his own directives to inhabit present moments of surprise. "We live forwards," William writes, "but we understand backwards."[45] It's worth unpacking the theory of temporal perception condensed into this statement in order to further understand how Henry explores and extends his brother's insights. William's foundational observation that consciousness moves like an ever-changing stream has important consequences for how time is qualitatively experienced. He writes: "*The knowledge of some other part of the stream, past or future, near or remote, is always mixed in with our knowledge of the present thing.*" The defining features of the stream of consciousness – its continuity and its movement – depend on how an experience of the present is at every moment shaped by "retrospective and the prospective sense[s] of time," by the "lingerings of old objects" and the "incomings of new." In short, our present perceptions are always inflected by "the germs of memory and expectation" (*PP*, 606).

William's recognition that the "instant field of the present" cannot be isolated from the past or future does not preclude his abiding efforts to access a realm of experience untethered from recollection or anticipation (*WII*, 1175). With the phrase "the specious present" James acknowledges that time is lived "prospectively as well as retrospectively," even while carving out a narrow window of experience that is ostensibly freed from recollection or anticipation (*WII*, 1181). The present is "specious" insofar as it has already melted into a remembered past by the time we try to focus on it. Yet James aims to reclaim that "just-past moment" from the archiving jaws of memory by expanding the interval that we call the present (*PP*, 638). According to his redefinition, the specious present describes the brief unification of attention, the "*duration* of which we are immediately and incessantly sensible" (*PP*, 613). The specious present, in other words, is an extended present; it has a duration that extends to encompass the length of time within which we are able to make immediate associations among incoming phenomena. For instance, James argues that a flash of lightning and the delayed thunderclap are apprehended within a *suspended present*, which spans our capacity to associate those phenomena as a single event.

This concept allows William to distinguish between two registers of recall: an immediate and unfinished process of recollection (by which we might connect lightning to a thunderclap), and the less-suspended process of memory we use to recollect events from a more remote past. The utility of this distinction is exaggerated by how a novel can collapse it: in the final sequence of *The Ambassadors*, Henry develops a distinctive syntax that makes it hard to differentiate between the two registers of recollection that William works to distinguish. With sentences that encompass a kind of "temporal double vision," Henry draws together and confuses time that has long past and time that has just past, pushing the speciousness of the present to its limits.[46]

Double Time

To parse the precise grammar of this double temporality, I borrow from the language of narratology, which may at first seem like a strange fit with William's psychology of time and with Henry's unconventional approach to narrative sequencing. Yet the terms Gérard Genette called "prolepsis" and "analepsis" – the narratological equivalents of a cinematic flashforward and flashback – are helpful for disentangling the dueling time structures that become entwined in pivotal episodes of *The Ambassadors* and in James's late novels more generally. Genette introduces these terms in a chapter titled "Order" to distinguish between something that happened previously (analepsis) and something that is anticipated in the future (prolepsis).[47] In Genette's usage, these terms are primarily tools for establishing linear order by classifying narrative action into clear categories of "earlier" or "later," events that took place "before" or "after" the narrated present. Contrastingly, I focus on distinctive moments of "proleptic analepses" in James where these categories collide to disturb the narrative order.[48]

Strether's encounter with the couple in the country is one of two extended scenes in *The Ambassadors* that are emphatically shaped by the temporal duality of "proleptic analepsis." In an earlier scene, the narrator shuttles disorientingly between the present moment of Strether's first meeting with Chad at the theater and the temporal perspective of a future when that initial encounter would come to lie in the protagonist's remembered past. At the very instant Strether realizes he is "in the presence of Chad himself," the narrative voice proleptically projects him into various future moments of analeptic reflection:

> Our friend was to go over it afterwards again and again – he was going over it much of the time that they were together, and they were together constantly for three or four days: the note had been so strongly struck during that first half-hour that everything happening since was comparatively a minor development. The fact was that his perception of the young man's identity – so absolutely checked for a minute – had been quite one of the sensations that count in life; he certainly had never known one that had acted, as he might have said, with more of a crowded rush. And the rush, though both vague and multitudinous, had lasted a long time, protected, as it were, yet at the same time aggravated, by the circumstance of its coinciding with a stretch of decorous silence. (*AM*, 89)

The narrator places Strether at several different intervals from the first "minute" he is flooded by "a crowded rush" of "sensations" – first, at the furthest temporal remove from the present into the period of "three or four days" spent in Chad's company after they meet; next, into the "half-hour" introduction at the theater; finally, returning to the "vague and multitudinous" rush of unarticulated feeling that fills the "stretch of decorous silence" marking the first moment of their meeting. From each of these projected perspectives, Strether can reflect on the overwhelming immediacy of the present in the past tense.[49]

When Strether happens upon Chad with Madame de Vionnet in the country, the narrator frames the chance meeting with similar formulations of proleptic analepsis: "Strether was to remember afterwards" and "was to reflect later" and "was to remember further still, in subsequent meditation," various recollections of an experience subsumed by wordless feeling in the true present of its occurring (*AM*, 310). Prolepsis and analepsis likewise converge in key episodes of *The Golden Bowl* and *The Wings of the Dove*: Maggie Verver "was to remember afterwards"; Kate Croy "afterwards imaged to herself"; and "it was not till afterwards that [Milly Theale] fully knew."[50] In *The Ambassadors*, the alternating focalizations of an anticipating, experiencing, and remembering Strether are further complicated by James's free indirect style, which entangles these perspectives and temporalities with that of a narrator who also implicates the reader:

> Since we have spoken of what he was, after his return, to recall and interpret, it may as well immediately be said that his real experience of these few hours put on, in that belated vision – for he scarce went to bed till morning – the aspect that is most to our purpose. He then knew more or less how he had been affected – he but half knew at the time. (*AM*, 311).

In this passage futural projections and retroactive reflections do double duty as metanarrative interjections. Incorporating future insight into past events, James's stuttering syntax tracks Strether's circuitous movements between experiencing and understanding, feeling and knowing. It ultimately remains unclear whether the benefit of foreknowledge belongs to the narrator, character, or both.

James adds another layer of interpretive complexity to this passage with his conspicuous use of "we" and "our." The plural pronoun and possessive draw attention to the reader's role in tracking the sentence's looping temporal and perspectival turns. The double temporality of the passage is redoubled again when the narrator overtly juxtaposes the time of reading with the time of narrative action. Proleptic analepsis hence collapses the period between Strether's "real experience" in the country and his interpretive recollection of it a "few hours" later in Paris. The narrative voice underlines the implications of this temporal economy for readers: since "we" have so efficiently compressed the narrative time span, the audience may be addressed more "immediately." By condensing hours, days, and weeks into compact clauses, Henry James's syntax achieves the narratological equivalent of William James's specious present. This is to say that proleptic analepses allow readers to experience "longer time-spaces" as a "short duration of which we are immediately and incessantly sensible," where intervals of varying length opened by projection and retrospection are felt as the same near-past and near-future that for William constitute a suspended present (*PP*, 631). In this way, Henry stretches the speciousness of the present to the time it takes to read his sentence.

Time at Sea

Studies of time in Henry James's novels frequently focus on the "past [that is] always present," "always spreading out," while relegating future potential into a "retrospective present."[51] As I've tried to demonstrate, William James's psychologies of time and feeling retrieve an equally vital future dimension of the countryside scene, from which the past and present are recast. The experience of surprise suffuses Strether's encounter with *éventualité*, to borrow Françoise Dastur's term – the potentiality of the unforeseen.[52] At the moment of its sudden dehiscence, surprise is not yet stabilized into determinate thought; only from a projected future moment can it be retrospectively woven into the fabric of time and understanding. Clearing previous frames of reference and reorienting the present, surprise opens the enlivening possibility that what is yet to come need not repeat what came before.

Strether's retroactive processing of his chance meeting with the lovers extends over the course of his return to Paris and over the remainder of the novel, reaching no final conclusion. But unlike the experience of traumatic repetition, each prospective and retrospective turn further loosens entrenched patterns of perception, allowing Strether to access more capacious middle ranges of thinking and feeling. As he apprehends the air of "fiction and fable" that pervades "the charming affair," he realizes that Chad and Marie's "detached and deliberate" lies are inseparable from "the deep, deep truth of the intimacy revealed" (*AM*, 311, 313). Refusing to rigidly divide truth from fabrication, or integrity from duplicity, Strether relinquishes any illusion that the pair's incalculable intimacy is fully knowable: the attachment can no more be condemned as dissolute than it can be valorized as innocent. Ultimately, Strether recognizes his culpability in providing "a common priceless ground for them to meet upon"; the admixture "of his art and his innocence" matches the couple's own (*AM*, 319).

Beyond acknowledging how "his intervention had absolutely aided and intensified their intimacy," Strether reproaches his own desire to fix ambiguous relations: "He had made them – and by no fault of their own – momentarily pull it for him, the possibility, out of this vagueness" (*AM*, 319, 313). Back in Paris, having recognized their mutual implication in "the situation," Strether and Marie are newly able to face one another in a state of exposed vulnerability. Cast adrift in the aftermath of this meeting, Strether "give[s] himself quite up" to drifting indeterminacy rather than anchoring himself to final conclusions (*AM*, 316). Having relinquished "command of the situation," Strether simply floats, "well in port, the outer sea behind him" (*AM*, 320, 327). There he "rest[s] against the side of his ship," treading water in "the iridescence of his idleness" (*AM*, 327). For the remainder of the novel, Strether stays "at sea," letting whatever comes wash over him, practicing immersive receptivity as his primary form of activity.

Strether plunges deeper still into aquatic tropes, comparing his experience to drifting down the "sacred river" of Xanadu in Coleridge's poem "Kubla Khan": "It faced him, the reckoning ... [he] would float to it doubtless duly through these caverns of Kubla Khan" (*AM*, 327). The Alph river of Coleridge's poem runs "through caverns measureless to man," tracing a "mazy" subterranean path through "ceaseless turmoil seething," erupting into "a mighty fountain" before sinking "in tumult into a lifeless ocean." Strether, like the poem's narrator, seeks a "mingled measure" where he can be "floated midway on the waves" between calm and "tumult."[53]

Critics have carefully attended to what Bill Brown calls James's "spatializing poetics of cognition," but reading William alongside Henry reveals how any metaphor that externalizes "thinking" must incorporate the strange temporality that coalesces into feeling.[54] For the Jameses, feeling unfolds according to a "law of successive aspects" or "successive takings."[55] Claiming the latter phrase as a touchstone for William's activist, pluralist philosophy (a phrase that variously refers to the processual dynamics of "takings-up," "taking-form," "takings-effect," and "'*takings*' by experience"), Massumi argues "it is a given" for James "that no event can lay down the law in a way that essentially predefines its succession."[56] Both Jameses evoke continuous multiplicity rather than sequential order with their watery figures of streams and oceans, waves and flows. William makes the relationship between his aquatic metaphors and time explicit when he writes, "We live, as it were, upon the front edge of an advancing wave-crest, and our sense of a determinate direction in falling forward is all we cover of the future of our path" (*WII*, 1172). On the crest of the wave, we are "a *that* which is not yet any definite *what*, tho ready to be all sorts of whats; full both of oneness and of manyness" (*WII*, 782–83). It is in this cresting "thatness," where subject and object, past and future are "as yet" undetermined, that Massumi finds an "inexhaustible reserve of surprise."[57]

Joan Richardson explicitly connects the ubiquitous maritime metaphors in *The Ambassadors* and the novel's pervasive use of the word "vague" and its variations ("vaguely," "vagueness," "waves," "wavering") to the figures of vagueness and flow that William James uses in *Principles* to characterize "the stream of consciousness."[58] William's project, in his own summation, is "the reinstatement of the vague and inarticulate to its proper place in our mental life" (*WI*, 164). For both brothers, vagueness marks the gap between floods of fluctuating experience and the expressive means available to represent that stream.[59] But whereas the psychologist remains invested in finding ways to conceive a bridging of this gap, Henry seeks a syntax that can represent the unbridgeable interval and actually incorporate this gap itself into his prose. Like William, Henry finds a model of such syntax in Emerson.

Moralist or Stylist

As I outlined in the introduction, William James credits Emerson with the primary insight that he brought first to the practice of pedagogy and then to his method of pragmatism: perception, judgment, and action "all depend on the *feelings* things arouse in us" (*WI*, 841). Emerson provides a counterpoint to the more instrumental directives of psychology, which points William toward new avenues for pursuing the "practical question of the conduct of life" (*EL*, 943).[60] As William writes to Henry, Emerson has thrown a paradoxically "practical light" on his path by illuminating those fleeting moments and fluctuating feelings that might otherwise be overlooked because they cannot be put to utilitarian ends.[61] Acknowledging the expressive limits of psychology, Emerson exemplifies for William what it means to go beyond a descriptive account "'about' this object or 'about' that," to both convey and perform the "flights and perchings" of thought (*PP*, 246, 243). William echoes Emerson's calls for a "vehicular and transitive" language better equipped to express "a feeling of *and*, a feeling of *if*, a feeling of *but*, and a feeling of *by*" (*EL*, 463; *PP*, 245). Henry's late novels seek a syntax that is up to this task. Though both brothers subscribe to what Henry calls "a religion of doing," it is the novelist who insists most forcefully that "to 'put' things is very exactly and responsibly and interminably to do them. Our expression of them . . . belong[s] as nearly to our conduct and our life as every other feature of our freedom" (*AN*, 347).[62]

While the brothers were growing up, Emerson was a fixture in their lives as Henry James Sr.'s close friend and as William's godfather. In life he loomed as an icon for the James boys, but it was only after his death in 1882 that William began to read Emerson with a keen attention that quickly came to inform every aspect of his thinking and writing. Henry, however, was not as immediately receptive to Emerson's literary influence. Early in his career he held up Emerson as a moral exemplar but took little account of his writing. Around the time that he was composing *The American*, Henry's critical writings characterize Emerson as an unworldly innocent who has successfully sheltered himself from the corrupting European influences that breed a numbed cynicism in an early protagonist like Newman. The same measures that afford Emerson "a ripe unconsciousness of evil" also leave him, in Henry's view, largely insensible to the nuanced complexities of more cosmopolitan cultural forms.[63] He suggests that Emerson's simplicity of vision remains uncontaminated by Europe and modernity to the detriment of his aesthetic sensibilities.

In an early review of a biography of Emerson, Henry reservedly praises "the wonder of Boston" for manifesting an overflow of feeling unhindered by form.[64] "Failing to strike us as having achieved a style," Emerson's "remarkable outburst of Romanticism on Puritan ground" is "not composed at all" and can be valued on "the strength of his message alone."[65] With his assertion that Emerson "never really mastered the art of composition," James upholds Matthew Arnold's contestation of "Emerson's complete right to the title of a man of letters."[66] Instead of directly engaging with Emerson's work, James presents a character study that depicts the writer as a passive conduit of natural wonders and moral lessons.

As previously discussed, critics who contest Emerson's literary merit tend to disparage and disqualify his contradictory and unsystematic prose. But James's appraisal is just the opposite, owing to the scarce attention he affords Emerson's essays. He focuses instead on the "private correspondence" that best captures the "texture of [Emerson's] history" – a texture he deems unvaryingly flat:[67]

> As most of us are made up of ill-sorted pieces, his reader . . . envies him this transmitted unity, in which there was no mutual bustling or crowding of elements. It must have been a kind of luxury to be – that is to feel – so homogenous.[68]

In privileging the private and personal over the compositional, Henry initially misses what William values first and foremost in Emerson: the distinctly unsettling force of sentences which William deemed "as fine as anything in literature" (*WII*, 38).

Countering claims of homogeneity, William embraces Emerson's heterogeneous prose for the way it sensitizes readers to what is familiar, frequent, close at hand. Far from separating his message from the medium, Emerson's "mission," according to William, was to find "the worthy form of each perception": "His genius was insatiate for experience, and his truth had to be clad in the right verbal garment. The form of the garment was so vital with Emerson that it was impossible to separate it from the matter" (*WII*, 1119). His vertiginous turns of syntax and sentiment repeatedly return readers to his touchstone question: "Where do we find ourselves?" (*EL*, 471). Giving himself over to the dizzying leaps and plunges of Emerson's sentences, William finds himself disoriented, but the process of reorientation renews his attention to the now and the near and to a "higher vision of inner significance" (*WI*, 848).

William's insistence that "Emerson's mission culminated in his style" offers a corrective to Henry's early dismissal of his formal flatness (*WII*, 1120). Over the years when Henry was composing his last three completed novels, William's letters narrate his "reading of the divine Emerson, volume after volume" as an experience of immersive enrichment.[69] Those volumes inspire him "to report in one book, at least, such impression that my own intellect has received from the universe."[70] In fact, William goes on to make such a report in every book he writes thereafter.

Reoriented by Emerson's writing, he reckons in each case with "accepting a universe unfinished, with doors and windows open to possibilities uncontrollable in advance" in place of an "absolutely closed-in world" (*WII*, 1054).

In May of 1903, as the centenary celebration of Emerson's birth approached, William wrote to Henry with redoubled fervor in anticipation of the address he was preparing to deliver in Emerson's honor:

> Emerson is exquisite! I think I told you that I have to hold forth in praise of him at Concord on the 25th ... You too have been leading an Emersonian life – though the environment differs to suit the needs of the different psychophysical organism which you present.[71]

Henry's response to his brother on the eve of the commemoration is twofold. Henry writes of his "longing to sit in the audience at Concord" and wishes him well with a metaphor of floating that owes as much to Emerson as it does to William: "May you be floated grandly over your cataract – by which I don't mean have any matter of *fall*, but only be a Niagara of eloquence, all continuously, whether above or below the rapids."[72]

In that same letter the expatriate commits to return to the United States after a thirty-year absence. Though he had written about America throughout his extended period away, to William, Henry expressed fear that distance and time had rendered his subject an abstraction. He determined that the only way to counter its growing impalpability was to return from whence he came so that "experience may convert itself, through the senses, through observation, imagination and reflection now at their maturity, into vivid and solid *material*, into a general renovation of one's too monotonised grab-bag."[73] Only by moving across the ground of his "birth-place" could he hope to recapture its "poetry of motion."[74] Here, Henry directly echoes Emerson's contention "that motion, poetry . . . affect[s] our convictions of the reality of the external world" (*EL*, 38).

During the years that William's correspondence with his brother featured Emerson most prominently, Henry was transitioning into what F. O. Matthiessen calls his "major phase."[75] Commentators have suggested multiple factors that potentially contributed to Henry James's distinctive late style. However, critics' marked emphasis on what Edmund Wilson first termed "the shock of recognition" in his late novels of consciousness has obscured the fact that those scenes of recognition are structured by the Emersonian temporality of "an everlasting Now": a temporal paradigm that reorients attention from moment to moment rather than fixing on a singular moment of breakage.[76] Though Henry determined early on that he knew what to expect from the Concord "moralist," his brother's correspondence and writing at the turn of the century introduced him to Emerson's oeuvre as if for the first time.[77]

Henry initially defines both Emerson and his innocent American protagonists by the unalloyed "unity" of their vision (*AN*, 171). His late novels depict a variegated field of perceptual receptivity shaped by the ongoing process that Emerson describes as rendering oneself "impressionable" to surprises (*EL*, 965). Newman bears an uncanny likeness to James's reductive depiction of Emerson's naïve New World sense of wonder, while Strether more closely resembles the Emerson who approaches life as a "series of surprises." Though Emerson celebrates "the impressionable man" as "the great man," he also acknowledges that sensitizing oneself to the point that "infinitesimal attractions" register as "new perceptions" entails precarious exposure (*EL*, 965, 331). Having been "surprised out of [his] propriety," Strether exemplifies the risks involved in cultivating a "way of life . . . by abandonment" (*EL*, 414).

Psychologies of Surprise

As William James attests, "each of us literally *chooses*, by his way of attending to things, what sort of universe he shall appear to himself to inhabit" (*PP*, 401). Strether chooses to inhabit an "a pluralistic, restless universe" by committing to dwell in the undefined realms of human relation (*WI*, 589). But his choice to give himself over to the unpredictable currents of experience is just one response to uncertainty. While the protagonist of an early novel like *The American* can only interpret an unexpected encounter in one way – as a traumatic shock – Henry James's late novels feature a remarkable range of reactions to the unsettling experience of surprise. Henry's emphasis on this interpretive variability dovetails with the work of several psychologists who developed William's model of emotion into a system of affects. A brief account of these theories of surprise will underline Henry James's own crucial contributions to a psychology of feeling.

William's transition from psychology to practical philosophy precludes any specific investigations of surprise in his first field of study, but a half century later, in his monumental work *Affect Imagery Consciousness* (1962), Silvan Tomkins gives pride of place to surprise because it confirms for him a foundational Jamesian insight: the experience of an emotion involves an interpretive act.[78] Yet the interpretive mechanism is feeling rather than cognition: bodily "excitations" are felt as an emotion. In the case of surprise, that recursive turn of feeling invites remarkable interpretive variety because surprise plays a role opposite to all the other affects; rather than supplying sensory information, its "resetting" function clears the perceptual apparatus, rendering it freshly receptive to incoming information, but also preventing the immediate coalescence of any interpretable message.[79] Instigating a momentary hiatus between a stimulus and our affective, cognitive, or motor response to it, surprise thus precludes an automatized behavioral feedback loop.

Surprise is the "ancillary to every other affect" because it primes a *capacity* for affectively charged experiences but carries no predetermined content. Reduced to its most basic mechanism, surprise is simply a "circuit breaker" that "orients the individual to turn his attention away from one thing to another." The experience of seizure retains a neutral "feeling tone" until the influx of new sensory information it has allowed is retrospectively processed; by the time the experience assumes a positive or negative charge, it is no longer surprise, strictly speaking. While Tomkins reserves the term surprise to designate the seizing and clearing of attention, he acknowledges how easily it is conflated or confused with other affects because it has already passed into something else by the time it can be reflected upon; on the extreme end of the affective continuum it might be felt as a shock, but it could just as easily segue into middle-ranging experiences of interest, confusion, or anxiousness.[80]

As Paul Ekman, a student of Tomkins, similarly observes, "Once you have determined the nature of the surprising event, you are no longer surprised."[81] Even the simple statement, "I am surprised," is a necessarily retrospective evaluation of a moment or an event that has already passed. How then can surprise be expressed in all its open-ended immediacy? Ekman, like Tomkins, limits himself to reading the signs of surprise that are registered in its distinctive facial expression of raised eyebrows and a dropped jaw.[82] Focusing on these physiological manifestations, both psychologists register the quasi-linguistic vocalization of surprise, the onomatopoeic "oh!" produced by the open-mouthed intake and audible exhalation of air.

Psychological studies of the language of emotion underline the difficulty of articulating surprise. The psycholinguist Barbara Kryk-Kastovsky organizes expressions of surprise on an "iconicity-conventionality scale" that places the spontaneous exclamations on one end and fixed idioms on the other. The "oh" sound is strongly iconic in the sense that it expresses with "possible universality" the "emotion experienced by a speaker faced by a sudden, unexpected turn of events."[83] As one moves toward the "conventional" end of the scale, the linguistic signs of surprise pass from direct reactions to retrospective "reports" of an "emotional (positive or negative) reaction to a new state of affairs."[84] Kryk-Kastovsky's enumeration of formulaic phrases like "I can't believe it!" or "Is that so?" underscores the highly mediated nature of surprise utterances that trail after the immediate experience. Meredith Osmond's study of preposition use in the "surprise group" of emotional expressions further specifies the strangeness of referring to "the moment of discovery of some situation," which "cannot be prolonged at will or recreated by recalling the moment of impact." We are surprised "at" rather than "with" something because the latter preposition implies a duration that is by definition alien to the experience.[85] As I will show, the poverty of these expressive possibilities becomes an engine of narrative innovation in the novels that epitomize James's late style.[86]

Verver's Issue

Henry James forecasts psychological and psycholinguistic insights into the nature of surprise by depicting Strether's efforts to stay suspended in the fleeting moment of seizure, but also by portraying a character on the other end of the spectrum who refuses to dwell in vague feeling and rushes instead to claim cognitive clarity. Adam Verver of *The Golden Bowl* reacts to incalculable forms of intimacy by circumscribing them into restrictive arrangements. Whereas Strether drifts aimlessly beneath Kubla Khan's city, Verver's mission is to establish his own Xanadu: "a stately pleasure dome," "girdled round" with "walls and towers" that hold the wilderness at bay.[87] Like Khan's stronghold, the bordering walls of the Verver estate demarcate strict divisions between inside and out; cultivated order fortifies against the chaos beyond and below.

With these characters, James exemplifies opposed approaches to navigating the experience of disorientation: Strether welcomes the dusky maze of confusion, while Verver seeks the dawn of clarity. Desperate to resolve "the vagueness [that has] spread itself about him like some boundless carpet," Verver declares "he should never sleep again" till he found the unnamed "something" he had been "vainly groping for" (*GB*, 152–53). I quote at length the extended account of Verver's emergent "something" because the passage epitomizes James's syntax of surprise, while also revealing how readily the experience of the unexpected gives way to something else – in this case, to wonder, the "passion" that Descartes championed as the emblem of rational discernment:

Light broke for him at last . . . As at a turn of his labyrinth he saw his issue,
which opened out so wide, for the minute, that he held his breath with
wonder. He was afterwards to recall how just then the autumn night seemed
to clear to a view in which the whole place, everything round him . . . lay
there as under some strange midnight sun. It all met him during these
instants as a vast expanse of discovery, a world that looked, so lighted,
extraordinarily new, and in which familiar objects had taken on
a distinctness that, as if it had been a loud, a spoken pretension to beauty,
interest, importance, to he scarce knew what, gave them an inordinate size.
The hallucination, of whatever he might have called it, was brief, but it
lasted long enough to leave him gasping. The gasp of admiration had by this
time however lost itself in an intensity that quickly followed – the way the
wonder of it, since wonder was in question, truly had been the strange delay
of his vision. He had these several days groped and groped for an object that
lay at his feet and as to which his blindness came from his stupidly looking
beyond. It had sat all the while at his hearth-stone, whence it now gazed up
in his face. (*GB*, 155–56)

Verver conjures the figure of a maze to announce his emergence from its
convolutions. In his account, the labyrinthine period of uncertainty ends
with his turn onto a suddenly expanded and clarified field of vision.

Yet the clear path Verver draws from confusion to "moral lucidity" is
interrupted by a gap that falls between the minute "he held his breath with
wonder" and the following sentence that begins with the distinctive
Jamesian locution: "He was afterwards to recall" (*GB*, 156). As in
The Ambassadors, Verver's perceptual reorientation takes place in an indeterminate interval between a sudden turn and a projected time "afterwards." From the retrospective vantage of this "afterwards," he can reflect
on the moment the "light broke for him" as a remembered past. These
proleptic and analeptic turns mark a syntax that gives place to experiences
which cannot be understood or articulated as immediately as they are felt.

Here, too, James's free indirect style makes it impossible to extricate
Verver's voice from the narrator's retrospective and projected viewpoints.
But unlike Strether, who remains enmeshed in the uncertain tangle of
temporalities and perspectives, Verver uses hindsight to recast his murky
"situation" as a solvable "riddle" that has been "all supremely cleared up"
(*GB*, 156). By the time he has exhaled his held breath, Verver has already
smoothed over any dislocations of time and perception to claim the "sharp
focus" of enlightened understanding. Yet just at the moment Verver denies
any lingering vagueness, his lock-and-key formulation raises the specter of
linguistic ambiguity by describing his "riddle" as a language problem
whose key is simply "the word" – a word that can't be named (*GB*, 156).

The phrase that stands in for the unnamed word is "his issue." Verver sheds light on this "issue" to the extent that he identifies a solution to the problem of his solitude following his daughter Maggie's recent marriage: he will marry her closest friend so that "Maggie would less and less appear to herself to have forsaken him" (*GB*, 156). Yet Verver's proposed antidote to Maggie's filial guilt obscures the darker underbelly of "his issue." The double valence of the word – invoking both his conflict and the offspring who is the site of his internal battle – points to the unarticulated core of Verver's problem: he must learn to view Maggie as his child rather than as the wife for which she has long stood as surrogate. The full depth of unspeakable incestuous desire must remain submerged beneath a carefully constructed edifice of cognitive clarity.

Reflecting on what happened in the moment he held his breath, Verver insistently frames his reconceived "issue" in the terms of wonder; the word is repeated three times in a single paragraph. "The wonder of it" lies in the all-at-once arrival of a resolution, but also in the "strange *delay* of his vision," with vision defined as full comprehension. Until the moment that "everything came together," Verver "groped and groped for an object that lay at his feet"; he figures the moment of recognition as an externalized encounter with an object of knowledge, one that "had sat all the while at his hearth-stone, whence it now gazed up in his face" (*GB*, 155–56). Verver seems to epitomize James's "spatializing poetics of cognition," but what precisely does he recognize in the face reflected back at him? Even as Verver decisively marks the end of the brief "hallucination" that delayed understanding, he relies on a phantasmic object encounter to usher uneasily cognized feelings into containable, domesticated forms. He stages a face-to-face encounter with himself, but one that only confirms a story of rational control over irrational desires.

Old and New World Wonder

Verver's description of his passage from bewilderment to cognitive mastery enlists tropes of New World wonder. He reenchants the rolling spread of his property "as a vast expanse of discovery." His explorer-gaze bestows "familiar objects" with "beauty, interest, importance" so that they appear "extraordinarily new," freshly vested with distinction. Framing the object encounter as a moment of "wonder," Verver can have it both ways: he can discover and lay claim to objects of value as if for the first time, but he can also imagine that he was in possession of them all along. Innocent amazement can coexist with cognitive control. By equating a poetics of wonder with a poetics of thought, Verver carries forward a Cartesian legacy that privileges cognition over feeling and disciplined wonder over unruly astonishment.[88]

Just as surprise is for Tomkins the ancillary of all other affects, wonder is for Descartes the "first of all the passions" because it is a precondition for all other passions, a state produced when our attention is piqued or gripped: "Wonder is a sudden surprise of the soul which brings it to consider with attention the objects that seem to it unusual and extraordinary."[89] While Descartes and Emerson both present surprise as a sudden seizure of attention that renders the soul susceptible to ongoing passionate engagement, they depart from one another in their respective valuations of that state of susceptibility. While Emerson values its open-ended indeterminacy, for Descartes evaluative judgment must be exercised to direct one's engagement toward desirable outcomes as efficiently as possible. We can't judge in advance whether the "novel" objects that surprise us are good or bad, but we can control the intensity of our response to them.[90] Descartes contrasts the temperate moderation of wonder (*l'admiration*) that is rightly regulated with the dangerous extremity of unbridled wonder, the excessive state he calls astonishment (*l'étonnement*).[91]

Properly controlled, wonder balances emotional engagement with cognitive appraisal. This more discerning species of wonder is valuable to the extent that it prepares the mind and body for "useful" action and inquiry in the pursuit of knowledge.[92] In the absence of careful calibration, the scales are tipped away from enabling utility and toward the disabling potential for astonishment to derail "the use of reason" and to immobilize activity. There is no way to know whether an object of wonder is "beneficial to us," but Descartes is clear that to be astonished (*étonné*) "can never be other than bad."[93] Those who make a "habit" of allowing themselves to be astonished may permanently lose the capacity for selective discernment: "Things of no importance are no less apt to arrest their attention than those whose investigation is more useful."[94] For wonder to serve as conduit of learning, the soul must be prepared for sudden surprises, yet Descartes requires a very different process of preparation than that of Emerson. The recommended Cartesian remedy for "excessive wonder" is "to acquire the knowledge of many things and to practise examining all those which may seem most unusual and strange."[95] Which is to say, those who struggle to restrain their intense responsiveness must anticipate potential sources of surprise and arm themselves in advance with foreknowledge of those things.

Descartes's wariness of the volatility of surprise has since fueled suspicion among philosophers who remain ready to condemn it as the enemy of rational judgment.[96] By challenging Descartes's assumption that learning relies on reason, Emerson reclaims the jeopardy of bad surprise – the state of disoriented suspension – as a site of potential discovery. James can then be said to follow Emerson in reversing the long-standing philosophical assumption that "vagueness" is anathema to knowledge. Like Emerson, Strether embraces open reception as a way of knowing: "All I know is reception" (*EL*, 491). Though Verver sounds like Descartes in his esteem of cognitive wonder, James foregrounds the facets of experience that are repressed – that Verver himself is actively repressing – when unknown quantities are dismissed as forms of knowledge.

As I noted in the introduction, Philip Fisher opens his study of wonder by making a counterintuitive argument that would seem to undermine the primacy of his key term: "both wonder and ... that favorite modern aesthetic category, shock" are best understood within the broader category of "the aesthetics of surprise and the sudden," defined as "the eliciting of notice."[97] James confirms the capaciousness of surprise in his late novels, but *The Ambassadors* and *The Golden Bowl* also show how easily it can be subsumed within those other more familiar aesthetic categories. When surprise is collapsed with shock, the experience of suddenness is coeval with rupture; when it is overshadowed by wonder, the goal of clear comprehension overwrites registers of experience unassimilable to the cognitive order. Yet the more subtle fluctuations of Jamesian surprise remain detectable in the circuitous temporal loops that shape his sentences, in the strange grammar of time that circumvents a linear path from ignorance to full understanding or dramatic revelation.

Critical Interest

In the prefaces to the New York Edition of his oeuvre, James works to bridge the gap between writing and reading. If a "novel is in its broadest definition a personal, a direct impression of life," as James declares, his ultimate aim is to "produce in the reader's mind" an impression that "must have much in common with the impression originally produced on his own mind by the subject."[98] James takes a two-pronged approach to transmitting this "impression of life." First, with the aim of absorbing the reader within the feeling that catalyzed the work in the first place, he returns himself and his reader to the scene of conception and composition; next, he establishes vital new connections between those past scenes of origin and the present scene of rereading and revision. The medium of connection between the novel's "productive germ" and its realized form will also, ideally, serve as the medium of transmission between author and audience (*AN*, 79). In each case, retrospection and preconception become sources of surprise that index the interval between past conception and present encounter; these surprises become sustaining sources of connection when they couple with an abiding interest in inhabiting these intervals.[99] The gaps that seemed to divide the reader and writer are recast as the sites where they are most likely to meet.

The prefaces define "life" as "all inclusion and confusion," while "art" is defined by "discrimination and selection" (*AN*, 120). The sudden "flush of life" that constitutes James's "first glimpse" of the inchoate novel in each case arrives all at once in an unguarded moment, swelling his field of attention to accommodate the overwhelming influx (*AN*, 99, 21). For James, converting life's confusion into the structured art of the novel is primarily a matter of containing the formlessness of "felt life" within a capacious yet controlled narrative shape: "really, universally, relations stop nowhere, and the exquisite problem of the artist is eternally but to draw, by a geometry of his own, the circle within which they shall happily *appear* to do so" (*AN*, 45, 5). An art that successfully draws such a circle achieves a "sublime economy" by coupling the startling expansion of relational possibility with the discriminating principle of selection James calls "interest" (*AN*, 120).

To separate out what is worthy of inclusion from what is not, James asks, "Up to what point is such and such a development *indispensable* to the interest?" (*AN*, 5). Here James refers to both his protagonist's and his reader's interest, which he hopes will become indivisible. As "interested and intelligent" witnesses and reporters, Jamesian protagonists "get the most out of all that happens to them and ... in so doing enable us, as readers of their record, as participators by fond attention, also to get the most" (*AN*, 62). James fosters this participatory attention by mapping the process of each novel's inception onto the process of its revision. By insisting on his receptive role in both these processes, James collapses the position of author and audience. Framing the task at hand as a shared project of reading, James extends "an earnest invitation to the reader to dream again in my company and in the interest of his own larger absorption of my sense" (*AN*, 345).

James narrates a reading experience animated by "surprises of re-perusal" (*AN*, 157). While he admits "a certain surprise" when "the march of [his] present attention coincides sufficiently with the march of [his] original expression," the surprise he felt at the novel-germ's unexpected arrival is more readily revived by the "frequent lapse of harmony between [his]

present mode of motion and that to which the existing footprints were due"
(*AN*, 75, 335, 336). The discrepancy James observes between the movements
of his past and present attention – "the high spontaneity of these deviations
and differences" between his "original tracks" and "present mode of
motion" – injects fresh vivacity into his present relationship with his past
work (*AN*, 336). These deviations activate an improvisational reading practice guided by his failure to "forecast chances and changes" that "could but
show for what they were as I went" (*AN*, 342).

While the idiosyncratic reading practice James describes might seem
available only to an author, he understands himself to be modeling a more
general critical method. The ideal form of "criticism" he imagines would
be intimately attuned to "arrests and surprise, emotions alike of disap-
pointment and of elation: all of which means, obviously, that the whole
thing was a *living* affair" (*AN*, 342). The job of the critic, in other words,
would be no different from his own: to revitalize the "felt life" that brought
the novel into being in the first place. This attunement to feeling would
ideally catalyze an "active, appreciative process" of analyzing the narrative
form it takes (*AN*, 336). Such "analytic appreciation" is guided by the
recognition that form and feeling shape each other at every stage (*AN*, 228).
For example, James describes the relation between scenic and non-scenic
elements of his novels like this: "We feel, with the definite alternation
[between scene and non-scene], how the theme is being treated. That is we
feel it when, in such tangled connexions, we happen to care" (*AN*, 158).
Invoking a united "we," James aligns himself with a more general critical
readership and invokes a future when the "finer idiosyncrasies" of those
"tangled connexions" will no longer be regarded as outside the scope of
criticism (*AN*, 157, 158).

Though James comes to his novels with the advantage of authorial
familiarity, he reads them for the surprises they yield, counterintuitively
suggesting that intimate acquaintance with a novel may in fact facilitate
rather than inhibit unexpected encounters. As his novels similarly
suggest, it is only after profound intimacy is established that unfathom-
able interest is uncovered. The ongoing "renewal of attention" James
demands depends less on the original newness of a first encounter than
on deep familiarity, the ground from which something else might
spring forth (*AN*, 336). James reads his novels with a penetrative care
that continually hits up against their opacity. Any insight James has
into the "accidents and incidents of [each novel's] growth" is only
useful insofar as it facilitates his sense of not knowing what he will
find when he reads them (*AN*, 7).

James's prefaces pioneer a critical practice that Tomkins will recommend a half century later. Coupling surprise with interest, the critic creates "necessary conditions for producing radical intellectual creativity."[100] This pairing proves so powerful because immediacy and duration can coexist and renew one another: surprise seizes attention, while interest holds attention to "maximize acquaintance with the object"; an otherwise fleeting interruption is extended, allowing "the individual to sustain attention to complex objects."[101] As acquaintance deepens, the increasing depth of relation proliferates possibilities for intimate familiarity to finally reveal unforeseen sources of "challenging novelty."[102]

CHAPTER 3

Nella Larsen's Novel Weather

"Then what do you love, you extraordinary stranger?"
"I love clouds . . . drifting clouds . . . there . . . over there . . . marvelous clouds!"

Charles Baudelaire

Whereas immersion in James's "tangled connexions" can illuminate unforeseen profusion for impressionable readers, extended exposure to Nella Larsen's turbulent *Quicksand* has left a century of critics hotly incensed or coldly unresponsive. Since its publication at the height of the Harlem Renaissance, *Quicksand* has persistently confounded with its incomprehensible protagonist and its inconsistent plot. The novel famously refuses to specify the unnameable "something" (a word repeated more than twenty times throughout the novel) that propels protagonist Helga Crane's movements from Alabama to New York, from America to Denmark, and back again.[1] Where we want narrative elaboration, we get anomalous gaps and ellipses; where we seek sources of psychological motivation and evidence of emotional depth, we are met with what scholars have termed Helga's "blank spots," or the novel's general "reluctance to utter."[2] For the majority of Larsen's early reviewers, the discontinuities of character and plot development in *Quicksand* prevented the book from achieving unity or "wholeness."[3]

Since Du Bois first championed *Quicksand* in an early review, the term "double consciousness" has been routinely invoked by defenders of the novel, who connect the apparent incongruities of its narrative to the psychological and political incongruities of a protagonist who struggles between "two unreconciled strivings; two warring ideals in one dark body."[4] However, several scholars have also emphasized that Du Bois's conception of "two-ness" is finally inadequate to account for the manifold psychic splits that must be navigated by the woman of mixed race whom Larsen figures as her subject.[5] Among the first to reclaim *Quicksand*'s significance after decades of neglect, Hazel Carby argues that Larsen's attempt to intervene in the "crisis of representation of the twenties" has the effect of unsettling her readers' formal expectations of the novel.[6] Carby roots this "crisis" in the artistic challenge facing Larsen, of finding a form that can adequately articulate an alienated state of consciousness at the nexus of racial, sexual, and class oppression.

Critics who extend Carby's efforts to move beyond Du Boisian "two-ness" in their readings of the novel have nevertheless remained dependent on the polarized categories that set "inside and outside" or "self and society" in opposition.[7] Though Larsen's critics have debated the limits of Du Bois's framework, the logic of doubleness abides insofar as *Quicksand*'s narrative contradictions ostensibly manifest the "duality" of a character whose internal states are at war with externally imposed demands for conformity.[8] This chapter will propose an alternate perspective for reading "double consciousness" in *Quicksand* by regrounding the term in Emerson's original definition as an antidote to binary thinking (*EL*, 3). Whereas "double" describes an oppositional split for Du Bois, Emerson had previously drawn out the relational dimension of the word – its etymological root in the verb *to fold* or *to join*, serving to bring distant phenomena into proximity and contact.

In typical fashion, Emerson's thinking about "double consciousness" supplies a dual meaning for the term that designates, on the one hand, the very problem of psychological "polarity" and, on the other, a possible strategy for exceeding the either/or of binary logic, for obviating the "old knots" that polarize and immobilize thinking in the first place (*EL*, 205 and 966, 943, 966). In the opening of "Fate" (1860), Emerson faults the "double consciousness" of his contemporaries as the mindset preventing them from solving "the question of the times," which is "the question of slavery."[9] If the dominant ideas of the time "are in the air" and constituting a political atmosphere, as Emerson continually asserts, the toxic tropes that make "racism and slavery possible" can easily "infect all who breathe."[10] A consciousness that "cannot span the huge orbits of the prevailing ideas ... and reconcile their opposition" is first defined as "double" in the sense that it is structured by a "stupendous antagonism" (*EL*, 943, 953). From the inflexibility of this limited response to cultural anxieties, Emersonian double consciousness is finally construed as a more capacious attunement to the double valence of "certain ideas ... in the air" – the same ideas stoking debates around compromise, secession, and emancipation at the fraught moment he is writing – which have the potential to dissolve or harden the single-minded infrastructures supporting slavery (*EL*, 965).

Du Bois expresses deep indebtedness to Emerson, and his seminal account of "two thoughts ... torn asunder" hews closely to the initial depiction in "Fate" of a mind torn between "two states of thought [that] diverge at every moment."[11] However, "Fate" proceeds to assert and dissolve so many antitheses – fate versus freedom, ideality versus materiality, tradition versus novelty, civility versus savagery – that by the essay's conclusion "double consciousness" has acquired a second meaning: it encompasses both the problem of twoness and the potential solution to intransigence that Emerson calls "impressionability," or a conscious susceptibility to atmospheric change. Knotted antagonisms within the individual and throughout the culture might be dissolved, Emerson suggests, by rendering oneself "impressionable" to countervailing premises that strobe into view within the "flux of matter" comprising social discourse (*EL*, 965). This is precisely analogous to how a mind alert to the nature of weather can register a continual and actionable collision between predictable patterns and contingent conditions. Emerson concludes by claiming that when we are attuned to the atmospheres around us, "every solid in the universe is ready to become fluid on the approach of the mind, and the power to flux it is the measure of the mind" (*EL*, 964). Using flux as a verb, Emerson implies that there's agency in applying pressurized diffusion to constants. With this recognition we are equipped to transform the "poles" of an antagonistic existence into connective and conductive "wires of thought" (*EL*, 965).

To trace the phrase "double consciousness" back to its original Emersonian usage is to retrieve a framework for understanding the strange atmosphere of uncertainty hovering around *Quicksand*'s evasive protagonist and amorphous plot.[12] Persistent critical focus on the antagonism between *inside* and *outside* in *Quicksand* misses an equally vital facet of the novel's form, which might be called Larsen's *literary atmosphere*; in this sense, to the novel's consideration of the politics of exclusion I want to add a consideration of its politics of transformation. Once readers are alerted to this fluid and nonbinary system of uncertainty, the novel's oppositional turns at the level of plot, character, and narrative consciousness might be conceptually keyed to the impersonal forces of moods and weather – the novel's primary manifestations of atmosphere. As I will contend, changes in atmosphere can momentarily dissolve the categorical integrity of binaries like *the self* and *the social* or *inner* and *outer*, which previously have organized (but not consistently clarified) most readings of *Quicksand*. At pivotal points in the novel, I argue, mounting pressures in the drama of the plot and the psyche of the protagonist find atmospheric release (which is not to say resolution); in these moments, plot is uncoupled from causal imperatives at the same time that Helga's consciousness becomes fully "impressionable" in the Emersonian sense, and thereby indistinguishable from its ambient surrounds. Rather than exclusively figuring Helga by her oppositionality, as a character defined by the political and narrative conventions she amplifies and bewilderingly exceeds, my reading instead derives Helga's significance from the novel's weather, her tempestuous arc offering an example of political and narrative mutability – and also perhaps a limit case of surprising literary form.

The Problem of Literary Atmosphere

Larsen's project converges with Emerson's where her prose heightens readers' attention to atmospheric dimensions of experience that can be felt even when they cannot readily be seen or articulated. While both writers cultivate this attention to atmosphere, it remains difficult to talk about these nebulous dimensions of their work because discussions of atmosphere have long posed particular difficulties for literary criticism. William Empson opens *Seven Types of Ambiguity* (1930) with a warning that indicates the problem: "It is very necessary for the critic to remember about the atmosphere." Yet by Empson's own admission, such atmosphere eludes description: "Criticism can only state that it is there."[13] While Empson recognizes the centrality of atmosphere to literary experience, he delimits his own critical task to the "verbal analysis" of "definite and detachable ambiguities."[14] By contrast, the ambiguity he associates with atmosphere has no clear definition, enveloping reader and text in a shared emanation from which there is no possibility of critical detachment.

Further efforts to solve the elusiveness of atmosphere, or even to address its operations, have foundered in the decades since. In the context of New Criticism, "atmosphere" is construed as a catch-all category, which broadly refers to "the general pervasive feeling which may be said to condition the treatment of the subject of any literary work."[15] Precisely *how* the atmosphere conditions the handling of the work remains largely unexplored. Tellingly, Cleanth Brooks and Robert Penn Warren's influential guide to teaching close reading relegates the term to a back appendix titled "Technical Problems," where it is defined as a "loose metaphor" for the "total feel" of a literary work.[16] The "glossary" that follows only reinforces the vagueness of this definition, describing "atmosphere" as "the general effect of the handling of the total work."[17] Framed in terms of its loose, metaphoric generality, atmosphere can find no place within a New Critical project that demands exacting specificity in its modes of interpretation. For Empson and the New Critics, "remembering the atmosphere" is limited to acknowledging that "analysis cannot hope to do anything but ignore it."[18]

Part of the difficulty of specifying literary atmosphere stems from a critical tendency to use the term interchangeably with a host of others, including "mood," "tone," "ambiance," "aura," "feeling," and most recently, "affect."[19] Mikel Dufrenne's *The Phenomenology of Aesthetic Experience* (1953) was first to equate "atmosphere" with the "affective quality" of an aesthetic encounter. The atmospheric immersion he idealizes merges audience and artwork in a primordial unity; when such a union is achieved, the "expressed world" of an aesthetic experience bypasses language and is "revealed only to feeling."[20] Affect theorists following Dufrenne have likewise subsumed those fugitive qualities most distinctive to atmosphere within the fundamental ineffability of affect.[21] As a result, affect theory's account of aesthetic atmospheres has, like New Criticism's, stalled against the critical impasse of becoming inapplicably general and necessarily inarticulate.

Larsen's attunement to the dynamics of atmosphere is hence easy to miss and hard to define because literary criticism has not yet developed a precise lexicon for describing the phenomena that might be encompassed by this elusive category of aesthetic experience. Yet Emerson, I would argue, does provide a uniquely nuanced and responsive vocabulary for investigating those atmospheric phenomena that are descriptively irreducible to vague abstractions or concrete objects. In contemplating "clouds and opaque airs," Emerson writes, "I shall see and comprehend my relations" (*EL*, 451). As I will demonstrate, in Emerson's usage "atmosphere" is never a vaguely metaphoric or synonymous placeholder for something other than itself: even when atmosphere floats in zones of indistinction between the literal and the figurative, it can always be palpably felt in ways that Emerson seeks to describe with as much precision as possible. Observing that "the web of relation" which enmeshes us in the universe is "atmospheric," the goal of Emerson's writing is to foster an "attitude of mind and reality of relation" that can likewise move "atmospherically" (*EL*, 336, 520). The kind of atmospheric relations that Emerson seeks to cultivate are at once cosmic and quotidian, intangible yet material. While he readily admits the difficulty of contemplating something as amorphous as atmosphere, he also holds that its subtle fluctuations become perceptible when we pay attention to its most everyday manifestations: in weather and in moods.[22]

Emerson's model of double consciousness as an impressionability to atmosphere provides a powerful framework for comprehending a protagonist whose identity alternates between self-divisive agency and pliant dispersion into history's sweeping currents, and for deciphering a plot that seems to harshly ground free-floating flux with the fixity of deterministic fate. The connections Emerson makes between meteorology and moods can point up crucial correlations between the shifts in Helga's volatile humors and the shifting weather patterns that backdrop her movements. Even as plot strictures appear to override Helga's commitment to contingency, *Quicksand*'s apparently inconsistent final sequence can be shown to unfold according to the same pattern of unpredictable atmospheric change that organizes all of the novel's pivotal scenes. The catalysts for action in the novel can never be located in a single causal factor; like the weather, *Quicksand* is patterned by the interpenetration of open and closed systems.

Larsen's investigation of these intersecting systems – the psychological with the social, the meteorological with the narratological – emerges when Helga's embrace of indeterminacy is conditioned by various constraints. These constraining conditions include what Judith Butler has described as "convergent modalities of power," which are difficult to frame beyond the "list of attributes separated by those proverbial commas (gender, sexuality, race, class)."[23] *Quicksand* shows these modalities of power to be complicit with the narrative conventions that threaten to flatten Larsen's unconventional protagonist into a categorical type. As I ultimately contend, Larsen juxtaposes the openness of a protagonist seeking atmospheric immersion with the closed boundaries of a novelistic frame in order to confront how the narrative constraints inherent to the novel form conspire with the deterministic logic of race and reproduction.

I locate Larsen's literary atmosphere in the drifting clouds that model Helga's mutability, but also in the strange and stifling final plot turn, which abruptly displaces flux with fixity. To read *Quicksand* "atmospherically," as I will demonstrate, is to reconsider the incongruous ending that has particularly baffled the novel's critics. For the majority of the novel, Helga's refusal of all circumscription precludes any typical framework that might shape her narrative trajectory into a legible arc. Living out a sequence of unrestrained possibilities, Larsen's protagonist escapes or exceeds all paths that would be reductively predetermined for her – by her family, her gender, or her race. It is therefore disconcerting when Helga's plot-defying itinerancy is, in the end, subjugated to conventional domestic constriction, "asphyxiating" in the "bog" of unhappy marriage and unwanted motherhood, betrayed by illusions of latitude and transformation (*Q*, 134). Measuring the force of *Quicksand* with Emersonian instruments, this chapter will conclude by asking whether the novel's stock ending is startling precisely because *Quicksand* has reconditioned its readers to expect a resilient open-endedness that typical novelistic closure betrays.

Atmospheric Events

Helga is tellingly introduced as someone who is "sensitive to atmosphere," and this sensitivity cues our attention to the way atmospheric change manifests at the level of character and plot (*Q*, 28). Larsen's working title for the manuscript, *Cloudy Amber*, underlines her investment in modeling characters and narrative events after phenomena that change state. *Cloudy Amber* references the intermediate color of Helga's skin and the pervasively overcast hue of the novel's backdrop, but clouds and amber also stand as more general emblems for transfiguring processes that are catalyzed by the rise and fall of temperatures and pressures. Just as shifts in air pressure and temperature form clouds from condensation and amber from sap, Helga's changes in mood and direction fluctuate between fluidity and fixity. Significantly, as the *cloudiness* of amber owes its opacity to trapped bubbles of air, Helga's attunement to the drift of clouds suggests that her own affective and imaginative idiom is primarily aerial.[24] Yet amber's process of transformation – from liquid tree sap into solid resin and a final fossilized form – also provides a potentially melancholic figure for how *Quicksand*'s fluidity of plot eventually threatens to harden into rigid conventionality.

    The impulsive choice that first catalyzes Helga's journeying serves to corroborate Emerson's meteorological maxim: "Life is March weather, savage and serene in one hour" (*EL*, 704). When Helga quits her teaching job without warning early in the novel, she insists on leaving her post in mid-March instead of waiting until the end of term, even as she ruins her chances of receiving a reference that would allow her to continue in the profession. In fleeing Naxos, a "Black Belt" college based on Booker T. Washington's industrial model of vocational schooling, Helga abandons an educational "machine" that "ruthlessly cut[s] all to a pattern."[25] The institution tolerates "no innovations, no individualisms," so that students are stripped of all "enthusiasm" and "spontaneity" (*Q*, 4). The structure of this opening sequence creates a loose pattern of pressurization and release repeated in each of the novel's subsequent scenes of sudden departure. Narrative form mirrors cloud formation (the inciting incident, the gathering storm): after an initial stage of condensation, dispersed energies begin to rise and concentrate into an amorphous but palpable mass. When atmospheric pressures are most volatile, Helga's clouded mood can no longer maintain its unstable state of suspension. Condensation prompts precipitation: from this first instance, each time Helga abandons a life she has been building, her embarkation is instigated by "an impetuous discharge," which releases accumulated pressures "with a surprising ferociousness" (*Q*, 5, 4). As weather systems accommodate collisions of natural forces, so the novel joins this scene to scenes that follow, each unfolding according to a predictable formal pattern which nevertheless is inflected by capricious contingencies.

At each point of departure, Helga casts her gaze upon the firmament, as if its aspect will provide guidance for how she should proceed. Out the window of the train that trundles her away from Naxos, she studies the "long, soft white clouds, clouds like shreds of incredibly fine cotton" streaking the early evening sky; the banded clouds seem to run parallel to the tracks, mapping out a flight path to the city along the "flying land-scape" of the sky (*Q*, 22). When Helga arrives in Chicago, and soon after in Harlem, she is drawn by "an uncontrollable desire to mingle with the crowd" (*Q*, 30). Every time she steps out into "the glimmering . . . swarming" street, the "tremulous clouds" both model and motivate her "aimless strolling" and wayward "drifting" (*Q*, 30, 32, 30). Paradoxically, the floating feeling of drift is also for Helga the feeling of belonging. Flitting cloud-like through the urban throngs, Helga observes, "oddly enough, she felt, too, that she had come home. She, Helga Crane, who had no home" (*Q*, 30). But in each new city, Helga's sense of itinerant freedom and home-coming is inevitably overtaken by a stifling claustrophobia. After a brief period of unconstrained belonging, a new weather front moves in. In every case, the air thickens with rising tensions and temperatures. Yet instead of culminating in a dramatic outburst or cathartic confrontation, these mounting atmospheric pressures are vented obliquely, into the negative space of Helga's tempestuous departures, which Larsen marks with abrupt chapter breaks. When the next chapter opens, the oppressive atmosphere has dispersed once more into liberated drift, and the cycle begins again.

I want to frame these opening scenes, and every other scene where Helga takes sudden leave of a stabilizing routine, as "atmospheric events."[26] Emerson defines an "event" as atmospheric in the sense that it comes over us like a passing mood or "mutable cloud" – immersive yet intangible, transformative but without a clear causal source (*EL*, 242). "Person makes event, and event person," he writes, but these mutual "changes pass without violence" (*EL*, 962, 546). There is no violence, Emerson maintains, because the functioning of the human body is itself atmospherically constituted. While his accounts of atmospheric encounters may be free of harmful aggression or overt brutality, they are characterized nonetheless by the same "ferociousness" that Larsen invokes in the opening scene. "If the Universe have [*sic*] these savage accidents, our atoms are as savage in resistance," Emerson asserts: "We should be crushed by the atmosphere, but for the reaction of the air within the body" (*EL*, 954).

For Emerson, our visceral relationship with atmosphere exemplifies forms of equilibrium and opposition that are not mutually exclusive. He asks, "Why should we fear to be crushed by savage elements, we who are made up of the same elements?" (*EL*, 967). To recognize that all entities share the medium of air is to drag together "the poles of the universe" and thus to attenuate "our own polarity" (*EL*, 953, 943). I read *Quicksand*'s various scenes of geographic departure and relocation as "atmospheric events" that unfold within the turbulent field of pressurization that both surrounds and comprises her, supplanting the controlled heightening of conventional plot points, where outer forces dictate the inner arc. This is to say that these events momentarily suspend Helga's experience of a polarizing split between inner and outer life, elementally suggesting that her breath and her environment swirl with the same stuff. But where Emerson upholds as "universal" the dynamic he describes as a "savage" push and pull between "two forces, centripetal and centrifugal," for Helga, the "savage strains" of atmosphere that permeate pressured moments in the narrative are always racially coded (*EL*, 565, 954, 565; *Q*, 59).

Larsen's Logic of Pathetic Fallacy

In its quotidian ordinariness, the weather in literature can pass unnoticed as the prosaic ground against which narrative action unfolds. When bringing *Quicksand*'s weather patterns to the fore as an apparently straightforward use of pathetic fallacy, the novel would at first suggest that its meteorological signs ought to be taken as a sentient reflection of Helga's otherwise indecipherable interior states. At first, this literary device appears to help us read our illegible protagonist by inviting us to look to the skies for referents when seeking to fill the "blank spots" of her character. As signs, the novel's weather can be taken as an externalized phenomenology of a seemingly impenetrable interior state. But as meteorologists and literary critics might agree, the vagaries of weather are hard to interpret.[27] In Emerson's words, "we cannot write the order of the variable winds. How can we penetrate the law of our shifting moods?" (*EL*, 1121).

The correspondence Emerson draws between wind and mood hinges on their shared volatility; however, this common inconstancy also indicates that neither meteorological nor temperamental flux can be systematized. While Emerson's essays are highly attuned to the unpredictable ways in which weather and moods inflect and refract one another, neither phenomenon provides a dependable key for deciphering the other.

Just as Emerson's weather signs resist coalescence into a psychological code, *Quicksand*'s instances of pathetic fallacy in fact intensify Helga's inscrutability rather than penetrating her opacity. Instead of projecting human emotions onto the natural world, Larsen seems to reverse the arrow and have her protagonist assume the nebulous qualities of clouds. Accordingly, Larsen's use of pathetic fallacy sheds no clarifying light on her protagonist's obscure inner workings beyond the insight that moods pass over her like clouds move across the sky: similarly variable, volatile, and obscure, their movements are dictated by impersonal forces like air pressure and temperature and remain unbounded by an individual consciousness. The vaporous phenomena that circulate throughout the novel serve only to corroborate that our protagonist is shaped by inconsistency: like the "tremulous clouds" she tracks with rapt fascination, Helga "drift[s] here and there with a sort of endless lack of purpose" (*Q*, 30). The weather doesn't so much reflect her internal state as appear coextensive with moods that likewise circulate aerially. Clouds provide an aptly fleeting model for a character, as well as for a narrative, that might at any moment lapse into formless flux.

"Our moods do not believe in each other," writes Emerson, and Larsen's heroine bears him out (*EL*, 406). A well-known passage from "Experience" aligning temperamental and celestial flux suggests one reason why Larsen perhaps ultimately chose to invoke groundlessness with her title:

> The secret of the illusoriness [of life] is in the necessity of a succession of moods or objects. Gladly we would anchor, but the anchorage is quicksand. This onward trick of nature is too strong for us: *Pero si muove.* When, at night, I look at the moon and stars, I seem stationary, and they to hurry. (*EL*, 476)

Looking to the sky, Emerson aligns the successiveness of moods with the onwardness of nature. The strength and necessity of these forces overtake us from within and without. Our impulse, he observes, is to anchor the self, but when we seek stationary "permanence," we find that the grounds of selfhood are "quicksand."

The self is groundless because our moods are no more intrinsic to us than the astronomical orbs passing overhead. In this passage it is the moon and stars that hurry across the sky, but just as often, Emerson describes watching clouds sweep across the "overarching vault" (*EL*, 337).[28] Whether he tracks meteorological or celestial phenomena, his primary concern is the challenge of recognizing the correspondence between their unceasing movement and our similarly dynamic "succession of moods." However, the onward trick of nature will remain too strong unless one can succeed in dissolving a desire for anchoring the self. In passages like these, Emerson models a process of reorienting one's habits of attention so that moods which once seemed yoked to personal identity might float without anchorage. To gaze aloft and discover the shared rhythms of inner and outer life is to feel seemingly firm ground give way to the precarity of quicksand.

Larsen's protagonist embodies two conflicting imperatives described in the Emerson passage above, which propel and arrest her flights. On the one hand, Helga seeks anchorage in a grounded sense of self and home; on the other hand, she aims to uproot herself from any defining categories of identity or place and to give herself over to the successive moods that keep her moving. When Helga first arrives in Harlem from Naxos, by way of Chicago, she feels "joy at seeming at last to belong somewhere," which springs from the feeling that "she had, as she put it, '"found herself"' (*Q*, 44). She finds herself defined by a sense of place: in Harlem her identity is "bounded by Central Park, Fifth Avenue, St. Nicholas Park, and One Hundred and Forty-fifth Street" (*Q*, 46). Soon, though, this geographically bound selfhood leaves her feeling "shut in, trapped" and "as the days became hotter and the streets more swarming," her "happiness" is subsumed by a claustrophobic "restlessness." With these changes in mood and temperature, the "crowds of nameless folk" that had earlier offered freedom and belonging now "encompassed her" with a sense of "estrangement" (*Q*, 47–48).

Instead of floating cloud-like through the throngs, Helga describes herself as stifled by the thick miasmic air of Harlem's boulevards, which "swallow[s] up all else like some dense fog" (*Q*, 53). When the suffocating feeling is heightened to an "excruciating agony," Helga suddenly determines that "it was of herself that she was afraid" (*Q*, 53, 47). Read straightforwardly, this line seems to mark an inward turn to reckon with the threat her own volatility poses to the stable life she has built in Harlem. And yet, Helga's subsequent efforts to shed the trappings of an anchored selfhood suggest that just as often she fears the prospect of being tied to a self that is proper to her.

In the same passage, Helga speculates that her "restlessness" is fueled by "her need of something . . . vaguely familiar . . . which she could not put a name to and hold for definite examination" (*Q,* 47). She reiterates this nameless longing on the eve of every flight, searching the skies for a nebulous "something" beyond herself. As the scene to which I now turn reveals, the only times her "ill-defined . . . vague yearning" is quelled are those moments when, in a state of ecstatic openness, she fleetingly glimpses the possibility that her "self" in fact partakes of that "something" she seeks (*Q,* 50). Caught in the throes of just such a moment one evening in Harlem, Helga is filled and indeed constituted by "the air of something about to fly" (*Q,* 56).

Moving Mosaic

I have described the novel's atmospheric events as unfolding according to a predictable pattern of accumulating pressures that require release. However, as the novel's signature scene exemplifies, Helga's experience of atmospheric immersion also oscillates unpredictably between antagonistic opposition to an invasive threat and ready yielding to an undulating stream. When Helga first sets out on a "sulky, humid night, thick furry night, through which the electric torches shone like silver fuzz," she sets herself "singularly apart from it all." "It is an atrocious night for cabareting," she declares, asserting a disdainful remove between herself and the Harlem crowds she initially embraced. Even as she resists getting swept up in the "gay, grotesque" atmosphere of Harlem's nightlife, Helga's sullen humor partakes of the "sulky" humidity, suggesting that she remains porous to her ambient surrounds (*Q,* 58). Once again, Larsen's use of pathetic fallacy confuses distinctions between an internal state and its external manifestation; the muggy swelter doesn't so much reflect Helga's interiority as permeate it, serving as a medium for moods that pass through our protagonist but are not intrinsic to her.

The same inundating air carries a cacophony of noise – "clanging trolley bells, quarreling cats, cackling phonographs, raucous laughter, complaining motor-horns, low singing" – which primes Helga's impressionability to the seductive sounds of a jazz cabaret (*Q,* 58). Descending from the street into "a vast subterranean room" that condenses and thickens the night's sultriness with "smoke and din," Helga's senses are immediately engulfed: "A glare of light struck her eyes, a blare of jazz split her ears. For a moment everything seemed to be spinning round" (*Q,* 58, 59, 58). Here, too, her first response is to defensively distance herself from sources of overstimulation.

But just at the moment when she is most insistent upon her singular apartness, Helga's apparent autonomy is sonically eroded. As a vehicle for music, the force of atmosphere overwhelms Helga's efforts to separate herself from "the familiar medley that is Harlem" (Q, 58).

In what is perhaps the novel's most cited passage, Larsen dramatizes Helga's absorption within a "moving mosaic" by unleashing a tumult of verbs floating free from clear markers of narrative focalization (Q, 60):

> They danced, ambling lazily to a crooning melody, or violently twisting their bodies, like whirling leaves, to a sudden streaming rhythm, or shaking themselves ecstatically to a thumping of unseen tomtoms. For a while, Helga was oblivious of the reek of flesh, smoke, and alcohol, oblivious of the oblivion of other gyrating pairs, oblivious of the color, the noise, and the grand distorted childishness of it all. She was drugged, lifted, sustained, by the extraordinary music, blown out, ripped out, beaten out, by the joyous, wild, murky orchestra. The essence of life seemed bodily motion. (Q, 59)

In the opening third-person articulation it remains uncertain whether Helga continues to hold herself "singularly apart" from the "they" who "danced." However, the clause that follows – "for a while" – opens an alternate temporal and spatial order dictated by a streaming rhythm that overflows all efforts to hold the ecstatic thumping at arm's length. Commingling with the stream, Helga enters a state of oblivion that effaces the difference between inhabiting and being inhabited. This merging of self and stream constitutes an atmospheric event to the extent that Helga discovers what Emerson attests to be "the secret of the world": a radical openness that displaces any divide between inner and outer life (EL, 962).

To discover that "person makes event, and event person," according to Emerson, is also to discover that "Life is an ecstasy" (EL, 962, 1116). As Branka Arsić argues, when Emerson asserts an ecstatic reciprocity between person and event, he is not marking out a rare and exceptional experience but is simply describing the way life is: "Life as such (of animals, plants, and humans) lives by leaving its posts, by being restless (being out of stasis)."[29] Immersed in the climate of the cabaret, Helga similarly glimpses the possibility that her own relentless restlessness, her aversion to stasis and her embrace of movement, is not an isolated subjective state but is in fact an essential condition of life: "The essence of life seemed bodily motion." The pileup of active verbs that blow, beat, and rip at the bounds of selfhood affirms the discovery that "life becomes an ecstasy [when] ... living functions as a process of leaving."[30] To leave, for Helga as for Emerson, is to abandon a settled self and to follow instead the flux of weather and moods.

While Emerson celebrates an ecstatic indistinction between persons and what lies outside of them, tropes of dissolved personhood quickly become fraught in *Quicksand*. There is, to be sure, a liberating inclusiveness in the assertion that *all* life – that of animals, plants, and humans – is bodily motion. However, for Helga to conflate the difference between forms of life is also to confront the way that black female sexuality has been burdened by a long history of association with primal animality and exoticism. The passage above and those that follow in *Quicksand* suggest how primitivist constructions insidiously inflect the possibility of ecstatic self-disappearance.

As soon as Helga gives herself over to the "wild" jazz rhythms, her mood of abandon is infiltrated by thumping tom-toms and feverish heat, such that an atmosphere of oblivion becomes indistinguishable from the savage air of some presumptive jungle scene. Even as she glimpses immersive communion with a world from which she has been estranged, this immediacy of relation is simultaneously mediated by overdetermined forms of cultural essentialism. Any release from subjective constraint she temporarily enjoys is swiftly countered by hardened clichés of racial and sexual identity. "Strangled by the savage strains of music," Helga "drag[s] herself back to the present with a conscious effort." The return to consciousness is accompanied by "a shameful certainty that not only had she been in the jungle, but that she had enjoyed it" (Q, 59).

Here, the ecstatic surge gives way to a flood of shame, so that consciousness manifests as self-contempt. Admonishing her implication in the "semi-barbaric" scene, Helga insists that she isn't "a jungle creature." But instead of rejecting wholesale this primitivizing trope, she defensively "cloak[s] herself in faint disgust" and turns an exoticizing gaze back onto "this oppressed race of hers" (Q, 59). While the club's "fantastic motley" will remain "in the heart of the jungle," Helga insists that she will escape (Q, 59, 62). Charged with the troubling dynamics of projection and internalization, the atmospheric exchanges between Helga's mood of disgusted shame and the climate of the club feel stiflingly airless. Suddenly desperate to escape the suffocating room, she staggers back into the equally stifling street, where she is left at the end of the chapter in a "crumpled" heap (Q, 62). In disavowing the primal sexuality that she associates with jazz, Helga also rejects her life in Harlem. At the opening of the next chapter, she has already set sail for the post-racial utopia she projects onto Denmark.

Grammars of Ecstasy and Essentialism

How are we to reconcile the convergence of ecstasy with essentialism in the cabaret scene, with its strange collision of moving sensation and hardened cultural clichés? Laura Doyle argues that the cabaret dance floor is the one place where "Helga *and* her narrator shed their vexed sense of [Du Boisian] double-consciousness."[31] But if Larsen's prose momentarily merges actor and action, narrator and narrated, the moment is so fleeting and its aftermath so divisive that Larsen seems more interested in vexing a two-dimensional understanding of double consciousness as a psychic split that might be momentarily spanned. Larsen's dramatization of the dynamics of shame foretells Frantz Fanon's revision of double consciousness several decades later as "third-person consciousness" (or triple consciousness).[32] With this phrase, Fanon signals his search for a grammar that expresses an elusive phenomen-ological experience: the feeling of hovering in "an atmosphere of certain uncertainty" around one's own body – a body shrouded by a thick mist of racist projections.[33]

    In terms that are resonant with Helga's cabaret experience, Fanon describes how any semblance of subjectivity is "battered down by tom-toms, cannibalism, intellectual deficiency, fetishism, racial defects, slave-ships."[34] When the atmosphere of uncertainty is saturated by these stereo-types, the subjecthood of a first-person "I" is displaced by a "crushing objecthood."[35] Suspended in uncertainty, a racialized consciousness is easily infiltrated by alienating images, just as Helga has internalized an objectifying gaze that equates black sexuality with jungle animality. When the founding self-relation is permeated by "shame and self-contempt," any openness to the atmosphere is felt as an open wound.[36]

    In the set-piece cabaret scene, Larsen's narrator performs the grammar of a third-person consciousness with fluctuations in focalization that cannot be located with any certainty either inside or to the side of the protagonist. When Helga is engulfed by the music's momentum, the narrative focalization appears intimately fused with her own, merging actor and action in the dynamic surge of verbs. Just one sentence before narrator and narrated merge in the declaration that all is "bodily motion," the focus can be seen to pull away from Helga, critiquing her obliviousness to "the grand distorted childishness of it all" (Q, 59). Alternately, the phrase might be taken as Helga's own critique, voiced just before her skeptical appraisal of the scene gives way to oblivion.

    When the prose moves in tune with jazz rhythms that are also jungle rhythms, it is difficult to ascribe the racially charged clichés to an identifiable and therefore containable perspective. Floating unanchored, released into atmospheric undecidability, disturbing stereotypes circulate like free radicals. The sinuous sentences that engulf Helga into the "swirling mass" also threaten to sweep readers into implicated relation with these racist formulations (*Q*, 59). The same air that promised bodily and psychic release becomes a medium for contagion. Without clear boundaries between focalizer and focalized, the disturbing discourse of savagery cannot be held at a safe remove. Larsen's feat in this passage is to create the narrative conditions under which *Quicksand*'s readers might breathe the same "atmosphere of certainty uncertainty" as their protagonist.

Helga's transatlantic flight from Harlem is fueled by her desire to find release from a claustrophobic climate pressured by racist stereotypes: seeking clear Nordic air, Helga leaves behind "the torrid summer . . . [that] had so oppressed her" and sets forth for Scandinavian shores. As the steam liner pulls away from the "cliff-like towers" of New York "into the open sea," the narrative focalization expands to cinematic scope; corporeal close-ups are replaced by a panoramic perspective that encompasses the expanse of the water and the vast firmament (*Q*, 63). "The problem of the color-line," to recall Du Bois's memorable phrase, seems dwarfed by the immensity and subtle gradations of "the western sky," with its "pink and mauve light . . . fad[ing] gradually into a soft gray-blue obscurity" at dusk, while at sunrise "the purply gray sky change[s] to opal, to gold, to pale blue."[37] As the boat skims along in "the serene calm of the lingering September summer," Helga "revel[s] like a released bird," floated aloft by the airy "feeling of happiness and freedom": "It had begun, a new life for Helga Crane" (*Q*, 64, 66).

Floated by "the air of something" in flight, dreaming of "life somewhere else," Helga is temporarily freed from identification with a specific "someone" (*Q*, 56). Her mood of open-ended yearning and unconstrained potential resembles the temperamental disposition that Emerson calls the "optative mood" (*EL*, 199). With this phrase, Emerson names a category of grammatical mood (related to the subjunctive) that expresses wishes, hopes, and desires which hinge on the conditional "if . . . then" structure. Though the verb form does not exist in English grammar, Emerson seeks equivalent expressions for this mood of future possibility, which he associates with America's literary and spiritual longings. Invoking the optative in relation to the problem of "double consciousness," he suggests its potential to resolve the problem of "polarity" by uprooting entrenched positions (*EL*, 205 and 966, 943). When one is "floated" into the optative mood, the modal logic of possibility displaces the static logic of identity; the assumed solidity of an established subject position is reduced to a "transparent atmosphere" (*EL*, 517). Holding up the poet and priest as exemplars of the optative mood, Emerson observes that these figures "cannot choose but to stand in awe . . . they eat clouds, and drink wind" (*EL*, 202).

We might imagine Helga in a similar posture of awestruck receptivity as she crosses the Atlantic. Comparing herself to a bird in flight, she likewise feels herself carried and filled by aerial elements, crane-like. Arsić's gloss of the optative as a "flight" and a "journeying abroad" underlines the resonances between Emerson's and Larsen's depictions of a self departing from itself in the act of leaving. When Emerson declares himself to be in flight or abroad, he is announcing "the moment in which thought is healed" in the sense that "'two' contraries" are reconciled.[38] Larsen's novel stresses the momentariness of this healing. Every time Larsen's protagonist faces the fresh horizon of a new beginning, promising prospects are rapidly constricted by the sutures she has tried to stitch around the "obscene sore" that throbs at the core of her being (*Q*, 29). Helga's optative "seeking for something" different from what she has left behind opens new possibilities, but also old wounds (*Q*, 50).

Race and Shame

If, as Emerson suggests, an impressionability to atmosphere can catalyze material state changes, Larsen is acutely aware of how easily "the power to flux" can congeal into fixed forms (*EL*, 964).[39] In effect, *Quicksand* tests Emerson's "solution" to the "stupendous antagonism" of double consciousness by investigating the conditions under which states of fluidity harden into stultifying solidity. In "The Transcendentalist," Emerson suggests that a "poet" writing in the optative mood might help dissolve antagonistic "states of thought" into the more fluid form of double consciousness (*EL*, 205). We can read his essays on "double consciousness" as exercises in finding an optative syntax capable of moving readers from the oppositional thinking that structures their introductions to the atmospheric awareness with which they conclude. Larsen also writes in an optative mood of longing, but its grammar of open possibility is constrained in *Quicksand*; the toxic coupling of "race and shame" repeatedly revives in Helga a "suspensive conflict" between "two unreconciled strivings": to escape limiting categories and to belong to a place and a people.[40]

Having disembarked in Denmark, Helga's optative flight is abruptly grounded by the indicative mood – the mood of declarative statements that affirm the "security and permanence in her new life" (*Q*, 77). Back on land,

no longer buoyed by her aerial sensibility, Helga announces her achievement of settled stability. And yet the "blessed sense of belonging to herself
alone and not to a race" does not last (*Q*, 64). Helga once again finds herself
under the shadow of "an indefinite discontent . . . like a storm gathering far
on the horizon" – a storm that breaks on another night of acute shame (*Q*,
81). But whereas the coupling of self-loss and self-consciousness in the jazz
club provokes her disidentification with racial clichés she associates with
Harlem, the spectacle of minstrel performers playing ragtime in
a Scandinavian circus prompts an identificatory journey of return.

Helga's faith in Copenhagen's colorblindness is punctured by the "ges-
ticulating black figures" on the vaudeville stage and the "delight" and
"avidity" with which the audience "drank [it] in" (*Q*, 83, 82, 83):

> She was filled with a fierce hatred for the cavorting Negroes on the stage. She
> felt shamed, betrayed, as if these pale pink and white people among whom
> she lived had suddenly been invited to look upon something in her which
> she had hidden away and wanted to forget. (*Q*, 83)

In the optative mood, the word "something" has previously referred to an
undefinable entity that is always on the way to becoming something else.
However, in the face of cavorting racial clichés, Helga's shame shuts down
its potential: "something" comes to signify "some characteristic, different
from any that they [the Danes] themselves possessed," "something in the
racial character" that is no less an exotic spectacle than the minstrels on
stage (*Q*, 83, 54). Though that difference is valued as a "precious thing," to
be "admired" rather than "despised," it is deemed essential; her shame
betrays the degree to which this essentialist thinking has become her own.
The performance leaves Helga "profoundly disquieted" and heralds the
end of a temporary calm: "Her old unhappy questioning mood came again
upon her" (*Q*, 83).

Shame manifests in Helga's expression of aversion toward the figures of
jungle animality and ragtime minstrelsy she encounters at the cabaret and
vaudeville circus (*Q*, 48, 63). Averting herself from these hackneyed figures,
Helga turns inward to confront a self-image inevitably inflected by the
same insidious tropes; detecting resemblances, Helga averts herself once
more in a gesture that disavows conformity with the racist stereotypes of
primal sexuality, grinning buffoonery, and in the final sequence, tragic
fallenness. As Stanley Cavell argues, this kind of aversive turn – an assertion
of non-conformity with externally imposed categories – is the signature
gesture of Emerson's essays. Cavell's account of Emerson's "aversive thinking" suggests instructive continuities between Helga's shame-induced

aversion and her final act of conversion – an act which many readers have dismissed as discontinuous with the rest of the novel. Emersonian aversion prompts a turn against "ourselves in our conformity," and this "gesture of departing from oneself" is the first act that sets us on the path of converting the conventional.[41] When we grow ashamed of "our fear of others' eyes," our aversive relationship to conformity is transformed into a conversionary force; Emersonian shame, according to Cavell, is "the condition under which anything new can be said."[42]

While shame opens expressive possibilities for Emerson, it often forecloses them for Helga. Even when *Quicksand*'s scenes of shame spur her to flight, racialized aversion tightens the paralyzing double bind Helga first articulates at Naxos: "She could neither conform, nor be happy in her unconformity" (*Q*, 7). Just as opposition and acquiescence commingle in our protagonist's stance toward racial essentialism, *Quicksand*'s final sequence enmeshes the conventional and the atypical at the level of plot. The capitulating forms of closure that overtake the novel's concluding pages are dissonant because they diverge from its previously unconventional itinerary. Having followed *Quicksand*'s idiosyncratic turns up to this point, we have learned, paradoxically, to expect the unpredictable. The novel's narrative gaps deliberately disrupt various Anglo-American master plots that are invoked only to be subverted. Larsen alternately employs and undermines the tradition of the tragic mulatta, the migration narrative, the return-to-roots saga, and the marriage plot, among others.

The last lines of Langston Hughes's epigraph to the novel – "I wonder where I'm gonna die, / Being neither white nor black" – suggest that Helga will suffer the double negation that conventionally condemns biracial heroines to a ruinous end. An archetypical figure in nineteenth- and early twentieth-century American literature, the "tragic mulatta" is a special case of the "fallen woman," whose mixed blood dictates her compromised entry into the world; the obstacles presented by this figure's inauspicious birth are often compounded by her experience of being orphaned, isolated, and variously abandoned. Helga's "painful isolation" is the product of her West Indian father's desertion and her Danish mother's death, but for the majority of the novel she assumes the role of abandoner, taking sudden leave of each person who tries in vain to hold her in place (*Q*, 24). Helga suffers the psychic and geographic dislocation of her "neither/nor" status, but Larsen's emphasis on the horizontal axis of her travels overwrites the vertical axis of fallenness. Moving with flâneur-like freedom through the crowd, Helga expands the narrow possibilities open to the tragic mulatta.[43] Similarly, her transatlantic traversals extend the arc of the migration narrative, which conventionally traces a journey from the rural South to the urban North.[44] Thus far, Larsen has twisted readily recognizable plots into unfamiliar forms, but in the concluding pages, the final plot twist is that narrative closure comes to us straight.[45]

Helga's sudden submission to sexual and racial norms she has hitherto resisted appears to confirm the novel's concession to convention. Having earlier left America to escape a racialized sense of self, Helga frames her return as a "surrender to the irresistible ties of race" (*Q*, 92). In the same way that Denmark failed to offer a post-racial paradise, her romanticized ideals of racial reconnection and belonging in Harlem are soon again disillusioned. Helga's peripatetic path has evaded romantic overtures and several proposals, but upon returning to New York, the "ecstasy" of an illicit embrace triggers the rhetoric of fallenness and infiltrates the final pages with "the suddenness of a dream" (*Q*, 105, 104).[46] At an uptown party she finds herself in the arms of the newly married Dr. Anderson who, as the former director at Naxos, unambiguously represents the oppressive past she has worked so hard to leave behind. In the throes of this sudden swoon, Helga's "irrepressible longing" – elsewhere described as a "strange ill-defined emotion, a vague yearning rising within her" – finds a clear object (*Q*, 106, 50).

Helga's desire for "consummation" is displaced by shamed "exposure" when her yearnings are unreciprocated (*Q*, 107). "Mortification" and "self-loathing" are felt all the more sharply because "she had deluded herself" into expecting mutuality (*Q*, 109). When Helga finds her "voluptuous visions" unshared, she laments that she has "ruined everything" (*Q*, 109, 108). Resembling the swooning fall into ruin that is the signature of the tragic mulatta plot, a novel that has routinely exceeded familiar narrative frameworks suddenly ushers in the tired tropes of fallenness, but also of religious revival, domesticating nuptials, and a final return to southern roots and Bible Belt piety. Larsen's capricious protagonist outstrips predictable plots for nearly the full duration of the novel, only to have the limits of such linear scripting imposed with a vengeance in its conclusion. Unsurprisingly, Larsen indexes this change in narrative register – from capriciousness to conventionality – with a change in the weather.

The Gathering Storm

Quicksand's inscrutable turns in plot and character development have invited a variety of interpretations, but critics have found near consensus on at least one front: the novel's "'surprising' or 'problematic' conclusion"

confounds explanation.[47] Deborah E. McDowell's introduction to the
critical edition of the novel surveys a long line of critics who have
"consistently criticized" Larsen's "unearned and unsettling endings" and
who attack her "difficulty with rounding off stories convincingly."[48]
A common theme that recurs in these assessments is the problem of
causality. As Mary Esteve asserts: "In the final episodes all bets are off.
Reader and writer have been abandoned to the cause of narratological
causelessness."[49] And yet, the argument could just as easily be made that
this abandonment occurs at the novel's outset. From its opening pages, the
novel refuses to satisfy our desire to identify clearly the catalysts propelling
Helga's movements. "Narratological causelessness" becomes the norm
insofar as she wanders cloud-like, defined by an "endless lack of purpose"
throughout the narrative, propelled by shifts in mood and the weather (Q,
30). Given that critical complaints regarding "*Quicksand*'s irritating
absence of psychological causation" are directed not only toward its ending, the novel's "enigmatic causality" bears further scrutiny.[50]

Guided by Emerson's model of double consciousness as an impressionability to atmosphere, my own reading of *Quicksand*'s complicated relation
to causation will draw out crucial continuities between the novel's stormy
climax and a plot propelled by moods and weather. The explanatory force
that this Emersonian framework can offer *Quicksand*'s conclusion belies
the claim that the novel's "surprise ending" dramatically breaks with
everything that came before.[51] If the ending comes as a surprise, as it has
for so many readers, it is because the preceding pages have trained an
expectation of endless open-endedness. When those expectations are
blocked by sudden closure, it is easy to attribute the startling sense of
disjunction to Larsen's lack of narrative control. Yet *Quicksand*'s weather
pattern – building pressures that find sudden release – continues until the
novel's last page. In reframing the novel's final sequence as an extension of
its ongoing series of atmospheric events, I will ask whether this final
soliciting of surprise also shows the limit case of a plot that pursues
unsettling surprise to the full disregard of narrative anchorage.

Having previously obfuscated with her unorthodox approach to
pathetic fallacy, Larsen finally volunteers a textbook example of the
literary device with a climactic storm that seems to straightforwardly
reveal Helga's internal state as well as her fate. Helga's shaming
rejection impels her to wander the Harlem streets on a blustery,
foreboding night. The amorphous vapors that have accompanied her
drift are displaced by "black clouds" that ominously gather to corroborate Helga's conviction that she has been doomed to suffer

a "dreary" destiny, as the ensuing downpour expresses her deluge of despair (*Q*, 110, 121). "Alone, isolated from all other humans, separated even from her own anterior existence," she gives herself over to elemental forces:

> Helga Crane, walking rapidly, aimlessly, could decide on no definite destination . . . Rain and wind whipped cruelly about her, drenching her garments and chilling her body . . . [A] sudden more ruthless gust of wind ripped the small hat from her head. In the next minute the black clouds opened wider and spilled their water with unusual fury. The streets became swirling rivers . . . she began desperately to struggle through wind and rain toward one of the buildings, where she could take shelter in a store or a doorway. But another whirl of wind lashed her and, scornful of her slight strength, tossed her into the swollen gutter. (*Q*, 110)

Once externalized, these meteorological signs of psychic upheaval become active agents of Helga's suffering. The clouds express their "fury" by unleashing "cruel" rain, while the "ruthless" wind "lash[es]" and "whip[s]" relentlessly. Tossing her into the gutter, the storm makes Helga's fall literal. Larsen's newly conventional use of pathetic fallacy reverts the novel into modes of character and plot development that unfold along the well-worn path of predetermined fate.

In *Narrative and Freedom*, Gary Saul Morson confirms that Larsen could not have chosen a more archetypal cue to foreshadow a pending "reversal of fortune" than the breaking storm.[52] The arrival of disaster affirms a kind of "backward causality," which pulls the ensuing sequence of events toward an unalterable conclusion.[53] "Choice becomes illusory," Morson explains, because the future – and the novel's ending – have been determined in advance.[54] The predictable plots that amass after the storm all conspire to confirm that Helga has become a plaything of fatalistic forces rather than the agent of her own actions. Yet Larsen undercuts the heavy-handed foreshadowing of fallenness by skewing the straight logic of determinism. Unleashing inexorable forces that overpower Helga's "slight strength," the storm acts as a closed meteorological and narrative system that drives her toward a predetermined end. However, there is a sense of hyperbolic melodrama that tonally shifts the scene from the pathos of tragic fate into a bathetic parody of fatalism. At the point where her agency seems completely obliterated and the scene's parodic tone assumes a graver cast, Helga seemingly undermines the inevitability of her fall by making a pragmatic decision. Lying "soaked and soiled in the flooded gutter," Helga determines "beyond all doubt that she had no desire to die, and certainly not there nor then . . . Death had lost all of its picturesque aspects" (*Q*, 110). In this moment, she decides to live rather than succumb to the prototypical death of "ruined" despair.

Understood as an emblem of fate, the storm indicates that the conventional plots of rebirth (religious, marital, and ancestral) are triggered by factors beyond the protagonist's control. Yet at the very moment Helga's agency appears most overwhelmed, Larsen provides unexpected access to her protagonist's pragmatic decision-making process. Opacity gives way to transparency, revealing her resolution to survive at all costs. Helga's decisions to convert, marry, and relocate south are pragmatic in the common sense that she is guided by practical rather than abstract considerations. But they are also properly pragmatist in the sense used by William James to describe his own decision to believe that life is worth living. Helga seems to counter her hopelessness by choosing to open a path into the future, even as inexorable plotlines close in on her. By highlighting this choice, *Quicksand*'s perplexing ending hinges on the same self-examining query that assumed life-or-death significance for James: what difference does it make if we understand our lives to be unfolding according to a predetermined plan or if we choose to believe that we inhabit a "pluralistic, restless universe" of chance (*WI*, 589)?

Pragmatist Conversion

As I have argued, Larsen's protagonist in effect tests Emerson's "solution" to the problem of psychological "polarity" by rendering herself "impressionable" to atmosphere. When her impressionability is finally met with an overwhelming atmospheric assault that waterlogs her wings, Helga's only recourse is to test the Emersonian approach further, extending it in the same direction that William James took his mentor's methods: toward pragmatism. James's emphasis on practical action and measured deliberation can make it easy to forget that he, like Helga, sought a strategy for survival in the throes of depressive despair.[55] James identifies his first pragmatic decision as his choice to live rather than remain in his self-described state of neurasthenic paralysis; this choice depends on a concurrent decision that is equally resonant with the commitment Helga makes at her lowest downturn: to believe in an open-ended universe that is "*still in the making*" over the determinist's "ready-made" reality (*WII*, 599). In *The Will to Believe* (1896) James argues that our very ability to choose life over death confirms that we live in an "unfinished world" where we are faced with "*genuine* option[s]" – momentous choices that make a difference, even if we can't know in advance what that difference will be (*WII*, 530; *WI*, 458). On these grounds he privileges the worldview of "indeterminism" over "determinism," or what Emerson calls "freedom" over "fate" (*EL*, 953). Yet the ending of *Quicksand* suggests that the "old knots" of this polarized debate are not so easily put to rest.

Larsen aligns Helga's choice between worldviews – fated or willful – with two models of the weather. When measured through the lens of determinism, weather represents predictable phenomena that can be prognosticated; when measured through the lens of indeterminism, it is a wholly unpredictable force.[56] The first framework suggests that weather constitutes a closed system of signs that needs only to be decoded, while the second charts a dynamic system where the signs may resist comprehension by remaining patternless. *Quicksand*'s storm scene stages a climactic confrontation between emblems of these opposing weather models and worldviews, which collide and then commingle in a symbolic landscape. The same wind and rain that seem arbitrarily intent on overpowering individual agency also feed James's principal metaphor of indeterministic flux – the swirling stream of experience – which is made literal in the flooded streets of Harlem. By emphasizing the pivotal *choice* Helga makes at the moment her will seems negated by inexorable forces, Larsen holds open the possibility that "genuine options" may still exist for her heroine in an unfinished narrative universe.

Helga's pragmatic process of decision-making culminates in her ecstatic conversion at the apex of the storm. Seeking refuge, Helga follows the sound of a refrain from Ezekiel – "Showers of blessings, / Showers of blessings" – into a storefront church (*Q*, 111). These hymnal showers at first appear as conspicuously overdetermined as the storm, but the rain in both cases ushers in an indeterminate flood – in this case, of tears. The Ezekiel verse bespeaks the providential plan of a creator who "will cause the shower to come down," but the rain assumes a more equivocal cast when it washes away the self.[57] The bellowing wind and "the wailing singing" merge with Helga's weeping as the chorus progresses from "All of self, and none of Thee," to "Some of self, and some of Thee," to "Less of self, and more of Thee" (*Q*, 111–12). Her deafening yells for mercy and "torrents of tears" "drown every other clamor," so that the hymn's final verse, which declares the sinner a conquered suppliant – "None of self, and all of Thee" – is not only articulated but also enacted by Helga's prostrate body.[58]

Emptied of selfhood, Helga is "penetrated" by the choir's singing just as she was overcome by the cabaret jazz. Where she retreated from ecstatic oblivion at the club, she now gives herself over to the "wild, ecstatic fury" within the church (*Q*, 112). In this emptied state of surrender Helga is opened once more to sexually and racially coded identifications with the music: "She felt an echo of the weird orgy resound in her own heart; she felt herself possessed by the same madness; she too felt a brutal desire to shout and sling herself about" (*Q*, 112–13). When "arms were stretched toward her with savage frenzy," she allows herself to be held as an "errin' sistah," a "Jezebel" and a "pore los' sinner" (*Q*, 114, 112). Giving herself over to revivalist designations of sin, it is unclear whether Helga tacitly accepts the congregation's judgment that she is a "scarlet 'oman" (*Q*, 112). As the bellowing wind and the wailing singing interpenetrate, the storm inside and outside converge in "a thunder-clap of joy" marking the instant "she was lost – or saved" (*Q*, 114, 113). At the moment "the thing became real," both protagonist and plot are suspended uncertainly between ruination and redemption, between a fated fall and the freedom of a new beginning (*Q*, 114).

The will to live and the will to believe in "some Power" go hand in hand for Larsen's protagonist, as for James; ecstatic revelation segues seamlessly into pragmatic deliberation (*Q*, 117). Resolving "for once in her life to be practical," Helga describes her conversion in terms of exchange, cost, and use value.[59] "Her resolution" to believe in a higher power is pragmatic to the extent that she asks what difference it would make to her daily existence (*Q*, 117). In each case, the choices she makes stave off literal and figurative falls. Helga is skeptically bemused by the frenzied worshippers praying for her soul until the moment "she fell forward" in nauseous dizziness; her conversion is also a decision to allow the members of the congregation to "clos[e] her in on all sides" and raise her up (*Q*, 113). After the service, she decides to seduce the Reverend Pleasant Green into marriage in the instant she is "seized with a hateful feeling of vertigo and obliged to lay firm hold on his arm to keep herself from falling" (*Q*, 115).

With Helga's capitulation to conjugal life with a "rattish yellow" preacher in the rural South, the novel seems to turn against its opening impetus by reversing the protagonist's catalyzing decision to cut all ties with Alabama, including her earlier engagement while still teaching at Naxos (*Q*, 118). But while a Bible Belt marriage once represented the unbearable constraints of conformity, now such an existence appears to offer a line of escape from worse fates. Proceeding pragmatically, for Helga, means calculating what it will take to stay standing. Without protection or resources, she determines that the "chance at stability" is "worth the risk" (*Q*, 117, 116). The following day, Helga marries the man she deems guarantor of her good standing and permanent belonging in the church community. Though she frames the union as a deliberate decision –

a safeguard against falling – with so few genuine options Helga admits she is "obliged" to grab hold of whatever will keep her literally and existentially upright.

Though Helga's conversionary embrace of life may bear some resemblance to a founding moment of pragmatism, there are telling points of departure between her pragmatic approach to survival and James's philosophical method. James's lectures on pragmatism call for his audience of east coast academics to inhabit "a tramp and vagrant world," which he compares to floating "adrift in space" (*WII*, 601). Larsen's protagonist is likewise characterized by her "vagrant primitive groping," but where James's figurative phrase served a rhetorical purpose for his listeners, Helga struggles to hold actual vagrancy at bay (*Q*, 95). While James argues for the necessity of "living in a state of relative insecurity," *Quicksand*'s depiction of pragmatic decisions made without a safety net reveals the risk of free fall when that state of insecurity is uncushioned by the qualifier "relative" (*WII*, 601). When Helga trades the precarity of drifting uncertainty for the "anaesthetic satisfaction" of a predictable life plan, her choice appears anathema to the pragmatist ideal of indeterminacy (*Q*, 118). Indeed, James explicitly objects to "anaesthetic revelation," which compromises full immersion in the stream of experience (*WII*, 350). For Helga, though, immersive experience risks submersion in quicksand. Seeking firm ground, she calculates "such a cost as she must pay for it" (*Q*, 116). In fact, the cost is much steeper than her pragmatic calculation could account for. Perhaps she evades an immediate fall, but Helga is soon laid flat by the labor of five consecutive pregnancies, and by the novel's final page she has become a spectral shadow, drained of all vitality by poverty and procreation.

Converting the Reader

The rapid-fire events that over the novel's last few pages leave Helga prostrate reinscribe the limits of a raced female destiny where domestic confinement is the only alternative to downfall and death. Belief in an open-ended future ultimately seems to make little difference in tempering or redeeming Helga's experience of the novel's punishing ending. However, I want finally to contend that for readers who have been training their attention to the novel's atmospheric events, it makes a distinctive difference whether or not Helga continues to interpret the nature of her universe as unfinished – whether or not she still willfully inhabits a universe shaped by surprise, even in the face of formal limits that would overwhelmingly consign her to existential and structural closure. Larsen's strategies for sustaining tension between open and closed narrative systems through the final sequence have the effect of maintaining the novel's structural continuity while overturning causal expectations around how it will end. At the point that readers are tempted to turn away in irritation from the wretchedness and roteness of *Quicksand*'s ending, an attunement to atmosphere may yet cause us to ask: what difference would it make if we took up the task of aversive thinking when Helga is no longer able?

Though readers have judged the oppressively airless conclusion to be incompatible with the rest of the novel, Helga observes a marked congruity between the conversion that catalyzes her return to the South and preceding aversive turns that share a pattern of atmospheric change. As Cavell notes in his reading of Emerson, "aversion" and "conversion" are both etymologically rooted in the verb "to turn," the action of upending an earlier conformity or compliance with convention.[60] In the storefront church, as in the jazz club and minstrel circus, Helga's aversion to the "contact of bodies" in "concerted convulsions" pressurizes the room with internal and external agitation, compressing her untenably between the hazily prescriptive social force of the crowd and the hazily aimless force of her own transitive convictions (*Q*, 113). The ecstasy of release is available only in "a gesture of departing from [her]self" – Emerson's definition of conversion.[61] Feeling the full exposure and precarity of habitually overturning her commitments, Helga makes her most dramatic departure from former selves and from Harlem to become the Bible Belt preacher's wife. In averting herself from a nonconformist past, she conforms with conventional domesticity, but by immediately invoking the novel's emblem of atmospheric drift, Helga frames this journey of return as a recommitment to her endless pursuit of "something else": on the day of her nuptials, the morning after her conversion, Helga watches "the wind scattering the gray-white clouds" and contemplates whether it is possible to secure her "well-being" while eluding final definition (*Q*, 116–17). For a time, the "unbelievably bright sky" stretches wide enough to encompass this possibility (*Q*, 120). Soon enough, though, the vivid expanse of the "Chinese blue sky" shrinks to a meager sliver: "'Pie in the sky,' Helga said aloud derisively . . . Pie – by and by. That's the trouble'" (*Q*, 120, 134). The last words Helga Crane speaks in the novel assert that the sky dissembles when we take it to promise future deliverance from present suffering.

As the sky narrows in visual aspect and symbolic credibility, the Alabama air grows increasingly unbreathable. At first Helga "eagerly . . . accepted everything" about her new life – "even that bleak air of poverty" and "the atmosphere of self-satisfaction which poured from her new husband like gas from a leaking pipe" (*Q*, 119, 122). It is only when she is bedbound, convalescing after the birth of her fourth child, that the air molders to the point of choking: "She had to admit that it wasn't new, this feeling . . . of asphyxiation. Something like it she had experienced before. In Naxos. In New York. In Copenhagen" (*Q*, 134). Her "suffocation" in the South "differ[s] only in degree" from previous experiences of similarly stifling conditions (*Q*, 134). In each place she flees to and from, the air of "novelty" is inevitably infiltrated by "the bleak air" of suffocating sameness (*Q*, 118, 122). When she resolves once more to "escape from the oppression, the degradation, that her life had become," the established pattern of atmospheric events alters in one crucial way: in the last instance, her "unconquerable aversion" – to stasis, to predetermination – is conquered in the sense that it finally fails to precipitate any further flight (*Q*, 135, 129).

In the novel's closing paragraph, Helga alternates between dreams of "freedom and cities" and practical questions of how to renew her strength and support her children. The narrative perspective remains closely aligned with her vacillating consciousness until the last sentence, which is set apart from the rest of the text by a blank line and a shift in focalization, as the narrator pulls back to announce the conception of a fifth child from a strangely detached distance (*Q*, 135). This new pregnancy is the last narrated event in Helga's story, and readers have compared the cold finality of its announcement with the finality of death.[62] The impulse for aversive overturning recalled by Helga on the previous page now comes to an abruptly unanticipated halt. Larsen highlights the contrast between this endpoint and previous pivot points by cutting off the narrative trajectory at its lowest downturn, rather than in the arc of flight. Instead of maintaining an indeterminate mode by scrolling the narrative forward, past this nadir and into the fresh in medias res reset of another chapter, the novel crashes all aspiration into a full stop, confirming its title by ending with a final description of Helga's dreams of freedom buried by the weight of reproduction without resources.

Frustrated critics have condemned Larsen for sacrificing her heroine "to the most conventional fates of narrative history: marriage and death."[63] But the very fact that so many readers have voiced dissatisfaction with *Quicksand*'s unfulfilled narrative trajectories makes clear that Helga's plunge feels anything but inevitable. By compromising both plot and protagonist to conventionality, Larsen creates the narrative conditions under which frustrated readers can imagine an alternate ending that resists the unsatisfying closure they are left with, willing Helga one more act of elusive escape. They might, in other words, be motivated to take up Helga's characteristic position, to continue seeking "something else," and to project this unpenned epilogue beyond the last page – creating a future where Helga's pursuit of vague yearnings remains uncircumscribed. Nancy K. Miller has traced a longer history of novels by women that likewise feature female protagonists who demand "something else" in place of the standard trajectory followed by so many heroines.[64] Such novels, she argues, often feature "implausible twists of plot," especially around their conclusions, which suddenly veer away from traditional endings as the protagonist contrives to avoid the predictable outcomes of conventional cultural narratives.[65]

Quicksand takes the opposite tack, but to a similarly unsettling effect. In averting conformity from the outset, Larsen casts as most "implausible" those "twists of plot" that come to us straight. Familiar forms of closure, such as religious rebirth, marriage, and the prodigal's return, have been expressly evaded and defamiliarized over the course of the novel. In this respect, Larsen has successfully untethered what Susan Stanford Friedman calls "the tyranny of plot" from "the tyranny of convention – the expected, the accepted."[66] When plot and convention do overlap at the end of *Quicksand*, it feels unprecedented and unacceptable to the degree that the preceding narrative events have shifted our anticipation and expectation of what the ending will be. Yet if she succeeds in unsettling expectations, Larsen also opens space for her readers to become implicated in her heroine's "unscriptable wish" for a story that would turn out differently.[67]

Under what conditions could Larsen have closed the novel without arresting all narrative drift and thus annulling its working title, *Cloudy Amber*? Is the protagonist's eventual entrapment inevitably forecasted, as the new title, *Quicksand*, suggests? Critical accounts of the ending invoke the title to describe an all-consuming force that sucks Helga under – defying escape, discontinuous with the rest of the novel's narrative terrain, and blankly stalling any explanation. *Quicksand* subsumes a variety of factors – social, political, personal, circumstantial, as well as "Helga's own vacillating inner self" – into a homogenous medium that conspires to pull her down.[68] When the motif of quicksand is interpreted as an undifferentiated, unidirectional force, the novel's individuated and heterogeneous narrative elements seem illusory, negated by the force of an inexorable, inhibiting, asphyxiated stopping point. Nevertheless, insistent dissatisfaction with *Quicksand*'s conclusion perhaps suggests it has generated imaginative possibilities that exceed the lone disappointing actuality we are left with. If a preferable narrative payoff can be conjured, even as a resentful compensation, the gap between the novel's working title and final title narrows. Even as protagonist and plot submerge into a sinkhole, Larsen affords an alternate view of quicksand that comes closer to clouds: a floating form of suspension fully amenable to ongoing state changes. In this sense, the novel invites the reader to adopt Emerson's double consciousness and likewise inhabit the gap or slippage between polarized elements (airiness and muck), polarized ontologies (drift and entrenchment), and polarized moral philosophies (uncertainty and determinism). If clouds and quicksand offer two naturally mutable analogs for the narrative traversals and transformations that give the novel its disorienting (surprising) form, these analogs also create paradoxical expectations, mixing open-endedness with closure in a way that seems to leave readers with conflicted criteria for evaluating whether the novel succeeds. This begs another question: at what limits do aesthetic returns diminish or degrade completely, when novelistic form presents (as *Quicksand* does) a causally opaque stew of transitive compulsion, provisional conversion, and picaresque effacement?

By the time Larsen was writing her first novel, scientists had definitively established that quicksand, like the weather, incorporates elements of open and closed systems. The saturated sediment acts like a solid until pressure changes initiate liquefaction. As early as 1910, scientists had proved the near impossibility of being sucked under by this liquefied soil.[69] The human body still floats in quicksand because it is of a lower density than the surrounding substance. But as Larsen's novel underlines, the delicate equilibrium that allows the body and its surrounds to remain in floating suspension is readily compromised by contingent material conditions. Similarly, studies of quicksand through the first half of the twentieth century revealed that a person could easily become stuck in an effort to escape; physical struggle only strengthened the suction force. Once a victim's liberty of movement is impeded, it is generally exposure to the elements that does the most harm. In other words, when fighting to stay afloat in quicksand, bad weather and physical exhaustion can prove a fatal combination, as it does for Helga.

Having tracked the patterns of meteorological flux over the course of the novel, an atmospherically attuned reader is finally equipped to conceive of a narrative universe in which "every solid . . . is ready to become fluid" (*EL*, 964). At the same time, *Quicksand*'s closing serves as a bracing reminder that the mind's "power to flux" can only take us so far toward transfiguring fixed forms into suspended solutions. Still, even as Larsen underlines multiple material constraints on the mind's transformative potential, those "suspensive conflicts" remain a necessary place to start (*Q*, 83).

CHAPTER 4

Gertrude Stein's Grammars of Attention

She was surprised by anything being something.

Gertrude Stein

Gertrude Stein tests our capacity to be surprised by a sentence. My previous chapters show modernist writers deepening the literary implications of surprise, beyond plot twist sleight of hand and toward more radical interruptions of expectation at the levels of readerly perception, literary syntax, and formal coherence. Yet Stein's commitment to excising all typical semblance of narrative tension or expectancy from her prose stands as uniquely rigorous. This differentiates her from Proust, James, and Larsen, whose work, in my analysis, catalyzes processes of disorientation and reorientation by overturning prior frames of reference. It would seem that for these previous works there are at least two basic requirements for the experience of surprise: first, a perceptual position must be established (before it can be unsettled); and, second, a referential frame must be in place (before it can be exceeded). For Stein, neither of these requirements holds, such that her readers are narratively denied both orientation and reference as anchoring points. Even Stein's most committed critics report challenges in training their attention upon writing that offers so few handholds; Stein untethers her words from conventional narrative forms (eschewing dramatic scenes, character arcs, or plot structures), but also from recognizable semantic association and grammatical arrangement. Since her prose first establishes no familiar baseline from which her language can contrastingly or unexpectedly depart, Steinian surprise must operate by an alternate mechanism.

For the first three decades of her career, Stein was principally concerned with surprising herself in the act of writing. The passage from which this chapter's epigraph is taken both describes and performs the process she applied in the cultivation and activation of this capacity:

> She was realising anything was something and the way she was telling about anything was the way she was one being surprised by the thing that was

148

anything. She was surprised by anything being something. She was realising anything was something. She was telling about anything telling about it in the way anything surprised her by being something ... She was telling everything in the way she had been surprised by something ... She was learning anything. She was liking knowing the thing she had come to be learning. She was surprised at the thing being existing the thing she had just learned was existing. She was surprised then.[1]

The stylistic and grammatical hallmarks of this passage – its repetitive circularity and its elusive generality – are instructive for understanding the special place of surprise in Stein's compositional practice. Invoking generically unspecified nouns that refer only to themselves – "something," "anything," "everything" – Stein detaches her verbs from external objects and foregrounds their present-tense movement. Significantly, these verbs are all in an active gerund form except for "surprised," which is already in the past tense by the time she is "realising," "telling," "learning," "knowing," or "liking." Even when Stein is in the middle of "being surprised," her report of the experience will always be retrospective.

Reading this passage as a description and performance of Stein's writing process, it's tempting to seek a patterned progression in her pursuit of "anything" and "everything." While she offers no straightforward path from "realising" to "telling" to "learning," "liking," and "knowing," these concatenated actions are punctuated by surprises that seem simultaneously to be their catalyst and product. The challenge is to keep the possibility of being surprised "alive" at every point of the process.[2] Any verb conjugated in the past tense signals a potential pitfall, since "liveliness" depends on immediacy; when one is "remembering," the words "will come out dead" (*N*, 13; *WL*, 293; *FA*, xi). In the pages that follow, I argue two points, one centered on a success and one centered on a failure: while Stein comes close to achieving a present-tense expression of surprise – making inscription and surprise simultaneous – when she writes as if she is her own sole audience, the breach of belatedness reopens between "telling" and "surprising" when her writing addresses an audience beyond herself.

In its most basic definition, surprise creates an affective gap, a sudden turning of attention. While my last chapter saw Larsen's surprising formal sequences *overturning* previous plots, the passage above exemplifies Stein's unusual technique of "insistence," an incremental process of *turning over* each word to make slight shifts in emphasis by gradually altering the structure of seemingly repetitive sentences, flooding her page with small circuit-breaking and attention-shifting syntactic interruptions (*WL*, 292). Each time Stein turns over the word "surprised," she reaffirms its "existing" – its moving, changing form of life. Even when "surprise" is not the word explicitly turned over, it remains the impetus of Stein's compositional strategy insofar as she strives to instill words with a life of their own; she treats them as evolving organisms that must adapt to the conditions posed by each new sentence.[3] Stein frames her method as a strictly routinized daily writing practice which allows for spontaneous encounters with "lively" words, sentences, and paragraphs that through the exercise of their verbal iterations can assert and reveal their expressive independence, as unembedded parts of speech that serve no grammatical or narrative purpose larger than the maximizing of new conjugative possibilities.

Such spontaneity for Stein depends on carefully cultivated "habits of attention," which she traces back to Emerson by way of William and Henry James (*WL*, 84). While critics have focused on Stein's engagement with the structure of attention she inherited from William James, who taught her psychology at Harvard, this chapter will examine her former teacher's influence alongside her seldom-studied turn to Henry James at a transitional moment in her career. While her writing was finding a wide audience for the first time, Stein was finding in the figure of Henry James, her fellow expatriate, a solution to what she described as "the problem of the external and the internal."[4] While Stein at first experiences her sudden celebrity as a distracting disruption of her previous routine, Henry James helps recast the relationship between her "inside" and "outside" audience in terms of continuity and integration rather than rupture and opposition. Instead of surrendering her long-standing compositional method (having lost much of her routinized privacy to the exigencies of public exposure), the Jamesian model allows her to reimmerse herself within the generative field of attentiveness she had long worked to cultivate – protective yet permeable, robust yet supple. Explicitly figuring both James and herself as generals, Stein understands herself in a literal, tactical sense to be doing what she has always done, but also to be "doing what American literature has always done": preparing with martial discipline to be seized by surprise (*WL*, 56).

The Problem of Attention

Stein studies often establish an irrevocable break between her "early" and "late" style. Of Stein's critics, Ulla Dydo has perhaps worked most closely with the vast collection of Stein papers housed in the Yale archives to trace "how experience becomes material for composition and yields the vocabulary for her writing."[5] According to Dydo's account, the unprecedented success of *The Autobiography of Alice B. Toklas* (1933) marked a defining split between "Stein's two voices": "the voice of words in meditation and the late, strident voice of personality that leads to audience writing, an aspect of personality display."[6] Likewise, foundational studies by Richard Bridgman, Robert B. Haas, and Donald Sutherland contend that Stein's concern with her public persona overtook the inwardly directed writing that she had earlier composed without consideration of any external audience.[7] For Dydo and others, the diversions of celebrity unambiguously compromise the integrity of Stein's formerly full, free voice.

Critics who mark the shock of success as a definitive break in Stein's creative trajectory organize their commentaries in terms that similarly structure discussions of what Jonathan Crary calls "the specifically modern problem of attention."[8] For Georg Simmel, Sigfried Kracauer, and other theorists of urban modernity, perception had become "fundamentally characterized by experiences of fragmentation, shock, and dispersal" by the later nineteenth century.[9] In his canonical articulation of the problem, "The Work of Art in the Age of Mechanical Reproduction," Benjamin diagnoses "reception in a state of distraction" across the modern masses; an earlier capacity for complete concentration has given way to a widespread failure of focus.[10] Just as Benjamin frames "distraction and concentration" as "polar opposites," Stein's critics pit the lure of diversion against the ideal of meditative focus.[11] Such critics charge Stein with dispersing her formerly undivided attention to the here-and-now of writing by capitulating to the external demands of her public.

In *Suspensions of Perception*, Crary tracks declarations of "a crisis of inattentiveness" across an array of psychological, sociological, and philosophical investigations from about 1880 to 1905.[12] Crary takes as his starting point Benjamin's claim that from the mid-nineteenth century on, "perception is fundamentally characterized by experiences of fragmentation, shock, and dispersal."[13] He argues that advances in understanding the perceptual apparatus in all its biological complexity were accompanied by a destabilized philosophical faith in perception itself as a reliable foundation for objective knowledge. Without any guarantees for the fidelity or completeness of subjective vision, the more particular concept of attention came to serve as "both a simulation of presence and a makeshift, pragmatic substitute in the face of its impossibility."[14] Crary frames his study with Benjamin's diagnosis of a "generalized crisis in perception," yet in surveying various discourses of attentiveness across the fields of psychology, philosophy, neurology, cinema, and photography, he uncovers "a sprawling diversity of often contradictory attempts" at explaining "the problem of attention."[15] Crary goes on to nuance Benjamin's claims of crisis in the context of these interdisciplinary debates, ultimately asserting "that attention and distraction cannot be thought outside of a continuum in which the two ceaselessly flow intro one another."[16] Tellingly, Crary cites John Dewey and William James to counter Benjamin's oppositional model and in so doing invokes the pragmatist sources of Stein's "genealogy of attention."[17] Rather than trying to exert control over the slips and contingencies of concentration and rather than treating her own distractibility as a crisis symptom, Stein asserts her place in a lineage of thinkers and writers who facilitate and heed the generative fluctuations of their own attention.

A number of critics have described how Stein's collegiate study of attention in the psychology labs at Harvard would bear a formative importance on her writing. As she recalls in *Autobiography*, "the important person in Gertrude Stein's life was William James" during this period.[18] In *The Principles of Psychology*, James elaborates a structure of attention characterized by its inherent distractibility, but also by its responsiveness to training. In his chapter on attention in *Principles*, James emphasizes the mechanisms of preparation and selection that can focus and hold perception. Primarily concerned in this context with increasing the "*clearness*" and speed of "intellectual *discrimination*" – with sharpening the capacity to concentrate – James only considers how distracting fluctuations of feeling warp his model of attention. Likewise, he frames unpreparedness – the encroachment of unforeseen factors into a perceptive experience – as an infringement on concentration (*PP*, 426).

As John Dewey forecasts, "the application of James's theory of emotion to his theory of attention would give some very interesting results."[19] In previous chapters I have argued that Emerson helps William James account for emotion in his pedagogical approach to attention and that Emerson likewise guides Henry James toward a literary critical model of attention that is vitalized by "felt life" (*AN*, 45). Here I want to trace this influence further by showing how the practice of attention that Stein describes as a process of *feeling writing* is shaped by the Emersonian inheritance that both the Jameses make available to her.[20] While studying with William equips Stein with the method of investigation he calls "introspection," it is from Henry that she learns to turn her introspective awareness outward. Drawing a line from Emerson, through Henry to herself, late Stein recognizes that composition is a practice of attention that does not exist in isolation; writing is a form of relation that puts her into contact with other writers, readers, and listeners who affirm generative continuities between her inside and outside audience, but also between the past and future of American literature.

Steinian Introspection

Stein's model of composition is less indebted to William James's psychological model of attention than it is to his introspective method of training attention to the movements of the mind – the method that would become the basis of his pragmatism. James's goal in his practice of introspection was to attune himself to unconsidered, unregistered facets of the stream of consciousness. At the same time, James acknowledges that we face insurmountable challenges in tuning unknown frequencies, in "focusing our attention on the nameless" (*PP*, 195). These challenges bring us back to where this book began: to the problems of belatedness and preconception. The stated goal of introspection is to cultivate "an immediate consciousness of consciousness itself" (*WII*, 1143). However, James acknowledges an inevitable "difference between the immediate *feltness* of a feeling, and its perception by a subsequent reflective act"; the "*feltness* of feeling" has already passed into another state by the time it is subsequently reflected upon (*PP*, 65). Always belated, introspection might more accurately be characterized as *retrospection*, an inferential process that relies on memory. James must then grapple with the question of whether introspection-as-retrospection necessarily reduces the moving, changing fluidity of consciousness to a static object of scrutiny excised from the stream.

The problem of preconception is even more debilitating for James than the problem of time. If the introspective method means to uncover something genuinely new, that discovery will inevitably exceed available frames of reference. The difficulty of contemplating certain psychic processes that can't readily be articulated, James observes, results in "a certain vacuousness in the descriptive parts" of psychology (*PP*, 195). Even the most fundamental introspective insight – that language is a rapid, continuous stream – is undermined by the fact that common descriptive language emphasizes the substantive parts of speech over the transitive parts. As a result, static, already-known entities can obscure through bias and outweigh through complacency what is dynamic or unfamiliar. As James's studies showed, it is exceptionally difficult to train attention to what is unanticipated because we have a limited capacity for perceiving phenomena that have not been "preperceive[d]" and "labelled" according to previous encounters (*PP*, 444). Eluding ready recognition or easy expression, unexpected encounters can have polarizing effects on attention: they might stimulate sensitivity and acuity, but just as often unexpected phenomena may fail to meaningfully engage perception, registering only numbly if not passing altogether unnoticed. Faced with these limits, as James readily concedes in a moment of understatement, *"introspection is difficult and fallible"* (*PP*, 191).

As I argued in my discussion of *Talks to Students* in the introduction, James reconceived his habits of introspective attention in the process of reading writers like Emerson. James's transition from the field of psychology to practical pedagogy and philosophy is rooted in the recognition that introspective insights matter most when they have concrete consequences in the day-to-day living of the person introspecting. For James, then, the truth value of all introspective findings came to be measured by the way they answer the pragmatist's guiding question: "What concrete difference will its being true make in any one's actual life?" (*WII*, 573). Introspection is thus retasked with discerning the difference that "our aesthetic, emotional, and active needs" might make in our daily existence (*PPII*, 312). As a means to more broadly salutary emotional and aesthetic discernment, the activities of introspecting into one's own consciousness and the act of reading literature become reciprocal processes that bridge life and art.

As James was first to admit, neither experimental psychology nor pragmatic philosophy was well equipped to fill the descriptive vacuum around uncharted regions of consciousness. However, where James identified the expressive limits of these fields in addressing consciousness, Stein tried to push her writing past such limits, transposing her teacher's introspective methods into a practice that demanded new forms for the expression of feeling. With these forms, Stein works to frame rather than fill the descriptive vacuum. In their common commitment to remaining responsive to those realms of experience that are recalcitrant to knowing or naming, James and Stein overlap with each other and with Emerson. Rather than requiring a wholly absorbed and linear concentration, the verbal whorls and lacunae of Steinian grammar quicken a more diffuse awareness, freeing both the path of the sentence and the attention of the reader from hewing to predetermined vectors. Instead of staving off distraction, interruption, and dispersal, this kind of attunement to urgently undirected registers of language recursively enfolds what James describes as "the peculiar *feeling* of attention" (*PP*, 440). In Stein's work, the peculiar feeling of monitoring one's own focus – of recursively paying *attention to attention* – can admit a sense of effortless floating and of effortful straining, the thrill of spontaneous suspension in Stein's language and the fatigue of realizing just how few resting places she offers. Stein's redefinition of the introspective method as a compositional method requires a moment-to-moment renewal of attention to the visceral act of writing. Her practice of *feeling writing* yokes James's method and object of introspection by registering *in* writing the bodily experience *of* writing. Accordingly, the process of composition becomes its own subject. Stein describes her introspective writing practice like this:

> Now what we know is formed in our head by thousands of small occasions in the daily life . . . All the thousands of occasions in the daily life go into our head to form our ideas about these things. Now if we write, we write; and these things we know flow down our arm and come out on the page. The moment before we wrote them we did not really know we knew them; if they are in our head in the shape of words then that is all wrong and they will come out dead; but if we did not know we knew them until the moment of writing, then they come to us with a shock of surprise. That is the Moment of Recognition.[21]

In Stein's account, our introspective findings can only come to us with "a shock of surprise" when we render ourselves vulnerably open to "all the thousands of occasions in daily life," without also taking in preconceived "ideas about these things." With her partitive construction, shock becomes a modifiable rather than monolithic entity. Here, Stein simultaneously experiences a sense of surprise and sense of shock at her own capacity to be surprised.

The "physical something" of inscription demands that cognitive knowing be suspended in bodily immediacy. A palpable feeling, which has not yet taken the shape of words, "flows down our arm" and onto the page. To hold "what we know" in nonlinguistic formlessness is to hold open a space for the experience and expression of something with a life of its own. For Stein, writing "comes out dead" when introspection precedes expression: "Whenever words come before the mind there is a mistake. This makes instant grammar."[22] It is only when the processes of introspecting and composing are simultaneous that we can have a surprising encounter with phenomena that are passing into writing for the first time.

The challenge of reading Stein can be attributed to the "disorienting democracy of attention" she affords to multiple registers of experience that we are not used to encountering at the same time, much less in the same sentence.[23] As Adam Frank has recently explained, "composition" for Stein designates the combination of words into sentences, and sentences into paragraphs, but also the arrangement of the material, sensorial, and emotional conditions of writing.[24] The forms of attention she highlights and demands are "compositional" in the sense that they bridge aspects of living and writing that authors conventionally hold apart for the sake of clarity and comprehensibility. She thus requires of herself and of her reader unusual attention to patterns of grammatical irregularity and unusual attention to the scenes and situations that generate writing and accommodate reading; these heightened forms of literary attention then also become subjects, to be folded back into the work itself. What might be dismissed as Stein's obscurity or abstraction may instead be seen as her refusal to obscure expressive multiplicity through editorial selection and her refusal to abstract the process of composition from its lived specificity.[25]

This is to say that writing is for Stein a literal composing of daily life, an aesthetic practice of quotidian attention and a quotidian practice of aesthetic attention that combine to require "new grammars for the new times in which she was living."[26] Rather than honing an internal focus by shutting out the external world, Steinian introspection shuttles between inner and outer impressions. This kind of busily syncretic engagement with the world seeks to incorporate "the irruption of the daily life" into the compositional field with a minimum of formal constraint.[27] Visiting Stein one summer in the French countryside, Thornton Wilder observes, "If her two dogs are playing at her feet while she is writing, she puts them into the text. She may suddenly introduce some phrases she just heard over the garden wall."[28] While these unexpected intrusions might unsettle and bewilder readers, they serve to continually refresh Stein's attention to "what happened . . . as it happened" (*WL*, 291). What could be construed as external encroachments on an introspective state actually prove vital to its cultivation. Stein's goal of inhabiting immediacy in writing finally cannot be achieved by isolating her process of composition from the everyday rhythms of living.

Grammar Studies

Stein develops a grammar that is particularly hospitable to daily rhythms during the intensive periods of language study she carried out on summer retreats from Paris to the Rhône Valley beginning in the mid-1920s. For months in the French countryside, Stein filled notebooks, or *carnets*, with collections of sentences, which she copied into larger *cahiers*, often reconstructing and rearranging these sample sentences into grammatical series that eventually form a variety of paragraph- and page-length sequences. These notebooks, excerpted in *How to Write* (1931), read like a kind of commonplace book. Rather than collecting the words or quotations of others, however, Stein gathers the commonplace features of her routines and encounters: the landscape, weather, animals, townspeople, cottage, and domestic activities that backdrop and inflect her scene of writing. While many writers jot observations that might serve as raw matter to be refined, Stein retains the unrefined immediacy recorded in her notebooks. To pick just one of many examples:

> What is grammar.
> Walking up and down.
> She got up sat down walked around and embroidered.
> When clouds resemble a horse.
> A leaf and a bird.
> Grammar is outlined.
> Resembles swinging.
> A grammar in out loud.
> Painted hot weather. (*HTW*, 77)

The statement Stein returns to again and again – *what is grammar* – does double duty as a challenge to her audience and to herself. Recurrently posing the question, Stein asks readers to reflect on unexamined grammatical conventions from which her sentences depart. At the same time, she prompts herself to generate new angles of response, often drawing on whatever is most immediately at hand. Her phrases are organized by the cadences of day-to-day activities like walking and embroidering, punctuated by the routine interruptions of mild forces beyond herself, like weather change. In this case, the logic of how sentences are shaped – how "grammar is outlined" – proceeds not by syntactic convention, but by following the stranger vectors of her attention as it joins clouds to horses to leaves to birds, based on associative conjunctions. Typical sentence actors like tense, predicate, and punctuation become inconstant, subsumed by fluctuation as Stein conjugates her attention restlessly across ground and sky, observation and reflection, interrogative and adverb. Her final lines yoke the aural register of "grammar out loud" to the visual and haptic registers of "painted hot weather." With these economical phrases, Stein manages to connect a striking range of sensory and aesthetic modalities.

This excerpt exemplifies Stein's goal of gathering a "grammar in collection," which displaces grammatical rules with a "list of what is to be done with it" (*HTW*, 56, 57). Conventional approaches to grammar assert limits on what makes sense to say. Yet Stein's studies reveal that these limits are not imposed absolutely and inflexibly by some static schema; instead, grammatical possibilities are narrowed by habits of articulation and association that become rote through repetition. Stein tracks these habitual accretions and begins to make them visible by testing unexamined standards of correctness and comprehensibility. For instance, by paring away conventional punctuation and clausal connections in the sentences quoted above, Stein suggests that these conventions are not essential; they are accrued over time through individual acts of expression and therefore can be renovated through new expressive acts. Breaking the relationship between words, sentences, and paragraphs into their component parts, Stein uncovers grammatical possibilities that refuse conformity with any authoritative system. Taking nothing for granted, she asks, "If you have a vocabulary have you any need of grammar except for explanation that is the question" (*HTW*, 60). Only by querying what communication *needs* from moment to moment are we "returned from grammar" as it is restrictively understood (*HTW*, 60).

When the exigencies of "communication" and "intuition" direct "successions of words," "grammar may be reconstituted" as "a conditional expanse" (*HTW*, 60, 39, 57, 55). Writing that is guided by both the contingent conditions and routinized rhythms of daily life produces grammatical constructions that shift in response to their environment. Dydo summarizes the guiding impetus of Stein's grammar studies like this: "A landscape moves as does a paragraph."[29] Or in Stein's own words, she aims to develop "Grammar in relation to a tree and two horses" (*HTW*, 111). As she elaborates in "How Writing is Written," she seeks "new constructions of grammar" in order to "get the sense of immediacy" one feels when "one feels anybody else."[30] The "feeling" of words "filled with moving" will dictate the shape of the sentences and paragraphs they form (*WL*, 161). Reconceived in the terms of relation and feeling, "grammar little by little is not a thing," but a process (*HTW*, 106).

Critical studies that mark a discontinuity in Stein's writing at the point she became famous tend to argue that the compromised quality of her compositional attention served to stall her grammatical invention; in response to her newfound popularity, Stein is seen to concede to more conventional formulations. A standard chronology of Stein's career identifies *Autobiography* as the end of Stein's "real writing" in 1933 and *Lectures in America* (composed in the spring and summer of 1934 and delivered to live audiences from the fall of 1934 into the spring of 1935) as the onset of a less inventive "personality writing" that would dominate the remainder of her career.[31] Yet when Stein's sudden success is taken to mark a decisive divide between two voices, it can be easy to ignore the pivotal work that followed *Autobiography* and preceded *Lectures*.

This before-and-after-*Autobiography* narrative would seem to find support in Stein's preliminary response to "the unexpectedness of onrushing impressions" that came with fame; declaring "there is no use in the outside ... [it] is no longer interesting," she initially tries to follow the recommendation made by Simmel and other intellectuals who declare a crisis of inattention, by erecting a protective barrier around everything that was "happening inside."[32] Though Stein's first reaction to literary celebrity was organized around the same dichotomies that structure discussions of "the modern problem of attention" – inner vs. outer, public vs. private, concentration vs. distraction – these terms did not remain polarized in her thinking for long.[33]

Stein's fears that the enervations of public exposure warranted defensive isolation could only be self-fulfilling; cloistering herself from outside contact, Stein also cuts herself off from everything that fed her compositional practice. But this strict separation between internal and external life proved untenable: she quickly found herself in the grip of a paralyzing writer's block that interrupted thirty years of writing every day. "I began to worry about identity," Stein later recalls, and in worrying about identity "I was not writing."[34] Grappling with these incapacitating apprehensions, Stein breaks her writer's block by working to establish a grammar of attention that foregrounds crucial continuities between her writing before and after she had an audience. In fact, the largely overlooked work Stein would produce in the months following the publication of *Autobiography* belies the tidy story of identity crisis that reduces Stein's late style to populist crowd-pleasing, while mourning her bygone capacity for concentration.[35]

Audience and Identity

The wide acclaim Stein received for *Autobiography* was accompanied by immediate requests for a sequel and promotional tour. Attempting to meet the demand for a follow-up, Stein began a short series of "Confessions" (as she termed them) that reflected back upon her own writing. These fragments of the soon-aborted sequel express Stein's estrangement from her former sense of herself as the "first and last audience" of her writing.[36] As Stein "began to think about how my writing would sound to others, how I could make them understand," she interrupts a formerly self-sufficient loop of affirmation between her own voice and ear. In one of her "Confessions," titled "And Now," she writes:

When the success began and it was a success I got completely lost. You know the nursery rhyme, *I am I because my little dog knows me*. Well you see I did not know myself, I lost my personality. It has always been completely included in myself my personality as any personality naturally is, and here all of a sudden, I was not just I because so many people did know me. It was just the opposite of I am because my little dog knows me. With so many people knowing me I was I no longer and for the first time since I had begun to write I could not write.[37]

With the proliferation of "so many people knowing" her, Stein loses confidence in knowing herself, the same confidence that supported and validated the private iconoclasm of her quotidian writing routine. Her despair at the scattering and dilution of an "I" that had, as she says, "always lived within myself and my writing" frames identity as something internal and intrinsic yet susceptible to uninvited transformation, which must be protected under peril of fragmentation and erasure.

The touchstone "I am I" phrase indexes Stein's ongoing negotiation of the relationship between authorial identity and audience. In the iteration above, the phrase hinges on the causal logic of "because" so that identity becomes dependent on the confirmation of an outside agent – her dog, her audience, her public. However, two other formulations of the phrase annul the false choice she poses here between public and private selves that can only be dispersed or consolidated. Tracking Stein's "I am I" motto back to its first pronouncement in 1929, and forward to its reiteration in the essay "Henry James" from 1934, I want to suggest that the grammar of interrogation and negation undoes the causal logic of this statement of identity. Stein's earlier and later "I am I" iterations voice her abiding commitment to a compositional "I," from which her dualistic thinking ("I am just the opposite") only temporarily departs.[38]

Stein's first "I am I" turns on an interrogative "what ... if ... then" construction. In a grammar study from *How to Write* titled "Saving the Sentence," she asks, "What is a sentence for if I am I then my little dog knows me" (*HTW*, 19). In this phrasing, the nature of identity and language are actively queried rather than simply asserted. Stein works toward a processual grammar through which both the self and the sentence can resist predetermined forms of expression. Through her grammar experiments she is "gradually com[ing] to find out" that "one has no identity that is when one is in the act of doing anything" (*WL*, 146). If using language is itself an "act of doing," as Stein's grammar studies demonstrate, then any stable foundations of selfhood evaporate in the present moment of composing. Accordingly, when Stein opens another grammar study with the assertion "I am a grammarian," her "I am" only exists in the specific and temporary activity of grammar experimentation (*HTW*, 105). Stein's pronouncement several pages later – "the subject is grammar" – acknowledges that her status as a writing subject is wholly constituted by her object of study; the grammar of the sentence determines the grammar of the self (*HTW*, 108).

In the winter of 1933, after months of uncharacteristic unproductivity, Stein began to draft a new study focusing on a set of American luminaries: Ulysses Grant, the Wright brothers, George Washington, and Henry James.[39] When Stein rephrases the "I am I" statement in the opening of the chapter on "Henry James," she is trying to return to the way that she "used to write" in a very different sense than in the grammar investigations of "And Now." Instead of attempting to recover some sanctity of subjectivity, Stein describes a writing self that is wholly permeable to what it perceives: "I am I not any longer when I see. This sentence is at the bottom of all creative activity" (*WL*, 275). In the immediate moment of perception, the distinction between the seeing "I" and the thing seen dissolves, and with it, any bounded sense of self. This dissolution of selfhood into the process of perception is not experienced as a threatening negation but as the vital basis of "creative activity." Here Stein's concept of identity is "just the exact opposite of I am I because my little dog knows me" insofar as she does not define herself by external recognition and does not protect an essential core self (*WL*, 275). In "Henry James" as in *How to Write*, the compositional "I" and the experiencing "I" mutually constitute each other in sentences where the activities of daily living and daily writing are intimately entwined.

These studies of luminaries, eventually published under the title *Four in America* (composed in 1933 and 1934, published posthumously in 1947), are premised on a set of "what if" thought experiments. Stein explores the relationship between fame, audience, and cultural identity by posing rhetorical questions that refuse to grant any grounding assumptions about the famous figures: what difference would it make if her four subjects had exchanged their respective military, political, religious, and creative pursuits for entirely different occupations. Considering her fellow writer, Stein asks, "What if Henry James had been a general?" – a hypothetical proposition that is far from arbitrary, since she often compared herself to a general.[40] The few critics who have commented on this work tend to read it as a record of struggle with fame, which resolved in a new kind of "audience writing" that allowed Stein to claim her place alongside the "representative Americans" who were her subject.[41] However, my reading of *Four in America* suggests a divergent way of evaluating this period of Stein's life, her study of James displaying not a conventional voice crafted to stabilize a crisis of identity but rather a return to writing the way she had "always done" (*WL*, 56).[42]

Stein conquers her writer's block by identifying the protective shield she had raised between herself and the world of audience expectations, a barrier that had severed the antennae of her creative scrutiny. In defending herself against a sense of exposure, she had also deadened her sense of thought and expression. In the process of completing *Four in America*, Stein conversely sought to stop defensively compartmentalizing the realms of inner and outer life, instead reasserting through the confident cadence of a familiar grammar that "the outside which is outside and the inside which is inside . . . are not existing" (*N*, 39). As Stein will go on to attest in her *Lectures in America*, the "very interesting" experience of beginning "to feel the outside inside and the inside outside" goes hand in hand with a new interest "in the relation of a lecturer to his audience," which Stein had finally decided to experience firsthand in America (*WL*, 205).[43] Stein pinpoints Henry James as an ideal proxy for examining her status as a cultural figure in the American literary field and distinguishes this chapter in *Four in America* by pursuing a highly intimate identification with its subject, in contrast to the more abstracted explorations of identity offered in other chapters. She describes the project in a letter:

> I am and have been very full of meditations about direct and indirect vision, and the relation between the writer and an audience either actual or not actual, I have just been writing about four Americans and one of them Henry James has cleared up a lot of things for me that is in trying to put him down.[44]

This passage describes a mental uncluttering, her focus on James sweeping away the obstacles to fluency, resetting her capacity to feel "full of meditations," the surplus of raw thoughts that could brim over into words. More specifically, her work on James dismissed the binary logic that opposed "direct and indirect vision" and sequestered her perceptual field. Instead of keeping the external world of readers at a hermetic remove, Stein introspects the feelings that circulate through and complexly entangle the "relation between the writer and an audience":

> As Henry James would say and what sensations. I am almost getting the better of these strange sensations and it is taking the form of meditations . . . that I know will interest you. I have just begun it and it will be all about audiences, a very fearful subject and it is taking form.[45]

Stein frames the James essay as a meditative exercise in giving compositional form to the "strange sensations" generated by the impact of audience on authorship. Through the process of triangulating her reading of James's literature and life with her new experience of being read by others, Stein gains the upper hand over "a very fearful subject," which becomes a source of interest as opposed to a site of blockage.

In turning to James, Stein is returning to the writer who provided her with an initial impetus to write and with the literary model for her first novella, *Q. E. D.* (1903).[46] From the time Stein made her initial foray into writing with a work that paid homage to the style and subject of *The Wings of the Dove*, James remained a formative figure whose work afforded a long-view comparative for her own authorial trajectory. In the unmooring storm of her new publicity, meditating on the writer who had spurred her first literary impulse allows Stein to articulate enabling continuities between the "way she used to write" and the uncertain future of her writing.[47] Looking back to look forward, Stein situates herself in what she describes as the "continuous present," a temporal order where sustaining connections with the past open onto future horizons of possibility.

Two Ways of Writing

By writing herself into relation with "James the General," Stein reaffirms that training attention does not mean tightening one's focus or honing one's interest to a more narrowly selective range. Instead of modeling militant concentration, Jamesian responsiveness more closely resembles the quality of attention she describes as "open feeling."[48] In *The Making of Americans* (1925), Stein defines "open feeling" as "that kind of being that has resisting as its natural way of fighting."[49] This counterintuitive definition provides one inroad for understanding her Henry James essay's idiosyncratic guiding question. Casting James as a general, Stein clarifies and develops her account of "open feeling," defining "feeling" as the primary way of "being" in the world, and asserting that a form of resistance comes from openly insisting on this "being" in the face of stifling forces. The James essay explores this form of resilient openness in explicitly military terms. Its martial premise unexpectedly allows Stein to consider the shock of her own new public exposure in terms other than assaultive attack and reactive defense. The model of attention she formulates in response to her "what if?" thought experiment allows a more complex reaction that blends the militant with the meditative, the protective with the permeable.

As James exemplifies, the general and the writer are both defined by their tactical command, by how they operationally ready and strategically equip themselves for the art of battle or the campaign of composition.[50]

The essay proceeds by laying out a series of agonistic dualisms, which are then systematically collapsed. As the title of the essay's opening section signals from the outset, seemingly antithetical pairings in fact form "DUETS," compositions for two voices that require the collaboration of both parts to make a relational whole. Stein opens by positing "two ways of writing," which might be contrasted as premeditated writing and spontaneous writing (*WL*, 278, 289). As she establishes first, the premeditated writer is guided by a preformed sense of what she will write and whom she writes for, the present process of writing thus incorporating a prior sense of conception and an anticipated sense of reception. Alternately, the spontaneous writer resides in a present uninflected by the past or future: her senses are entirely occupied by the immediate act of writing. Stein begins by privileging spontaneity over premeditation, but by the essay's close she discovers that Henry James "is a combination of the two ways of writing" – improvising and strategizing – that she initially held to be opposed (*WL*, 291).

In the immediate aftermath of *Autobiography*, Stein is compelled to defend her writing practices – and by extension, her self – against unknown forces that threaten to breach her compositional consciousness. Yet her meditations on James make clear that the task is not to patrol the borders of attention with redoubled vigilance. James's successful command of the art of writing depends on his capacity to deliberately plan and then creatively improvise in the face of unexpected exigencies. As Stein describes, his careful preparations for everything "that could happen or not happen" allow James to respond to "what happened as it . . . happened" (*WL*, 291). Though James is thoroughly "prepared" for "winning a battle and a war," he can also throw cautious preparation to the wind when the moment calls for more adaptive response (*WL*, 293). Having "no care for plans" and "no wishes" for any particular outcome, he simultaneously "controls something" and "controls nothing" (*WL*, 287, 294). For Stein, James embodies the impulse toward "settlement in place" even as he "could adventure to wander away from being a general" (*WL*, 297). Echoing Emerson, she suggests that the roles we find ourselves playing – writer, military leader, celebrity – are as impermanent as the moods we pass through from one minute to the next.

The process of investigating James's "two ways of writing" provides Stein with evidence that she too writes "both ways" at once (*WL*, 276, 287).

When framed as an exploratory investigation, the essay appears more immediately indebted to the principle of spontaneity. Refusing a preconceived stance toward her subject, Stein proceeds haltingly, often bafflingly, feeling her way from one line to the next. For instance, she opens by approaching the pressing "question of audience" as a kind of classroom call-and-response, a perverse Socratic dialogue where the queries receive no authoritative answers:

> What is an audience.
> Everybody listen.
> That is not an audience because will everybody listen.
> Is it an audience because will anybody listen.
> When you are writing who hears what you are writing.
> That is the question.
> Do you know who hears what you are writing and how does that affect you or does it affect you.
> That is another question.
> If when you are writing you are writing what some one has written without writing does that make a difference.
> Is that another question.
> Are there, is there many another question. Is there.
> On the one hand if you who are writing know what you are writing, does that change you or does it not change you.
> That might be an important question.
> If you who are writing know what it is that is coming in writing, does that make you make you keep on writing or does it not . . .
> Perhaps yes perhaps no.   (*WL*, 276–77)

This tortuous line of inquiry exemplifies the generic slipperiness of *Four in America*. Readers seeking sustained arguments or conventional portraits may find passages like this one more readily recognizable as some kind of poetry, where its gaps and recursions of syllogistic absurdity scan as expected genre features, and not as an aberrant rebuke of essayistic form. Stein moves in the "perpetually provisional" mode she shares with Henry James's figure of the "restless analyst," but also with William James's equally restless investigator: the pragmatist.[51] Instead of marshalling final conclusions, Stein weighs each query and proposition according to the defining question of pragmatism: what difference does it make to one's experience? In the lines quoted above, Stein repeatedly returns to this refrain, while never conclusively determining "what does or does not make any difference" (*WL*, 309). Instead, she follows both Jameses in shifting the object of her ongoing meditation, away from the instrumentalism of answers and toward how the act of questioning "affects" and "changes" her.

This is not to say that Stein's groping provisionality precludes preparation. Her correspondence and "Confessions" following *Autobiography* reveal that she had been planning this study for months, and she had been preparing this analogy for years to the extent that she frequently framed the act of composition in military terms. Besides comparing herself to a general, Stein often drew analogies between marshalling words into sentences and marshalling troops into battle. In *How to Write*, "a grammar is fought" with "the weapons of precision," and the "positions of the troops" depend on intimate acquaintance with the contours of landscapes and sentences: "Battles become hills. Hills a grammar" (*HTW*, 59, 72, 89). Those grammar studies yield discoveries that Stein will rediscover in relation to James. "Premeditation" is not opposed to meditative writing, she observes, since premeditated composition is simply "meditated before meditation" (*HTW*, 32). Both "prepared unpreparedness" and "premeditated meditation" are open to "surprise attacks," which are not warded off but embraced as a source of "start startle startled abundance" (*HTW*, 32, 60, 55). Combining martial discipline with adaptive improvisation, Stein prepares herself to be surprised by the unknown future of her writing and its place in literary history.

Stein calls James a general but also claims him as her "forerunner," which in its original usage referred to an advance guard that cleared the way for the army approaching the battlefield.[52] In this capacity, he opens a path for her embrace of the fact that writing, like "war is a surprise" – a refrain she repeats in *Four in America*.[53] Stein's treatment of James in *Lectures in America* suggests that he clears a way forward but also guides her back to Emerson. Through James, Stein regains a balanced sense of preparatory control and spontaneous abandon and can confidently situate her work in a lineage of writers who approach the act of composition as an extension of the Emersonian insight that "life is a series of surprises."

Floating American Feelings

Stein writes her essay on James in anticipation of the lecture tour of America, which marked her first return to the United States in three decades – exactly thirty years after Henry James's own long-delayed tour of his homeland.[54] In James, Stein finds a fellow American abroad who similarly struggled with ambivalent feelings about literary celebrity and the United States. Both writers situate themselves as distanced rather than immersed observers of their home country, suggesting that it was the "improvised European" who could see most clearly what it is to be an American.[55] Yet at pivotal points in their respective careers, the expatriates each conceded the importance of reorienting their purview, updating a potentially abstracted national landscape around a fresh set of on-the-ground experiences. The striking parallels between the homecoming journeys that followed underscore James's importance as Stein's forerunner and guide.[56]

Following James's American tour in 1905, James began to contemplate the mammoth project of revising his vast body of work for the New York Edition. Stein was one of the few subscribers to this Edition, and James's prefaces offered her a powerful model for reflecting back on a body of work and imagining the future forms it might take. At this moment of retrospection, James reflected on the place of his largely unread later fiction in the American cultural imagination and in literary history more generally. To this end, as he writes to William, he planned "to write a *book* of 'impressions' (for much money)" as he traversed the country, eventually publishing that record of his tour as *The American Scene* in 1907.[57] Rather than rooting his narrative persona in home soil, this work opens with a flood of maritime metaphors like those that circulated through *The Ambassadors*. The "repentant absentee" arrives back in New York on a "warm wave" that breaks "over the succession of aspects and objects according to some odd inward rhythm."[58] Like Strether, James cultivates a "fluidity of appreciation," which allows him to "float" with "a certain recklessness in the largest surrender to impressions."[59]

Whereas James figures himself and Strether as vessels floating among sensations and impressions, Stein observes an unnameable "something" irreducible to character or consciousness that "floated up there" above James's paragraphs (*WL*, 56). In "What is English Literature," the first of the lectures she presents in America, Stein identifies a "disembodied" drift in James's novels as the essentially "American thing" that defines the "future feeling" of his writing against stagnated European literary traditions (*WL*, 56, 54, 56). The "American feelings" she detects hovering around his writing are formally manifest in the way a "whole paragraph was detached from what it said from what it did, what it was from what it held" (*WL*, 53). The paragraph's content no longer determines its form; rather, the form becomes constitutive of its content. In this way, James opens the way for Stein's poetic project of making the process of composition its own subject.

In Stein's account of her own American tour, James serves as a mediating figure who permits her to locate herself in a cohesive American tradition, while carving out her distinctive place within it.

> In the American writing the words . . . began to detach themselves from the solidity of anything, they began to excitedly feel themselves as if they were anywhere or anything, think about American writing from Emerson, Hawthorne Walt Whitman Mark Twain Henry James myself Sherwood Anderson Thornton Wilder and Dashiell Hammett and you will see what I mean . . . words left alone more and more feel that they are moving and all of it is detached and is detaching anything from anything and in this detaching and in their moving it is being in its way creating its existing. This is then the real difference between English and American writing and this then can then lead to anything. (*N*, 10)

As Steven Meyer observes, Stein awards Emerson pride of place as the origin of her literary lineage by positioning his name at the opening of the line and following it with the lone comma in the sequence – a grammatical marker that both sets him apart from the group and distinguishes him at its head.[60] The otherwise unpunctuated list demonstrates that the connective tissue adhering this American genealogy is finally its "lack of connection": the writers share a "disembodied way of disconnecting something from anything and anything from something" (*WL*, 56).

For Stein, the discontinuity and disconnection that comes from relentless unsettlement finds its source in Emerson. Asserting that she is "doing what American literature had always done," Stein traces her compositional method of detaching words from "the solidity of anything" back to Emerson's essays (*WL*, 56; *N*, 10). "The poetic American thing" in this Emersonian tradition is "a space of time that is filled with moving": words "excitedly feel themselves" mobilized "in every and in any direction" (*WL*, 97; *N*, 10, 14). Stein attributes her vibratory excitement to the open horizon of imaginative possibility that characterizes what Emerson calls "this new yet unapproachable America": its expansiveness can "lead to anything" (*EL*, 485). Whereas British literature is circumscribed by "daily island life" on a bounded land mass tethered to a long cultural tradition, American writing exceeds geographical and historical strictures (*WL*, 33–34). Though "the words used are the same words," they are mobilized in their American usage by an unconstrained immensity and vitality (*N*, 14).

Although Emerson first manifests this American dynamism in writing, Stein credits James with inaugurating "the method of the twentieth century."[61] James serves as Stein's most immediate point of connection to the Emersonian lineage she lays out, but also as her point of departure from it. Even as she esteems James for the "future feeling" of his writing, she faults him with stopping short of detaching this feeling wholesale from narrative form: James still insisted on subjugating the free flow of this feeling to "a beginning and a middle and an ending" (*WL*, 55; *N*, 25). In decisively cutting all ties with character and plot, Stein claims to have done "more with the paragraph than ever had been done" (*WL*, 56). She describes a continuous process of "breaking the paragraph down" and reconstituting it to make the words themselves the plot and characters so that "all the action is there in the play of one word next to another one."[62]

Surprise Encounters

Stein's lectures work to close the gap between herself and her audience by continually situating herself as a reader of literature, viewer of art, or spectator of theater. For example, in the talk titled "Pictures" Stein recalls standing before paintings that "give me pleasure and hold my attention" – from "a panorama of the battle of Waterloo" she saw when she was eight, to gold-framed oil paintings hanging in the Louvre, to Cézanne's landscapes.[63] Having aligned listeners to her particular perspective on these artworks, Stein introduces excerpts of her idiosyncratic literary portrait of Cézanne. Where her audience may expect portraiture to have a referential relation to its subject, Stein's portrait investigates the feelings that inflected her perceptual encounters with her subject: "And was I surprised. Was I very surprised. Was I surprised. I was surprised and in that patient." Having reoriented readers and listeners around her introspective process, she turns them back on their own experience of reading and listening by asking, as if posing an ultimatum, "Are you patient"?[64]

Patience, Stein suggests, is required to cultivate the form of familiarity – with paintings, but also people – which might yield new discoveries:

> When you have looked at many faces and have become familiar with them, you may find something new in a new face you may be surprised by a different kind of a face you may even by shocked by a different kind of a face you may like or not like a new kind of face but you cannot refuse a new face. You must accept a face as a face. And so with an oil painting.[65]

Stein's insistence that "you cannot refuse a new face" is itself a refusal of the kind of familiarity that forecloses surprise. While "most people are more predetermined as to what is the human form and the human face," painters such as Cézanne or Picasso model an uncompromising attention to "something new."[66]

A journalist reporting on Stein's lecture tour attested to her success in bridging the speaker-listener divide by attuning the audience's attention to incremental "differences" among sentences "which seem so much alike": "When you think she has been saying the same thing four or five times, you suddenly know that she has carefully, link by link, been leading you to a new thing"; this newness emerges as the product of a gradual remaking of one's habits of attention, "link by link," "from sentence to sentence."[67] As one reader of Stein elaborates, her work requires us "to invent new ways of reading" that somehow reconcile the "long stretches that tax one's attention" with "constant surprise."[68] As I have aimed to show in this chapter, Stein "taxes" our attention precisely to the point that "the same thing" reveals itself as "a new thing."

Coda
Surprised by Silence
(Listening with John Cage)

For John Cage, the exacting process of learning to read Gertrude Stein was formative. Stein's work presented an indeterminate art experience that required and cultivated new intensities of attention from its audience, an aesthetic commitment that would shape Cage's theoretical attitudes and creative practice for the rest of his life. Under the tutelage of Stein's prose, Cage began to see "composition as process," a recognition of how life's daily contingencies constantly recondition art with unpredictable inflections. In light of the mercurial force that webs of context exert upon a text, all fixed notions of what a literary or musical text is – how its production and reception can fill mutable durations and what fissures of expansion and infarction it can unknowingly admit – must for Cage, via Stein, be tenaciously explored through the application of surprising pressures.

Stein reported having discovered new forms of compositional attention while working in a Harvard lab from 1893 to 1897. A half-century later, Cage found himself likewise at Harvard, steeped in his readings of Stein and primed to have his own powers of introspective awareness tested. Stein's writing was teaching Cage to consider the spaces that emerge between words, and during a visit to an anechoic chamber (a room that is free from echo) on campus at Cambridge, a parallel exercise was facilitated in sonic space. In this room, specially built to absorb all sound, Cage for the first time understood silence to be as plastic a medium as is language. He would recount this foundational moment of discovery many times over the course of his career, recalling how he entered the chamber

> not expecting in that silent room to hear two sounds: one high, my nervous system in operation, one low, my blood in circulation. The reason I did not expect to hear those two sounds was that they were set into vibration without any intention on my part.
>
> That experience gave my life direction, the exploration of non-intention.[1]

At this particular point in time (under the aesthetic influence of Stein) and this particular point in space (through the research auspices of Harvard), Cage was prepared and positioned to have his acts of noticing radically redirected along unforeseen vectors. The chamber's total absence of ambient noise gave unavoidable primacy to a completely new field of awareness – *self*-awareness literalized in the most bodily sense. An indifferent apparatus within Cage's body spoke, and Cage heard it palpably for the first time – a thrumming of nervous and circulatory systems that signaled not merely a new objective category of sound but a new subjective capacity for perceptual attention itself. In this powerful recalibration, the distracting and desensitizing affects of intention were stripped away, opening for Cage a new sensory frequency upon which non-intended effects could surface or materialize. This channel is what his life's work would henceforth seek to tune, so the ears of audiences might likewise hear unpredicated frequencies and be similarly seized in unprecedented ways.

Crucial to the anechoic encounter was the unwilled and unexpected aspect of its circumstances. Just as the emergent sounds manifesting in the chamber's silence came to Cage as a surprise so too did those spontaneous sounds ungovernably reorient his attention. Whereas reading Stein required a certain kind of training – giving strenuous attention to the fidelity and lapses of his own attention – the chamber created the experiential conditions under which Cage's attention could be turned back on itself with minimal effort, could be turned back on itself irrespective of effort, even. Cage was exporting a Steinian program of introspective self-awareness from the realm of language into the realm of music, employing unpunctuated silences in his compositions in order to challenge listener attention, just as Stein had forced readers to consider intervals, absences, and fugue-like repetitions on the page. But Cage was also pushing this program further. As he contended, music may have inherent formal advantages over prose when seeking new angles within what Joan Retallack has described as our "geometries of attention."[2] To listen to music is already to attend to the nonreferential because music, as Cage defines it, is "a language already without sentences, and not confined to any subject."[3] Recognizing, as did William James, that people have "great difficulty" in "paying attention to something they don't understand," Cage saw music's lesser emphasis on understanding as key to the open receptivity of its audience.[4] "Music is about changing the mind," he affirms, "not to understand, but to be aware."[5] This underlines Cage's emphasis on process – his conviction that edification evolves from the simple act of listening reflexively, not from arriving at a referential interpretation. And as Cage's investigations continually prove, the listening mind can become most acutely and instructively aware of itself through contact with its most immediate surroundings, a bare common soundscape, when music is construed as silence.

While unfeasible to recreate the space-specific experience of the anechoic chamber on a larger, public scale, Cage's experiments with silence sought to open for audiences a similarly transformative space in time. Conceived in 1947 as his first "silent piece," *4'33"* was later deemed by Cage to be his most important work (*S*, 98). Structured only by three noteless time brackets whose indicated durations add up to four minutes and thirty-three seconds, the ostensibly empty score offers no guidelines for its performers. Correspondingly, *4'33"* could command no specific response from its audience, with no positive auditory object to engage or gratify attention. Yet as decades of Cage listeners confirm, to turn attention toward his silence is to provoke a heightening, attention turning back upon the self as it interpolates that silence. From the sudden exposure of this moment, in which the intentions of the composer and performer are swallowed by negativity, *4'33"* compels a surprised and sensitized vantage, as the silence speaks an implicit directive: notice anew where you are, what you see, what you hear.[6]

Amid such a milieu, Emerson's foundational question – "Where do we find ourselves?" – can again be profitably and ceaselessly rearticulated (*EL*, 471). At the Woodstock, New York premiere of *4'33"* in 1952, the attention of Cage's audience was surely redirected to details beyond the normal purview of concertgoing: the still figure of pianist David Tudor opening and closing the piano lid, as he marked the three periods of silence; the creak of chairs in the concert hall, beneath the shifting of suddenly self-conscious bodies; the uncertain coughs and throat clearings, felt as disruptions, but disruptions of what? In Cage's recollection of that night, "You could hear the wind stirring outside during the first movement. During the second, raindrops began pattering the roof, and during the third people themselves made all kinds of interesting sounds as they talked or walked out."[7] When I play *4'33"* in my classrooms, the expectations of a conventional performance are not in place to be overturned for students, as they would be in a hall filled with musicians and concertgoers (some "prepared" to hear Cage, some unsuspecting). But the disparity between iterations of *4'33"* is precisely the point. The plastic form of Cage's composition – its explicitly defined yet flexible structure – frames as the performance whatever happens in the given temporal span. The piece serves as a repeatable approximation of Cage's Harvard experience – a holding place, a bounded chamber in space and time within which the unexpected sonic textures of silence are given rise, a heightened zone where consciousness invites new contact with its encasing environment.

Against the human tendency for perceptual orientation, once learned, to remain fixed, *4'33"* spurs a "figure/ground swerve" that can disrupt and reorganize the patterning within a field of experience: "What was previously ground," (that is, ambient noise), "becomes figure" (that which is supposed to comprise the musical object of attention), while "what previously lay dormant outside the scope of our attention becomes possibility."[8] By inverting customary contexts and habits of hearing, Cage dismisses the standard formal impetus of art that would "bring order out of chaos," relegating the aesthetic predictability of order and instead seeking "a way of waking up to the very life we're living" (*S*, 12). Sounding like Stein, and like William James, Cage expands and recircuits the operations of attention, drawing passive and unreflective reception into more complicated self-scrutiny and charging the spaces of self-scrutiny with "the irruption of the daily life."[9] By paring the border between art and life to the most permeable and flexible threshold possible, Cage exposes his audience to the experience of living in an uncertain universe of chance, joining a lineage of pragmatism and a lineage of surprise – four-and-a-half bounded minutes of disorienting art serving to reinvigorate for audiences again and again the daunting and perpetual conditions of life.

* * *

4'33" represents the culmination of an intensive five-year period of pragmatist investigation initiated by Cage's experience as an instructor at Black Mountain College, a hub of cultural innovation and educational reform in North Carolina's Blue Ridge Mountains. The liberal arts college was founded in 1933 on John Dewey's pedagogical premise that experiential learning is the engine of aesthetic innovation and democratic participation. The school's founder, John Andrew Rice, and its most formative faculty member, Josef Albers, were equally committed to practical Deweyan methods for dissolving boundaries between teacher and student, art and life. As a member of the school's advisory board, Dewey visited the campus throughout the 1930s and affirmed its exemplary approach to "learning by doing."[10] By the time Cage joined the faculty in 1948, Black Mountain's classrooms and studios had served for over a decade as sites where Dewey's mandate could be activated, as articulated in the "Black Mountain College Prospectus."

The prospectus reads as a pedagogical manifesto, but instead of proclaiming the revolutionary newness of the school's educational program, it opens with the distinctly pragmatist claim that "Black Mountain College" is simply "a new name for some old ways of thinking" about teaching (*WI*, 479). As the prospectus establishes:

> Black Mountain College is heretical because it has practised from its founding (1933) two of the simplest and oldest principles on which higher learning – when it has been higher – has rested:
>
> I. that *the student*, rather than the curriculum, is *the proper* centre of a general education [...]
> II. that a faculty fit to face up the student as the centre have to be measured by *what they do with what they know* [...][11]

These two "base principles" provide Cage with a nonhierarchical, action-oriented model for experiencing teacher-student reciprocity, which in turn allows him to reconceive and restage the artist-audience relationship. While Cage's silent pieces exemplify one cycle of audience-centered experimentation that emerges from his time at Black Mountain, the school's pedagogical influence is even more overtly evident in his efforts to reinvent the lecture form as what he calls a "structured silence."[12] In keeping with the spirit of the prospectus, Cage's lectures are less about conveying knowledge than about transforming the channel of conveyance, premised on the pragmatist notion that ideas "exist in things and in actions" – or more precisely, in "what happens between things." The act of lecturing therefore succeeds for Cage only to the extent that it newly charges the physical and mental space passing between speaker and listener. In this charged space, which per the prospectus is "where the life of [ideas] is to be sought," the *raisons d'être* of Black Mountain's institutional legacy and Cage's experimental legacy align.[13]

In the foreword to a collection of his writings, titled *Silence* (1961), Cage reflects on the method of composing and lecturing he honed at Black Mountain: "My intention has been, often, to say what I had to say in a way that would exemplify it; that would, conceivably, permit the listener to experience what I had to say rather than just hear about it" (*S*, ix). Through his teaching, Cage began investigating whether the experiential immediacy of music could in fact be lexically achieved; through the performative genre of the lecture, Cage and his students could mutually inhabit a new kind of productive transmission in real time. Cage's unsettling use of the lecture form – like Emerson's and Stein's before him – "*enacts* the struggles" to "give present life" to words which otherwise "are always *past*," irretrievably inert once written or inattentively spoken.[14] Cage best encapsulates this aspiration in his "Lecture on Nothing": "Each moment / presents what happens. / How different / this form sense is / from that / which is bound up with memory" (S, 111).

Written in 1949 and delivered in 1950 (two years before the debut of *4'33"*) at The Club, an artists' loft at 39 East Eighth Street in New York, "Lecture on Nothing" is Cage's first major public incorporation of the pragmatic and pedagogic concerns developed at Black Mountain – an intellectual inquiry "enacted and undergone" *with* his audience in the Deweyan sense, rather than "externally imposed."[15] Toward this aim, the lecture opens with a series of enigmatic statements that exemplify Cage's use of paradox: "What we re-quire / is / silence; / but what silence requires / is / that I go on talking . . . But / now / there are silences / and the / words / make / help make / the silences. / I have nothing to say / and I am saying it / and that is / poetry / as I need it" (S, 109). Cage's koan-like repetitions and reversals provide meditative means for going "beyond the logical mind," insistently overturning any expectation that the lecture will educate by authoritative assertion.[16] By having "nothing to say" and ostensibly no message to deliver, Cage privileges the exploratory, present-tense act of "saying" over preconceived content or linear argument: "Slowly, / as the talk goes on, / we are getting nowhere / and that is a pleasure" (S, 118).

Dewey recognized that putting "enactment into practice" is not "self-explanatory"; a judicious apparatus of explanation is what makes enactment legible.[17] In "Lecture on Nothing," these two modes continuously converge in the lecture's reflexive metacommentary on its own unfolding structure and method. Cage draws attention to his medium, comparing the relationship between music and silence to the relationship between words and silence. Cage observes that in either medium, his mode of composition remains largely the same: "This is a composed / talk, / for I am making it / just as I make / a piece of music" (S, 110).[18] Whether verbal or musical, the compositional process is for Cage "a discipline," which if properly practiced may generate "rare moments / of ecstasy" (S, 111). In this practical conjoining of discipline with ecstasy, Cage invokes the same principles that I have shown modernist pragmatists deriving from the practices of Emerson throughout this book. In my introductory discussion of William James's lectures on education, I briefly compared his portrait of experienced teachers to experienced musicians, the latter for whom rigorous preparation more familiarly enables virtuosic improvisation. Noting that his method for creating a sonata informs his method for creating a lecture, Cage affirms and embodies the mutual reliance of these two professions – one stereotypically enactive, one stereotypically explanatory – on balancing methods of pedagogical preparation and performative realization.

"Lecture on Nothing" both describes and performs how disciplined structures give rise to "rare moments" of ecstatic discovery. After his opening string of disorienting paradoxes, Cage reanchors his unmoored audience with a detailed explanation of the talk's unconventional composition. He outlines the "rhythmic structure" used to divide and subdivide the talk's "space of time" into measures and units, just like a sonata's formal conventions; on the page, these breaks are marked with blank spaces that separate his words into four columns (*S*, 112).[19] Cage continues with a holistic account of the lecture's construction and organization: "You have just / ex-perienced / the structure / of this talk / from a / microcosmic / point of view. / From a macrocosmic / point of view / we are just passing the halfway point / in the second / large part. / The first part / was a rather rambling / discussion of / nothing, / of form, / and continuity ... / This second / part / is about structure" (*S*, 112–13). By breaking from the conventions of lecturing while reflexively guiding that departure, Cage simultaneously unsettles and leads his audience, disarming expectations while creating new uncertainty about where his remarks may ramble next. As he explains, the talk's meticulous, almost mathematical, structure permits a free-ranging approach to its content, or lack thereof: "Most speeches / are full / of / ideas. / This one / doesn't have to have / any. / But at any moment / an idea / may come along" (*S*, 113). Instead of imparting previous discoveries or precedent lessons, Cage's "Lecture on Nothing" invites the arrival of "something" unforeseen, speaker and listener collectively probing the present space where they are, mutually open to what may emerge, as it were, ex nihilo (*S*, 126).

The lecture form that grows from Cage's time at Black Mountain employs methodical arrangements, yet he describes his "technique / of handling materials" as a "discipline" of removing authorial intention (*S*, 114). As he elaborates in an interview, "the discipline is a discipline of the ego," a means of forgetting or jolting free of the self, to access "something outside, over which I have no control."[20] Cage's challenge as a lecturer, then, is to assert a rigorously structured process of discovery, while simultaneously effacing himself from it.[21] Here we might recall that Richard Poirier's "pragmatist poetic space of enactment" is also a space of effacement, "where action, not entity, is all."[22] Cage's "rhythmic reading" of the penultimate section of the "Lecture on Nothing" works in this same way to displace his "entity" as speaker with the incantatory action of speaking (*S*,

109). He repeats one passage "some fourteen times" (with small Steinian variations), concluding with a winking refrain: "Originally / we were nowhere; / and now, again / we are having / the pleasure / of being / slowly / nowhere. / If anybody / is sleepy, let him go to sleep" (*S*, 123, 109). Cage cultivates a hypnogogic state with these reiterations, a strange sleepy "nowhere" (graphically represented by a blank page), where the borders between subject and object of speech might begin to blur.

Cage's account of "being slowly nowhere" closely resembles Dewey's account of "undergoing" an aesthetic experience. Dewey wrote the lectures that would become *Art as Experience* during the same year Black Mountain was founded, suggesting that the practical possibilities of art education modeled by the college also exerted a strong reciprocal influence upon his experiential aesthetics. Dewey could not have anticipated a work like "Lecture on Nothing," and Cage, amazingly, would not be directly exposed to Dewey's art lectures until the late 1980s. Yet their mutual affiliation with Black Mountain helps explain the close affinities between their pragmatic aesthetics.[23] As Dewey writes, "the unique distinguishing feature of esthetic experience is exactly the fact that no such distinction of self and object exists in it, since it is esthetic in the degree in which organism and environment cooperate to institute an experience in which the two are so fully integrated that each disappears."[24] By effacing himself in his "rhythmic reading," Cage creates the conditions of integration and disappearance Dewey describes. The degree to which he succeeds in dissolving the self-object distinction is of course unpredictable, and any attempt to direct the experience would be anathema to his ethos of "non-intention." As Cage recalls, at least one audience member forcefully rejected "the pleasure of being slowly nowhere," interrupting his sleepy refrain to loudly exclaim: "John, I dearly love you, but I can't bear another minute" (*S*, ix). This interruption forcefully returns Cage to his specific authorial identity and threatens to lay bare the fact that a certain hierarchical relation remains in the lecture hall – his audience the assailed recipients of his (sleep-) imposing performance. On the other hand, by challenging that authority and breaking from the decorum of staying silent, this audience member exerts her own participative agency, charging the space anew with a surprising circuit break, and wonderfully fulfilling Cage's hope that "at any moment / an idea / may come along."

While the merging of artist and audience is Dewey's measure of a fully realized aesthetic experience, Cage's lecture ultimately comes to rest on a more modest methodological claim: "All I know about method is that when I am not working I sometimes think I know something, but when

I am working, it is quite clear that I know nothing" (*S*, 126). Upholding uncertainty as the only consistent condition in which useful work unfolds, and extolling a definition of method that serves to overturn any passive sense of knowing, Cage echoes Black Mountain's teaching philosophy, as articulated by the college's founder, John Andrew Rice: "Our central consistent effort is to teach method, not content; to emphasize process."[25] Through practices that explore "the restriction and freedom of absence, the plastic fullness of nothing, the point a circle begins and ends," Cage is compelled above all, as were the students and faculty of Black Mountain, to "a program for more work" (to recall William James once more).[26] On that note: like a lecture or a sonata or a novel, a work of criticism must at some point stop its work and risk moving, Cage-like, into that temporary state of knowing something – until the next work prompts each of us, as reader, writer, or teacher, "to draw a new circle" (*EL*, 414).

Notes

Introduction

1. Ralph Waldo Emerson, *Essays and Lectures* (New York: Library of America, 1983), 10. Hereafter cited internally and in notes as *EL*.
2. "Works and Days," in *Ralph Waldo Emerson: The Major Prose*, ed. Ronald A. Bosco and Joel Myerson (Cambridge, MA: Harvard University Press, 2015), 525.
3. Michael Clune, *Writing Against Time* (Stanford, CA: Stanford University Press, 2013), 3.
4. Harold Bloom, *Wallace Stevens: The Poems of Our Climate* (Ithaca, NY: Cornell University Press, 1980), 60–61.
5. See Michael North's "The Making of 'Make It New,'" *Guernica*, August 15, 2013, <www.guernicamag.com/the-making-of-making-it-new/>, for the complex genealogy of "this common shorthand for modernist novelty." As the phase assumed the status of a slogan, he shows, it came to signify an oversimplified concept of newness: "Make It New was not itself new, nor was it ever meant to be."
6. Ralph Waldo Emerson, *The Topical Notebooks of Ralph Waldo Emerson*, vol. 2, ed. Susan Sutton Smith (Columbia: University of Missouri Press, 1993), 164.
7. "Innovate, v.," *OED Online*, accessed Aug 7, 2015, <www.oed.com/Entry/96310>.
8. John Dewey, "Emerson: The Philosopher of Democracy," *International Journal of Ethics* 13.4 (1903): 406.
9. Dewey had already begun to put psychological principles to practical and pedagogical use in *Psychology* (New York: Harper and Brothers, 1890), a study written "expressly for use in class-room instruction" (iii). As Dewey argues, "surprise is one of the most effective methods of arousing attention." Introducing "the unexpected in the midst of routine" serves to refresh and expand the "variety and mobility of psychic life": it is for Dewey "the very contrast" between habitual rhythms and interruptive surprises that reorients the student into a posture conducive to learning (127).
10. For a concise overview of scholarly debates around Emerson's relation to pragmatism, see the introduction of Gregg Crane's "Intuition: The 'Unseen

Thread' Connecting Emerson and James," *Modern Intellectual History* 10.1 (2013): 57–86.

11. William James, *The Principles of Psychology*, vol.1 (New York: Dover, 1950 [1890]), 434. Hereafter cited internally and in notes as *PP*.

12. William James, *Writings, 1878–1899* (New York: Library of America, 1992), 837. Hereafter cited internally and in notes as *WI*.

13. Elisa New, *The Line's Eye: Poetic Experience, American Sight* (Cambridge, MA: Harvard University Press, 1998), 6, 7.

14. New, *Line's Eye*, 7; *EL*, 7.

15. For persuasive revisions of Bercovitch's account of Emersonian nationalism, see Lawrence Buell, *Emerson* (Cambridge, MA: Harvard University Press, 2003), 270–75; see also Branka Arsić, *On Leaving: A Reading in Emerson* (Cambridge, MA: Harvard University Press, 2010), 248–51. The collection of essays titled *The Other Emerson*, edited by Branka Arsić and Cary Wolfe, (Minneapolis: University of Minnesota Press, 2010), likewise contests what Buell identifies as "the doctrine of individualism" frequently attributed to Emerson (1). In Chapter 1, I will consider a paradigm of Emersonian self-loss that contrasts starkly with the Emersonian "imperial self" presented by Bercovitch in *The Puritan Origins of the American Self* (New Haven, CT: Yale University Press, 2011 [1975]), 175.

16. John Dewey, *Art as Experience* (New York: Penguin, 2005 [1934]), 29.

17. *WI*, 856; William James, *Writings, 1902–1910* (New York: Library of America, 1987), 1124. Hereafter cited internally and in notes as *WII*.

18. Dewey, *Art as Experience*, 5. Nancy Bentley argues that both James and Dewey were theorists of what she calls "neurological modernity" (a phrase she borrows from Ben Singer) in *Frantic Panoramas: American Literature and Mass Culture* (Philadelphia: University of Pennsylvania Press, 2009), 247–87.

19. Dewey, *Art as Experience*, 5, 8.

20. Dewey, *Art as Experience*, 29, 27, 29, 32.

21. Dewey, "Emerson," 411.

22. Dewey, *Art as Experience*, 181.

23. Dewey, *Art as Experience*, 151.

24. Dewey, *Art as Experience*, 151.

25. Dewey, *Art as Experience*, 181.

26. Dewey, *Art as Experience*, 182, 55, 182.

27. Dewey, *Art as Experience*, 102.

28. Dewey, *Art as Experience*, 359.

29. Benjamin also draws on the work of Henri Bergson and Georg Simmel to diagnose the withering of experience in a shock-saturated modern age, but he privileges the historicity of Freud's framework of shellshock (even as he

dehistoricizes Freud's theory when he generalizes it beyond the conditions of war that provide its context).

30. Freud quoted in Walter Benjamin, "On Some Motifs in Baudelaire," in *Illuminations*, trans. Harry Zohn (New York: Schocken, 1969), 161. Hereafter cited internally and in notes as *M*.

31. I borrow the phrase "the crisis of experience" from Martin Jay, who argues that "no one became so acute and persistent a diagnostician of the crisis than Walter Benjamin" in *Songs of Experience: Modern American and European Variations on a Universal Theme* (Berkeley: University of California Press, 2005), 329.

32. Sigmund Freud, *Beyond the Pleasure Principle* (New York: Dover, 2015 [1920]), 6, 7. Following the atrocities of World War II, Benjamin's declaration that "shock experience has become the norm" seems to prophesy the traumatic course of history, figured as a closed circuit that does not allow for contingency or change (*M*, 162). From this vantage, some strains of contemporary trauma theory have claimed that all history is structured by trauma. Here trauma becomes "an inherent latency of the event that paradoxically explains the peculiar temporal structure, the belatedness, of historical experience: since the traumatic event is not experienced as it occurs, it is fully evident only in connection with another place, and in another time," per Cathy Caruth's influential definition in *Trauma: Explorations in Memory* (Baltimore: Johns Hopkins University Press, 1995), 8.

33. Benjamin in fact explores various permutations of "shock experience" over the course of his career and takes different – often contradictory – approaches to theorizing it. Susan Buck-Morss traces some of those contradictions in "Aesthetics and Anaesthetics: Walter Benjamin's Artwork Essay Reconsidered," *October* 62 (1992): 3–41. See also Miriam Bratu Hansen's *Cinema and Experience: Siegfried Kracauer, Walter Benjamin, and Theodor W. Adorno* (Berkeley: University of California Press, 2012), especially 103–6 and 119–21. In "The Work of Art in the Age of Mechanical Reproduction" (1936) (which I discuss in Chapter 4), an essay published several years before "On Some Motifs in Baudelaire," Benjamin swings between two seemingly antithetical versions of shock, alternately highlighting its capacity to diminish or rejuvenate experience, both lamenting and celebrating the destruction of the aura by new technologies. My point here is that "Motifs" is the only essay where Benjamin frames shock in terms of Freudian trauma. Within this framework, Benjamin decries modern breaks with prelapsarian plenitude, but other writings declare his allegiance with avant-garde efforts to harness aesthetic shock, exploding the homogeneity of history and making way for revolutionary change.

34. Franco Moretti, "Homo Palpitans," in *Signs Taken for Wonders: On the Sociology of Literary Forms* (New York: Verso, 2005), 116. Moretti argues

that Benjamin's broad application of Freudian shock fundamentally misunderstands urban experience by presuming a rigid system of expectations and a singular event that violates them. His discussion of Balzac's novels of "urban personality" elaborates the way that "city life" tends to unfold along a continuum, mitigating extremes and extending a range of "intermediate possibilities" (126, 117). City dwellers who adopt "ever more pliant and provisional attitudes" are protected against crises and can perceive "surviving potentiality," even in the midst of "sudden catastrophe" (117, 118, 117).

35. Giorgio Agamben, *Infancy and History: The Destruction of Experience*, trans. Liz Heron (London: Verso, 2005), 41.

36. Philip Fisher, *Wonder, the Rainbow, and the Aesthetics of Rare Experiences* (Cambridge, MA: Harvard University Press, 1998), 1.

37. Fisher, *Wonder*, 20.

38. *EL*, 150, 954, 91; Ralph Waldo Emerson, *The Early Lectures of Ralph Waldo Emerson, 1833–1836*, ed. Stephen Whicher and Robert Spiller (Cambridge, MA: Harvard University Press, 1951), 6. Hereafter cited internally and in notes as *EAL*.

39. *EL*, 266; Emerson, "Works and Days," 525; *EL*, 490; "Works and Days," 523.

40. Here I echo Eve Kosofsky Sedgwick's influential account of reparative reading, which clears space for the realization "that the future may be different from the present," so that the reparatively positioned reader can also entertain such "ethically crucial possibilities as that the past, in turn, could have happened differently from the way it actually did"; see *Touching Feeling: Affect, Pedagogy, Performativity* (Durham, NC: Duke University Press, 2013), 146. Both this introduction and this book as a whole are indebted to the reading methods modeled by Sedgwick in her criticism and classroom.

41. New, *Line's Eye*, 12.

42. New, *Line's Eye*, 11, 13.

43. New, *Line's Eye*, 10.

44. Joan Richardson, *Pragmatism and American Experience: An Introduction* (New York: Cambridge University Press, 2014), 112.

45. Richardson, *American Experience*, 122.

46. Richardson, *American Experience*, 110, 108.

47. Richardson, *American Experience*, 110.

48. Emerson's relationship to pragmatism has been hotly contested. My goal here is not to prove Emerson's status as a "proto-pragmatist" contra Stanley Cavell and others but rather to suggest some of the important ways that James's and Dewey's readings of Emerson inflected their thinking; see *Emerson's Transcendental Etudes* (Stanford, CA: Stanford University Press, 2003), 215

and 232. For one angle on the debate, see Richardson's *Pragmatism and American Experience*, which makes the case that Cavell himself is a pragmatist, "in spite of his demurrals about being so designated" (9).

49. Dewey, *Art as Experience*, 355.
50. Dewey, *Art as Experience*, 354.
51. Dewey, *Art as Experience*, 357.
52. Dewey, *Art as Experience*, 356.
53. Dewey, *Art as Experience*, 356.
54. Lisi Schoenbach, *Pragmatic Modernism* (New York: Oxford University Press, 2012), 10.
55. Schoenbach, *Pragmatic Modernism*, 24. Here Schoenbach extends Joan Richardson's insight that the founders of pragmatism registered Darwinism in its conception of language and thinking as life forms that are, as Richardson says, "constantly undergoing adaptation and mutation" (quoted in *Pragmatic Modernism*, 153n14). Richardson's studies of pragmatism examine daily "habits of mind" cultivated by William James, Dewey, and others in their efforts to accommodate Darwin's insight that we are "accidental creatures inhabiting a universe of chance;" see *A Natural History of Pragmatism: The Fact of Feeling from Jonathan Edwards to Gertrude Stein* (New York: Cambridge University Press, 2007), 131; *American Experience*, 3.
56. Emerson discusses the phrase in "The Method of Nature" (1841).
57. Dewey, *Art as Experience*, 361.
58. Dewey, *Art as Experience*, 361.
59. Emerson underlines his ongoing investment in this phrase by titling his 1860 collection of essays *The Conduct of Life*.
60. Dewey, "Emerson," 184.
61. Dewey, "Emerson," 184.
62. Dewey, "Emerson," 185; *EL*, 311.
63. Dewey, "Emerson," 185.
64. Dewey, "Emerson," 186.
65. As the essays collected in *Emerson's Transcendental Etudes* make clear, Cavell has devoted much of his career to remedying Emerson's exclusion from philosophical conversations.
66. While Emerson's method of moving from old beliefs to new perceptions can be discerned most readily in pragmatism, his model of surprise also forecasts key developments in psychologies of emotion that I take up in Chapter 2.
67. Ralph Waldo Emerson, *Emerson in His Journals*, ed. Joel Porte (Cambridge, MA: Harvard University Press, 1982), 556. Hereafter cited internally and in notes as *EJ*.
68. Emerson, *Topical Notebooks*, 164.

69. Ralph Waldo Emerson, *Journals and Miscellaneous Notebooks of Ralph Waldo Emerson*, vol. 8, *1841–1843*, ed. William H. Gilman and J. E. Parsons (Cambridge, MA: Harvard University Press, 1970), 12.

70. For a particularly generative reading of this visit and Emerson's treatment of past writings as "textual specimens" (181), see the chapter titled "The Emerson Museum" in Lee Rust Brown's *The Emerson Museum: Practical Romanticism and the Pursuit of the Whole* (Cambridge, MA: Harvard University Press, 1997), 59–168. As Brown observes, Emerson found himself reading "a version of precisely the kind of writing to which he had long aspired" (60). See also Paul Grimstad's chapter "The Method of Nature" in *Experience and Experimental Writing: Literary Pragmatism from Emerson to the Jameses* (New York: Oxford University Press, 2013), 17–41.

71. Ralph Waldo Emerson, *Journals and Miscellaneous Notebooks of Ralph Waldo Emerson*, vol. 5, *1835–1838*, ed. Merton M. Sealts (Cambridge, MA: Harvard University Press, 1965), 39.

72. Ralph Waldo Emerson, *Journals and Miscellaneous Notebooks of Ralph Waldo Emerson*, vol. 7, *1838–1842*, ed. A. W. Plumstead and Harrison Hayford (Cambridge, MA: Harvard University Press, 1969), 90.

73. Brown, *Emerson Museum*, 121.

74. Julie Ellison, *Emerson's Romantic Style* (Princeton, NJ: Princeton University Press, 1984), 175. Arsić's "Appendix" to *On Leaving* opens with a survey of critics, including Ellison, Cavell, and Richard Poirier, whose "engagements with Emerson's logic, grammar, and rhetoric" have countered the "widespread prejudice" that his writing is "contradictory" and "unmethodical" (*On Leaving*, 293). My reading of Emerson is everywhere inflected by the work of these critics and by Arsić's own study.

75. Ellison, *Emerson's Romantic Style*, 77.

76. The reviewer is quoted in the introduction of Ralph Waldo Emerson, *The Later Lectures of Ralph Waldo Emerson*, vol. 1, *1843–1854*, ed. Ronald A. Bosco and Joel Myerson (Athens: University of Georgia Press, 2010), xxvi.

77. Ellison, *Emerson's Romantic Style*, 13.

78. Ellison, *Emerson's Romantic Style*, 168.

79. Ralph Waldo Emerson, *The Journals and Miscellaneous Notebooks of Ralph Waldo Emerson*, vol. 4, *1832–1834*, ed. Alfred R. Ferguson (Cambridge, MA: Harvard University Press, 1964), 288; *EL*, 581.

80. On abandonment in Emerson see Arsić's *On Leaving* and Sharon Cameron's "The Way of Life by Abandonment: Emerson's Impersonal," in *Impersonality: Seven Essays* (Chicago: University of Chicago Press, 2007), 79–107.

81. "This affirmation of the ethical imperative to act, even within the framework of a less than absolute surety is a fundamental premise" of Emerson's writing argues David M. Robinson in *Emerson and the Conduct of Life: Pragmatism*

and *Ethical Purpose in the Later Work* (New York: Cambridge University Press, 1993), 156. Eduardo Cadava echoes and extends Robinson's argument in *Emerson and the Climates of History* (Stanford, CA: Stanford University Press, 1997), 69.

82. Susan L. Dunston, "Ethics," in *Emerson in Context*, ed. Wesley T. Mott (New York: Cambridge University Press, 2014), 172.

83. Dunston, "Ethics," 177.

84. Dunston, "Ethics," 174.

85. Silvan S. Tomkins, *Affect Imagery Consciousness*, vol. 1, *The Positive Affects* (New York: Springer, 1962), 273.

86. Adam Frank, "Some Affective Bases for Guilt: Tomkins, Freud, Object Relations," *English Studies in Canada* 32.1 (2006): 13.

87. Brian Massumi, interview by Mary Zournazi, "Navigating Movements: A Conversation with Brian Massumi," in *Hope: New Philosophies for Change*, ed. Mary Zournazi (New York: Routledge, 2002), 218.

88. Emerson, *Journals*, vol. 8, 254.

89. Emerson, *Journals*, vol. 5, 178.

90. Emerson, *Journals*, vol. 5, 178.

91. Emerson, *Journals*, vol. 5, 245.

92. "Surprise, n.," *OED Online*, accessed July 3, 2009, <www.oed.com/view/Entry/194999>.

93. With this claim I build on Christopher R. Miller's *Surprise: The Poetics of the Unexpected from Milton to Austen* (Ithaca, NY: Cornell University Press, 2015), which leaves off chronologically where this book begins. Having made the compelling case that surprise was "the presiding spirit of eighteenth-century prose fiction and aesthetic discourse," Miller begins his epilogue by identifying Emerson as the writer who brings surprise to its "apotheosis" in the nineteenth century (223). Following this brief but suggestive assertion, Miller observes that "shock" replaces "surprise" as the touchstone term in the twentieth century (226). I argue that Emersonian surprise abides in modernist forms that have been subsumed under the rubric of shock.

94. Arsić, *On Leaving*, 88. With this last formulation Arsić describes Emerson's investment in moments "when everything has been left . . . but nothing has been gained or attained" (88).

95. Nella Larsen, *Quicksand and Passing*, ed. Deborah McDowell (New Brunswick: Rutgers University Press, 2004), 28 (hereafter cited internally and in notes as *Q*); Arsić, *On Leaving*, 145.

96. Gertrude Stein, *The Making of Americans* (Normal, IL: Dalkey Archive Press, 1995 [1925]), 296.

97. See Gertrude Stein, *Writings and Lectures, 1911–1945*, ed. Patricia Meyerowitz (London: Peter Owen, 1967), 25–27. Hereafter cited internally and in notes as *WL*.

98. Cage publishes a lecture by that name in *Silence: Lectures and Writings* (Middleton, CT: Wesleyan University Press, 1961), 18–56. Hereafter cited internally and in notes as *S*.

99. Irving Howe, *The American Newness: Culture and Politics in the Age of Emerson* (Cambridge, MA: Harvard University Press, 1986), 1.

100. Richard Poirier, *Poetry and Pragmatism* (Cambridge, MA: Harvard University Press, 1992), 5.

101. Poirier, *Poetry and Pragmatism*, 4.

102. Poirier, *Poetry and Pragmatism*, 178.

103. Poirier, *Poetry and Pragmatism*, 6.

104. Richard Poirier, *The Renewal of Literature* (New Haven, CT: Yale University Press, 1988), 98.

105. Poirier, *Renewal of Literature*, 98, 97.

106. Poirier, *Renewal of Literature*, 99, 98.

107. Poirier, *Renewal of Literature*, 98.

108. Poirier distinguishes "difficulty" from "density," his word for uses of language that make their complexity felt by way of allusive inflection rather than announcement (*Renewal of Literature*, 134).

109. Poirier, *Renewal of Literature*, 107, 98.

110. Poirier, *Poetry and Pragmatism*, 175.

111. Poirier, *Poetry and Pragmatism*, 180.

112. Poirier, *Poetry and Pragmatism*, 180–81.

113. The conference was held at the CUNY Graduate Center, organized under the direction of Morris Dickstein, who published the proceedings in *The Revival of Pragmatism* (Durham, NC: Duke University Press, 1998). Cavell's contribution, "What's the Use of Calling Emerson a Pragmatist?," was republished in his 2003 collection, *Emerson's Transcendental Etudes*. Poirier inverts Cavell's question with the title of his talk: "Why Do Pragmatists Want to Be Like Poets?"

114. Grimstad, *Experience*, 3. Grimstad finds unexpected affinities between Poirier's definition of pragmatism and Cavell's definition of modernism. As he argues, both critics are invested in the "tuition by which, in composition, intuitions turn into shareable meanings" (14).

115. In Richardson's account, Cavell represents a "transcendentalist strain" of pragmatism; see *American Experience*, xi, 18, 126, 140.

116. Richardson, *American Experience*, 127.

117. Richard Poirier, interview by Giorgio Mariani, "Poetry, Pragmatism, and American Literature: An Interview with Richard Poirier," *College Hill*

Review 5 (2010), <www.collegehillreview.com/005/0050201.html>; *Poetry and Pragmatism*, 8.

118. Dickstein, *Revival of Pragmatism*, 15.
119. Dickstein, *Revival of Pragmatism*, 15.
120. Morris Dickstein, "The Rise and Fall of 'Practical' Criticism: From I. A. Richards to Barthes and Derrida," in *Theory's Empire: An Anthology of Dissent*, ed. Daphne Patal and Wilfrido Corral (New York: Columbia University Press, 2005), 62.
121. See, for instance, Nicholas Gaskill's account of the New Critics' strong ideological opposition to pragmatism in "What Difference Can Pragmatism Make for Literary Study?," *American Literary History* 24.2 (2012): 374–89. Dickstein's introduction to *The Revival of Pragmatism* tells a similar story.
122. Henry Steele Commager, *The American Mind: An Interpretation of American Thought and Character Since the 1880's* (New Haven, CT: Yale University Press, 1950), 97.
123. Poirier, *Poetry and Pragmatism*, 11.
124. Poirier, *Poetry and Pragmatism*, 184.
125. Poirier, *Poetry and Pragmatism*, 184.
126. Poirier, *Poetry and Pragmatism*, 179.
127. Cleanth Brooks, "The Language of Paradox," in *The Well Wrought Urn* (London: Dennis Dobson, 1947), 3.
128. Poirier, *Poetry and Pragmatism*, 171–72.
129. Poirier, "Interview."
130. Poirier, *Poetry and Pragmatism*, 191.
131. *WII*, 509; William James quoted in *Poetry and Pragmatism*, 130.
132. Poirier, *Poetry and Pragmatism*, 191.
133. Poirier, *Poetry and Pragmatism*, 25.
134. Poirier, *Poetry and Pragmatism*, 25.
135. Poirier, "Interview"; *Poetry and Pragmatism*, 25.
136. Poirier, "Interview."
137. Ross Posnock, "Reading Poirier Pragmatically," *Yale Review* 80 (1992): 168; Poirier, *Poetry and Pragmatism*, 95.
138. Poirier, *Poetry and Pragmatism*, 95.
139. Poirier, *Poetry and Pragmatism*, 94.
140. Richardson, *Natural History*, xv.
141. Richardson, *Natural History*, 16.
142. Richardson, *Natural History*, 17.
143. Reuben A. Brower, "Reading in Slow Motion," in *In Defense of Reading: A Reader's Approach to Literary Criticism*, ed. Richard Poirier and Reuben A. Brower (New York: Dutton, 1962), 4.

144. Brower, "Reading in Slow Motion," 4.
145. Brower quoted in Richardson, *Natural History*, 240; Brower quoted in Steven Meyer, *Irresistible Dictation: Gertrude Stein and the Correlations of Writing and Science* (Stanford, CA: Stanford University Press, 2001), 396n22. Richardson's *A Natural History of Pragmatism* extends Poirier's Emersonian line back to Edwards, while Meyer's *Irresistible Dictation* expands it to include Alfred Whitehead and Wittgenstein. Meyer situates himself as "part of a current reassessment" of pragmatism in literary studies "due largely to the efforts of Richard Poirier" but cites Poirier only in his preface and in footnotes (xix). His lone direct citation from Poirier is a Wittgenstein quote that Poirier uses in the Hum 6 essay to further hone Brower's definition (and to strengthen the connection Meyer draws between Stein and Wittgenstein): "I really want my copious punctuation marks to slow down the speed of reading. Because I should like to be read slowly. (As I myself read.)," Wittgenstein quoted in Poirier, *Poetry and Pragmatism*, 209; quoted in Meyer, *Irresistible Dictation*, 396n22. Fittingly, Poirier's presence in Meyer's text feels more like an absence; Poirier is indirectly credited with employing Wittgenstein and with clarifying Brower, but where Wittgenstein's and Brower's voices appear, Poirier's does not.
146. Posnock, "Reading Poirier," 161.
147. Poirier, *Poetry and Pragmatism*, 27, 26, 27.
148. Poirier, *Poetry and Pragmatism*, 129.
149. Poirier, *Poetry and Pragmatism*, 129.
150. Poirier, *Poetry and Pragmatism*, 130.
151. Posnock, "Reading Poirier," 161, 169.
152. As one of the first critics to pay thanks to Poirier, Posnock has been working longer than most to expand the purview of his pragmatist lineage. Across his books, Posnock has put Emerson and James into contact with an expansive circle of American and European philosophers, writers, and artists, including members of the Frankfurt School (in *The Trial of Curiosity*); Du Bois, Alain Locke, Hurston, and Ellison (in *Color and Culture*); and Philip Roth (in *Philip Roth's Rude Truth*).
153. Ross Posnock, *Renunciation: Acts of Abandonment by Writers, Philosophers, and Artists* (Cambridge, MA: Harvard University Press, 2016), 9.
154. Posnock, *Renunciation*, 8.
155. Posnock, *Renunciation*, 2.
156. *EL*, 414; Emerson quoted in Posnock, *Renunciation*, 2. Tellingly, Posnock published an excerpt from the introduction to *Renunciation* under the title "I'm Not There," *Daedalus* 143.1 (2013): 85–95.
157. Posnock, *Renunciation*, 2, 8. Forgetting himself and letting the material guide his investigations into its depths does not for Posnock entail

"indulging in imitative form"; while he tries "to minimize mimetic reciprocity," or *stylistic* enactment, Posnock remains invested in the critical and creative possibilities of what might better be described as *structural* enactment (9).

158. Posnock, *Renunciation*, 9, 8.

159. Posnock, *Renunciation*, 8.

160. Posnock, *Renunciation*, 10; "'Don't Think, but Look!': W. G. Sebald, Wittgenstein, and Cosmopolitan Poverty," *Representations* 112.1 (2010): 114; *Renunciation*, 2. The phrase "an open intellectual experience" is from Adorno's "The Essay as Form" (which Posnock describes in *Renunciation* as "a very Emersonian essay") (10). Posnock previews the method he will employ in *Renunciation* in an earlier essay, which outlines his approach to "receptive reading" – a phrase he also takes from Adorno writing in an Emersonian mood – as "nearly the opposite of the familiar postmodern adversarial relation of critic to text"; "miming the motion" of the text under study in this "nonargumentative" mode, Posnock discovers "a broad associative weave of linkages and also an intimacy between [his] critical method and [his] peripatetic principal figures"; see "Cosmopolitan Poverty," 14.

161. Posnock, *Renunciation*, 10.

162. Posnock, *Renunciation*, 8.

163. Posnock, *Renunciation*, 7.

164. As one student observed, reading Richardson on Stevens required the same quality of careful, recursive attention as reading Stevens himself. While some students expressed frustration with the painstaking process of unpacking dense formulations, many others found that the density of the critical prose rewarded rereading and became an ideal bridge in mood and sensibility for improved comprehension of the equally dense primary texts. At the very least, these works of pragmatist criticism prepared students to read more slowly.

165. Poirier, *Poetry and Pragmatism*, 30.

166. Posnock, "Reading Poirier," 169. As Posnock concludes, Poirier has "taught us to regard his gaps not as defects but as invitations for future tropings," an invitation he takes up (169).

167. Two studies of literary pragmatism written under Posnock's influence seem poised to fill the gap he identifies. Paul Grimstad names Posnock as the model who informs his mode of reading in the acknowledgments that open *Experience and Experimental Writing* (ix). Immediately invoking his mentor's mentor, Grimstad situates his study in relation to Poirier's line of "poet-pragmatists" and claims as his own Poirier's definition of writing "as a dramatization of how life may be created out of words" (Poirier quoted in

Grimstad, *Experience*, 2). Looking to Poirier, Grimstad establishes a generatively reciprocal relation between experimental approaches to composition and pragmatist understandings of experience. His chapters extend Poirier's lineage by arguing that Poe and Melville join Emerson in prefiguring pragmatism. However, when his introduction stages a debate between naturalist and skeptical views of experience, Grimstad displaces Poirier, installing Cavell as the voice of skepticism and as Dewey's interlocutor. Poirier is in fact doubly displaced when Grimstad makes Dewey the articulator of Emersonian pragmatism in this debate. Here, squaring Poirier's "evasions of Dewey" seems to require sidelining Poirier altogether.

The book that has done the most to correct Dewey's neglect in literary studies, Lisi Schoenbach's *Pragmatic Modernism*, further exemplifies the difficulty of bringing Dewey and Poirier into contact. Schoenbach cites Posnock's influence, and the literary lineage she traces parallels Poirier's line of poetic pragmatism, yet she ultimately looks to her former teacher Richard Rorty to frame the relation between pragmatist and modernist aesthetics in terms of "recontextualization." Schoenbach's suggestion that literary pragmatists like Henry James and Stein took a recontextualizing approach to modern change counters a long tradition of modernist literary criticism that relies on what she calls "the ideology of the break" (a phrase that echoes Poirier's insight that modernist reading habits, inflected by a Benjaminian story of modern "breakdown," assume "an unprecedented break in cultural continuity") (*Pragmatic Modernism*, 13; *M*, 181; *Renewal of Literature*, 97). Establishing lines of literary pragmatism by way of Rorty rather than Poirier, Schoenbach's study does not look to Emerson as a point of origin or as a methodological inspiration (Poirier repeatedly calls out Rorty's "close to total avoidance of Emerson," *Poetry and Pragmatism*, 41). As some of the more recent considerations of pragmatism and literary studies, Grimstad's and Schoenbach's studies seem to widen rather than bridge the gap between Poirier's and Dewey's pragmatist projects. My study locates common ground by interpreting Poirier and Dewey through their pedagogical commitments.

168. John Dewey, *Experience and Education* (New York: Simon and Schuster, 1938), 35.
169. John Dewey, *Democracy and Education, 1916: The Middle Works of John Dewey, 1899–1924*, vol. 9, ed. Jo Ann Boydston (Carbondale: Southern Illinois University Press, 2008), 262.
170. Dewey, *Democracy and Education*, 284, 43.
171. Dewey, *Democracy and Education*, 44; *Experience and Education*, 25.
172. Poirier, *Poetry and Pragmatism*, 167.

1 Marcel Proust's Perceptual Training

1. Originally published as the preface to Proust's 1906 translation of John Ruskin's *Sesame and Lilies* (1865), "Sur la lecture" first appeared in *La Renaissance latine* (1905). I follow Adam Watt in treating "Sur la lecture" as "a seed from which Proust's novel grew"; see *Reading in Proust's* A la recherche: *'le délire de la lecture'* (Oxford: Oxford University Press, 2009), 3. Proust invokes Emerson in the preface of his 1904 translation of Ruskin's *The Bible of Amiens* (1882), which also suggests that Proust found in Emerson an alternative to the Ruskinian model of reading. Whereas Ruskin embraces all-consuming encounters with books that displace the outside world, Proust's Emerson offers a powerful method for more fully inhabiting the novelist's here and now. In an essay on Proust's philosophical influences, Thomas Baldwin argues that parts of the *Recherche* that are often mistaken for "a modernistic inversion of Ruskin" in fact "turn out to be a very close fit with the words of Emerson"; see "Philosophy," in *Proust in Context*, ed. Adam Watt (Oxford: Oxford University Press, 2013), 77. By way of example Baldwin compares the narrator's description of a landscape viewed through the window of a train en route to Balbec in *A l'ombre des jeunes filles en fleurs* to Emerson's account of "seeing a face of country quite familiar, in the rapid movement of the railroad car" in *Nature* (Emerson quoted in "Philosophy," 78).
2. Marcel Proust, *On Reading*, trans. Jean Autret and William Burford (London: Souvenir Press, 1972), 17. Hereafter cited internally and in notes as *OR*.
3. Emerson, *Topical Notebooks*, 164.
4. Charles Baudelaire, "The Life and Work of Eugène Delacroix," in *The Painter of Modern Life and Other Essays*, ed. and trans. Jonathan Mayne (London: Phaidon, 2003), 53.
5. By elaborating how Emerson and Proust read Plotinus, I aim to recover their shared commitment to perceptual practice, readily overlooked in reductive accounts of their Platonic idealism. Just as Plotinus tasked himself with enriching philosophical understandings of Plato, this chapter means to deepen critical interpretations of these writers' engagement with both Platonic and Neoplatonic traditions – traditions which would not, in any event, have been distinguishable for Plotinus. The term "Neoplatonism" wasn't coined until the early nineteenth century, and the newness of the phase of Platonism that Plotinus initiated has been long debated. Plotinus understood himself to be an interpreter and defender of Plato's work rather than an innovator.
6. Georges Poulet develops Proust's account of reading into a literary critical approach that paves a middle road between "extreme proximity and extreme detachment" in "Phenomenology of Reading," *New Literary History* 1.1 (1969): 63. Instead of holding the book myopically near or at a distanced remove, we

might allow ourselves to be permeated by "an existence which is not mine, but which I experience as though it were mine" (60). This strange merging of "me" and "not me" for Proust "provokes a certain feeling of surprise" that suspends the "astonished consciousness ... of the critic" between sudden seizure and reflective delay (58–59, 63). In *Philosophy as Fiction: Self, Deception, and Knowledge in Proust* (New York: Oxford University Press, 2004), 141–45, Joshua Landy describes the *Recherche* as a "formative" novel that succeeds at the level of syntax and style in training its audience in this kind of readerly attention.

7. Reino Virtanen, "Proust and Emerson," *Symposium* 6.1 (1952): 123.

8. Jean-Yves Tadié's biography of Proust tantalizingly reports that on his deathbed, Proust jotted a note paraphrasing Emerson from memory: "There's nothing so frivolous as dying," *Marcel Proust* (New York: Viking, 2000), 777. This anecdote suggests that Proust had Emerson in mind even on the last night of his life, but it also perhaps reductively keeps alive his image as an iconic dispenser of pithy aphorisms.

9. Proust used four selections from Emerson as epigraphs in the essays comprising *Les Plaisirs et les jours* (1896), cited him twice in *Jean Santeuil* (written between 1896 and 1900 and published in 1952), made six references to him in *Pastiches et mélanges* (1919), and mentioned him in various letters and reviews. He read Emerson's essays in the following translations: Emile Montégut, *Essais de philosophie américaine* (1851); I. Will, *Sept essais d'Emerson* (1894); and Jean Izoulet-Loubatières, *Les Sur-Humains* (1895).

10. Virtanen, "Proust and Emerson," 136, 133.

11. Everett Carter, "The Emersonian Proust," *Comparative Literature Studies* 29.1 (1992): 49.

12. See Murphy's excellent discussion of Emerson in *Proust and America* (Liverpool: Liverpool University Press, 2007), 64–111.

13. Emerson was likely first exposed to Plotinus through Ralph Cudworth's *The True Intellectual System of the Universe* (1678), and he read Thomas Taylor's Plotinus translations: *An Essay on the Beautiful* (1792), *Five Books of Plotinus* (1794), and *Select Works of Plotinus* (1817). He also encountered Plotinus in his extensive readings of Coleridge and Goethe (who translated Plotinus's writings on art). For discussions of Emerson's debt to Plotinus, see Stanley Brodwin, "Emerson's Version of Plotinus: The Flight to Beauty," *Journal of the History of Ideas* 35 (1974): 465–83; J. S. Harrison, *The Teachers of Emerson* (New York: Haskell House, 1966 [1910]), 3–31; and chapter 4 of F. I. Carpenter, *Emerson and Asia* (Cambridge, MA: Harvard University Press, 1968 [1930]).

14. Studies of the diffusion of Neoplatonism in France at the turn of the twentieth century have focused on Plotinus's philosophical inheritors – chiefly Henri

Bergson – rather than his literary interlocutors. Rose-Marie Mossé-Bastide's *Bergson et Plotin* (Paris: Presses Universitaires de France, 1959) presents the first comprehensive account of Bergson's engagement with Plotinus, and critics have continued to elaborate and extend her reading. Luc Fraisse connects Bergson's investment in Neoplatonism to Proust by calling Proust "un Plotin des temps modernes," parenthetically noting that Bergson taught the *Enneads* at the Collège de France in *L'éclectise philosophique de Marcel Proust* (Paris: Presses Universitaires Paris-Sorbonne, 2013), 578. Given how often Proust's novel is read in Bergsonian terms, it is perhaps surprising that scholars have not pursued the connection. Yet René Wellek warns against assuming any easy affinity between Proust and Bergson – Proust himself denies his indebtedness – suggesting that "we must rather consider Neoplatonism" for Proust's "historical antecedents"; see *History of Modern Criticism, 1750–1950*, vol. 8, *French, Italian, and Spanish Criticism, 1900–1950* (New Haven, CT: Yale University Press, 1992), 64. Eve Kosofsky Sedgwick has closely examined this antecedent in tracing an intricate web of Neoplatonic connection woven throughout the *Recherche*. My reading is cued by Sedgwick's observation that "the Neoplatonic tradition remained for Proust the profoundest reservoir for such ideas and images [of replenishment], as it also was for such of his favorite authors as Emerson"; see *The Weather in Proust* (Durham, NC: Duke University Press, 2011), 7.

15. Arsić, *On Leaving*, 340n38; *EL*, 663.
16. Arsić, *On Leaving*, 340; *EL*, 38.
17. Arsić, *On Leaving*, 316.
18. Emerson, *Later Lectures I*, 299; Pierre Hadot, *Plotinus, or, the Simplicity of Vision*, trans. Michael Chase (Chicago: University of Chicago Press, 1998), 34.
19. Frederick Copleston, *A History of Philosophy*, vol. 1, *Greece and Rome* (New York: Image Books, 1993 [1946]), 471; quoted in Robert Richardson, *Emerson: The Mind on Fire* (Berkeley: University of California Press, 1995), 348.
20. Ralph Waldo Emerson, *The Later Lectures of Ralph Waldo Emerson*, vol. 2, *1855–1871*, ed. Ronald A. Bosco and Joel Myerson (Athens: University of Georgia Press, 2010), 356.
21. Marcel Proust, "Contre Sainte-Beuve," in *Marcel Proust: On Art and Literature 1896–1919*, trans. Sylvia Townsend Warner (New York: Caroll & Graf, 1997), 19.
22. Robert Richardson, *First We Read, Then We Write: Emerson on the Creative Process* (Iowa City: University of Iowa Press, 2009), 32.
23. In asserting Proust's commitment to cultivating the numinous in the present moment, I follow critics who refuse to equate Proustian memory with a capacity to revive thoughts of the past and who describe *mémoire involontaire* as a "secular" epiphany. See, for example, Joshua Landy's

assertion that "voluntary memory is really not memory at all" in *Philosophy as Fiction*, 110. Also see Vincent Descombes's contention that "the literary experience invoked by Proust under the name of experimentation is a variety of religious experience" in *Proust: Philosophy of the Novel*, trans. Catherine Chance Macksey (Stanford, CA: Stanford University Press, 1992), 292.

24. Plotinus, *An Essay on the Beautiful*, trans. Thomas Taylor (London: printed for the author, 1792), 44, 41, 43.

25. Plotinus, *Enneads* IV.3.8.15–16, quoted in Hadot, *Simplicity of Vision*, 22. My reading of Plotinus is indebted to Pierre Hadot, whose translations I draw on periodically. When quoting Plotinus from Hadot's translations, I have included citations from the Loeb edition of the *Enneads*. When not attributed to Hadot's or Taylor's translations, Plotinus quotations are from *Enneads*, trans. A. H. Armstrong, 9 vols., Loeb Classical Library (Cambridge, MA: Harvard University Press, 2014).

26. Marcel Proust, *Finding Time Again*, trans. Ian Patterson (London: Penguin, 2003), 200. Hereafter cited internally and in notes as *FT*.

27. Plotinus, *Five Books of Plotinus*, trans. Thomas Taylor (London: printed for Edward Jeffrey, 1794), 261; *Beautiful*, 35.

28. Hadot, *Simplicity of Vision*, 29.

29. In the 1849 republication of *Nature*, Emerson replaced Plotinus's epigraph with his own poem, which insistently incorporates earthly existence into every echelon of spiritual ascent. The poem reads, for example, "striving to be man, the worm / Mounts through all the spires of form" (*EL*, 5).

30. Plotinus, *Beautiful*, 40–41. The fact that Emerson "carefully indexed and thoroughly digested" Plotinus's writings on aesthetics is noted by Harrison in *The Teachers of Emerson*, 146.

31. Plotinus, *Five Books*, xxx; *EL*, 25 and 128.

32. Plotinus, *Enneads* I.1.11, 8, quoted in Hadot, *Simplicity of Vision*, 30.

33. Plotinus quoted in Hadot, *Simplicity of Vision*, 76.

34. Plotinus, *Five Books*, 249–50.

35. As Richard Poirier observes in relation to this passage, "our reading-writing brings into existence a moment in which we are actively there, but also a moment in which self-present identity is reportedly lost" (*Renewal of Literature*, 201). At the moment Emerson announces the self's disappearance, he also performs the rediscovery of an "I" that partakes of what it encounters and describes.

36. Hadot, *Simplicity of Vision*, 29.

37. The place of organic "life" and the physical body in Emerson's writing has been much contested. Although my claim that transparent vision is inseparable from physiological processes of perception may appear to be in tension with

Emerson's relegation of "nature and art, all other men and my own body" to the category he designates "NOT ME," I read this apparent negation of the body within a larger rhythm of "systole and diastole" that patterns Emerson's attempts to record "the upheaving principle of life everywhere" (*EL*, 8, 287; *EJ*, 111). It is only by continually abandoning his "own body" that Emerson can find fresh embodiments for "the great and crescive self" (*EL*, 487). A year later, in "The American Scholar," Emerson softens his logic of negation so that "NOT ME" is redesignated *"other me"*; see Brown, *Emerson Museum*, 191.

38. Plotinus, *Enneads* I.6.9.3–9.
39. Plotinus, *Enneads* I.6.9.24–26.
40. Plotinus, *Beautiful*, 38, 9.
41. Emerson closes the first chapter of *Nature* with an encounter emphasizing the potential for novelty to spring forth from familiarity: "The waving of the boughs in the storm, is new to me and old. It takes me by surprise, and yet is not unknown" (*EL*, 11).
42. No critic has been more attentive to Emerson's perception of "the extraordinary of the ordinary" than Stanley Cavell (*Transcendental Etudes*, 39).
43. Plotinus, *Beautiful*, 31.
44. Proust quoted in Sedgwick, *Weather in Proust*, 2.
45. Plotinus, *Select Works of Plotinus*, trans. Thomas Taylor (London: Black and Son, 1817), 506.
46. Plotinus, *Beautiful*, 41–42.
47. Hadot, *Simplicity of Vision*, 20; Plotinus, *Beautiful*, 40.
48. Plotinus, *Beautiful*, 24.
49. Emerson invokes Taylor's translation of Plotinus's phrase in "Illusions," in "The Over-Soul," in an essay on Swedenborg, and in various letters and journal entries.
50. Marcel Proust, *The Guermantes Way*, trans. Mark Treharne (London: Penguin, 2003), 79 (hereafter cited internally as *G*); *OR*, 19.
51. Marcel Proust, *The Way by Swann's*, trans. Lydia Davis (London: Penguin, 2003), 14, 13.
52. Proust, *Swann's*, 14.
53. Proust, *Swann's*, 14.
54. *FT*, 183; Emerson, "Works and Days," 525.
55. Charles Baudelaire, "The Painter of Modern Life," in *Baudelaire: Selected Writings on Art and Artists*, ed. Patrick Edward Charvet (New York: Cambridge University Press, 1981), 392.
56. Charles Baudelaire, "Salon de 1859," in *Oeuvres complètes de Charles Baudelaire: Curiosités esthétiques* (Paris: Michel Lévy frères, 1868), 258.
57. Baudelaire, "Delacroix," 53. For Emerson's influence on Baudelaire, see Margaret Gilman, "Baudelaire and Emerson," *Romantic Review* 34.3

(1943): 221–22; Bernard Howells, "'La vaporisation du moi': Baudelaire's *Journaux intimes,*" *French Studies* 42.4 (1988): 424–42; Dudley M. Marchi, "Baudelaire's America—Contrary Affinities," *Yearbook of General and Comparative Literature* 47 (2000): 37–52; and Arsić, *On Leaving,* 70–79.

58. Baudelaire, "Delacroix," 53.
59. Baudelaire, "Delacroix," 47.
60. Baudelaire, "Delacroix," 49.
61. Gilman, "Baudelaire and Emerson," 214.
62. Christopher Isherwood, "Translator's Preface," in Charles Baudelaire's *Intimate Journals,* trans. Christopher Isherwood (Mineola, NY: Dover, 2006), 10.
63. Baudelaire's *Journaux intimes* combines two sets of notes titled "Fusées" and "Mon coeur mis à nu." There is evidence that Baudelaire had intended to compile these pages into what he described as "un grand livre sur moi-même, mes Confessions" ("a big book of myself, my Confessions"), *Baudelaire: Correspondance,* tome 2, *1860–1866* (Paris: Gallimard, 1973), 182 (my translation).
64. Charles Baudelaire, "Salon of 1846," in *Baudelaire: Selected Writings on Art and Artists,* ed. and trans. Patrick Edward Charvet (New York: Penguin, 1981), 51.
65. Baudelaire, *Intimate Journals,* 109.
66. Baudelaire, "Delacroix," 59.
67. Baudelaire, *Intimate Journals,* 63.
68. Leo Bersani argues something similar in his discussion of Baudelaire's conflicted responses to the experience of "unanchored identity": "Baudelaire's work gives us images of this psychic fragmentation at the same time that it documents the resistance to all such ontological floating"; see *Baudelaire and Freud* (Berkeley: University of California Press, 1977), 2, 4. We might recall how Emerson likewise invokes images of unanchored drift to document his struggle with life's exposure to uncertainty. My claim is that both writers respond to this unmoored condition by reorienting their aesthetic projects around surprise.
69. Jean-Paul Sartre, *Baudelaire,* trans. Martin Turnell (New York: New Directions, 1967), 22.
70. Charles Baudelaire, *Journaux intimes: Fusées; Mon coeur mis à nu* (Paris: Les Éditions G. Crès et Cie, 1920), 21.
71. Sartre, *Baudelaire,* 27.
72. Sartre, *Baudelaire,* 135.
73. Sartre, *Baudelaire,* 27.
74. Baudelaire, "Delacroix," 47.

75. Baudelaire, "Delacroix," 47.
76. Baudelaire, "Delacroix," 47, 46; "Painter," 402.
77. Baudelaire, "Delacroix," 53, 46.
78. Howells, "'La vaporisation du moi,'" 432.
79. Baudelaire, *Intimate Journals*, 90.
80. Baudelaire, "Painter," 399.
81. Baudelaire, "Painter," 420.
82. Baudelaire, "Painter," 417.
83. Baudelaire, "Painter," 399.
84. Baudelaire, "Painter," 399, 401.
85. Charles Baudelaire, *Paris Spleen*, trans. Louise Varese (New York: New Directions, 1970), 58.
86. Baudelaire, "Painter," 400.
87. Baudelaire, "Painter," 403.
88. Baudelaire, "Painter," 403.
89. Baudelaire, "Painter," 403.
90. Baudelaire, "Painter," 400.
91. Following critical convention, I'll periodically refer to Proust's narrator as "Marcel."
92. Hadot, *Simplicity of Vision*, 32.
93. Proust's final volume thus confirms Emerson's contention that "noble creative forces" are unleashed when "we have successive experiences so important that the new forgets the old" (*EL*, 954).
94. Marcel Proust, *Remembrance of Things Past*, vol. 2, *The Captive*, trans. C. K. Scott Moncrieff (New York: Random House, 1932), 559.
95. Bercovitch, *Puritan Origins*, 160; *The American Jeremiad* (Madison: University of Wisconsin Press, 2012 [1978]), 183.
96. Bercovitch, *American Jeremiad*, xi.
97. Bercovitch, *American Jeremiad*, 92.
98. Bercovitch, *Puritan Origins*, 164, 175.
99. Cavell argues Emerson's writing is "the reverse of" possessive: "it is the exercise not of power but of reception" (*Transcendental Etudes*, 17).
100. Plotinus, *Enneads* V.8.4.9–12.
101. Plotinus, *Select Works*, 54; *Five Books*, 71.
102. Plotinus, *Enneads* V.8.9.3–7.
103. On Plotinus's "thought experiments," see Sara Rappe, *Reading Neoplatonism: Non-discursive Thinking in the Texts of Plotinus, Proclus, and Damascius* (New York: Cambridge University Press, 2000), 79–90.
104. Andrew Delbanco, *The Puritan Ordeal* (Cambridge, MA: Harvard University Press, 1989), 248.

105. Delbanco, *Puritan Ordeal*, 26.
106. Delbanco, *Puritan Ordeal*, 26.
107. Emerson quoted in Delbanco, *Puritan Ordeal*, 238.
108. Delbanco, *Puritan Ordeal*, 238.
109. Delbanco, *Puritan Ordeal*, 217, 71.
110. Delbanco, *Puritan Ordeal*, 26.
111. Delbanco, *Puritan Ordeal*, 1, 4.
112. New, *Line's Eye*, 6, 11.
113. New, *Line's Eye*, 11.
114. New, *Line's Eye*, 6.
115. Christopher Looby, "Scholar and Exegete: A Tribute to Sacvan Bercovitch, MLA Honored Scholar of Early American Literature, 2002," *Early American Literature* 39.1 (2002): 1. The symposia commemorating the reissuing of Bercovitch's first two books are published in *Early American Literature* 47.2 (2012): 377–441 and *Common-Place* 14.4 (2014).
116. Looby, "Scholar and Exegete," 6.
117. Christopher Looby and Cindy Weinstein, "Introduction," in *American Literature's Aesthetic Dimensions*, ed. Christopher Looby and Cindy Weinstein (New York: Columbia University Press, 2012), 2, 31n14.
118. Looby and Weinstein, "Introduction," 6.
119. Looby and Weinstein, "Introduction," 6.
120. Felski quoted in Looby and Weinstein, "Introduction," 5.
121. Looby and Weinstein, "Introduction," 31n14.
122. Looby and Weinstein, "Introduction," 31n14.

2 Henry James's Syntax of Surprise

1. Henry James, "Anthony Trollope," *The Century Magazine* 26.3 (July 1883): 395.
2. *The Portrait of a Lady* (1881) can be considered a transitional work in James's oeuvre insofar as it combines the characteristics of his earlier paradigm of expatriate shock with his later, more integrative model of surprise.
3. Henry James, *The Ambassadors* (New York: Norton, 1964 [1903]), 310. Hereafter cited internally and in notes as *AM*.
4. Henry James, *The American* (London: Macmillan, 1878), 34. Hereafter cited internally as *A*.
5. Richard Poirier, *The Comic Sense of Henry James: A Study of the Early Novels* (New York: Oxford University Press, 1960), 45.
6. Poirier, *Comic Sense*, 64.
7. Leon Edel, "Afterword" *in* Henry James's The American (New York: Signet Classics, 1963), 328.

8. Peter Brooks, "The Turn of *The American*," in *New Essays on* The American, ed. Martha Banta (New York: Cambridge University Press, 1987), 62.

9. Percy Lubbock, *The Craft of Fiction* (New York: Peter Smith, 1947 [1921]), 176.

10. Lubbock, *Craft of Fiction*, 176.

11. Nicholas Dames, "Wave-Theories and Affective Physiologies: The Cognitive Strain in Victorian Novel Theories," *Victorian Studies* 46.2 (2004): 210.

12. Lubbock, *Craft of Fiction*, 1.

13. Henry James, *The Art of the Novel: Critical Prefaces* (New York: Charles Scribner's Sons, 1962), 45. Hereafter cited internally and in notes as *AN*.

14. For an exemplary study that navigates between cognitive and psychoanalytic understandings of feeling, see Jane Thrailkill, *Affecting Fictions: Mind, Body, and Emotion in American Literary Realism* (Cambridge, MA: Harvard University Press, 2007).

15. As I will further elaborate in specific discussions of each theorist, I use the terms "emotion" and "feeling" in accordance with William James's theory of emotion, while my references to "affect" follow Silvan Tomkins's lead (who is himself working in a Jamesian tradition). Influenced by this body of work, I contest the rigid distinction that a poststructuralist strain of affect theory asserts between affects understood as physiological sensations and emotions understood as psychological states. Rei Terada neatly distills this mind/body divide when she defines "emotion" as "a psychological, at least minimally interpretive experience whose physiological aspect is affect," *Feeling in Theory: Emotion after the "Death of the Subject"* (Cambridge, MA: Harvard University Press, 2001), 5. In Terada's work (as in James's), a third term – feeling – mediates between these two domains of experience.

I discuss Brian Massumi's nuanced work with William James's model of emotion in this chapter, but in a more Deleuzian mood, Massumi defines the unstructured, free-flowing "autonomy" of affect against "the tawdry status of a private 'emotion,'" its enslavement to bounded formations of signification, "subjective content," and linear narrative; see *Parables for the Virtual* (Durham, NC: Duke University Press, 2002), 219, 28. It becomes crucial, Massumi concludes, "to theorize the difference between affect and emotion" so that "psychological categories" will not "slip back in," thus "undoing the considerable deconstructive work that has been effectively carried out by poststructuralism" (27, 28). The very term *emotion* has been "contaminated by centuries of association with rhetoric" that equates it with stationary beliefs, behaviors, and identifications, as Charles Altieri observes in *The Particulars of Rapture: An Aesthetics of the Affects* (Ithaca, NY: Cornell University Press, 2003), 50. The apparently antithetical relation between affect and emotion has thus come to rest on precisely the reductive Cartesian division that it purports to undo but more often simply inverts.

Both Henry and William James are interested in forces that exceed subjectivity and signification, but for Henry the chief question is how to represent these intensities in narrative form. Like his brother, Henry rejects the separation of corporeal flows from psychological structures that affect theorists so often insist upon. I therefore want to distinguish the immersive feeling that circulates in the central scenes of James's late novels from free-flowing affective states that exceed all narrative structures.

16. Martha Nussbaum, "Exactly and Responsibly: A Defense of Ethical Criticism," *Philosophy and Literature* 22.2 (1998): 348.

17. Kaja Silverman, "Too Early/Too Late: Subjectivity and the Primal Scene in Henry James," *Novel* 21.2/3 (1988): 159. See also Kevin Kohan, "James and the Originary Scene," *Henry James Review* 22.3 (2001): 229–38; George Smith, "The Last Phase: Henry James and the Psycho-Painterly Style," *Henry James Review* 30.1 (2009): 62–67; and William Veeder, "James and the Consolations of Time," *Henry James Review* 17.3 (1996): 230–41.

18. William James, "What Is an Emotion?," *Mind* 9.34 (1884): 203; *PP*, 503.

19. James's "visceral theory of emotion" is revised and reformulated over the ten-year period between the initial 1884 publication of "What Is an Emotion?" in *Mind* and his later publication of "The Physical Basis of Emotion" in *Psychological Review* 101.2 (1894): 205–10. However, its basic tenets remain intact in James's major statement on "The Emotions" in *The Principles of Psychology*, vol. 2 (New York: Dover, 1950 [1890]) (hereafter cited internally and in notes as *PPII*). James's theory of emotion is often discussed as the "James-Lange Theory," which links two similar hypotheses regarding the origin and nature of emotion that William James and Carl Lange were developing independently through the 1880s.

20. Richard P. Blackmur, "Introduction," in *The Art of the Novel: Critical Prefaces by Henry James* (New York: Charles Scribner's Sons, 1962), xxv.

21. Ruth Yeazell's *Language and Knowledge in the Late Novels of Henry James* (Chicago: Chicago University Press, 1976) powerfully instantiates the terms of knowledge and recognition in James criticism.

22. Kohan, "James and the Originary Scene," 234.

23. Ross Posnock, *The Trial of Curiosity: Henry James, William James, and the Challenge of Modernity* (New York: Oxford University Press, 1991), 242.

24. Silverman, "Too Early/Too Late," 80. "Afterwardsness" is Jean Leplanche's translation of *Nachträglichkeit*. See Kent Puckett, "Before and Afterwardsness in Henry James," in *Narrative Middles: Navigating the Nineteenth-Century Novel*, ed. Caroline Levine and Mario Ortiz-Robles (Columbus: Ohio State University Press, 2011), 80–83.

25. Puckett, "Before and Afterwardsness," 81.

26. Puckett, "Before and Afterwardsness," 82.

27. Puckett, "Before and Afterwardsness," 83, 94.

28. Leo Bersani and Adam Phillips, *Intimacies* (Chicago: University of Chicago, 2008), 21.

29. Bersani and Phillips, *Intimacies*, 23 (emphasis added).

30. Bersani and Phillips, *Intimacies*, 22, 24, 25 and 26, 24.

31. Bersani and Phillips, *Intimacies*, 28.

32. Bersani and Phillips, *Intimacies*, 28.

33. Bersani and Phillips *Intimacies*, 30.

34. Massumi, *Parables for the Virtual*, 25.

35. James quoted in Brian Massumi, *Semblance and Event* (Cambridge, MA: MIT Press, 2011), 1.

36. Massumi, *Semblance and Event*, 11.

37. Massumi, *Semblance and Event*, 10.

38. Massumi, *Semblance and Event*, 10, 11.

39. Massumi, *Parables for the Virtual*, 231. A decade after Massumi first voiced his Jamesian motto he returns to the bear episode and offers a slight variation on the dictum: "Participation precedes cognition" (*Semblance and Event*, 32).

40. Massumi, *Parables for the Virtual*, 221, 233, 231, 220.

41. Massumi, *Parables for the Virtual*, 214, 231, 233.

42. Massumi, *Parables for the Virtual*, 233.

43. Massumi, *Semblance and Event*, 16.

44. Massumi, *Parables for the Virtual*, 221. Massumi outlines his critical practice in his introduction to *Parables*: "If you know where you will end up when you begin, nothing has happened in the meantime. You have to be willing to surprise yourself writing things you didn't think you thought . . . You have to let yourself get so caught up in the flow of your writing that it ceases at moments to be recognizable to you as your own" (18).

45. James quoted in Massumi, *Semblance and Event*, 32.

46. Paul Armstrong, *The Challenge of Bewilderment: Understanding and Representation in James, Conrad, and Ford* (Ithaca, NY: Cornell University Press, 1987), 94–95. As Armstrong insightfully observes, "James depicts *in tandem* the immediacy of the present experience and the mediating musings of the future which reflects back on it as part of the past" (94).

47. See Gérard Genette, *Narrative Discourse: An Essay in Method* (Ithaca, NY: Cornell University Press, 1980), 40–54. My reading is informed by Dorrit Cohn's discussion of analeptic prolepses in relation to *The Golden Bowl* in "'First Shock of Complete Perception': The Opening Episode of The Golden Bowl, Volume 2," *Henry James Review* 22.1 (2009): 5–8.

48. Genette points to Proust's *Recherche* as his single example of a novel featuring "proleptic analepses," noting that its "complex anachronies ... somewhat disturb our reassuring ideas about retrospection and anticipation," *Narrative Discourse*, 83.

49. As Philip Fisher notes, "what narrative adds" to an unexpected "all-at-once" experience, which would otherwise remain an "extremely short-lived unique moment of being," is a protracted breakdown of "the sequence of recognitions that took place in fractions of a second of time," *Wonder*, 25–26. In James's late novels, this brief "sequence of recognitions" can only be discerned from the perspective afforded by retrospect.

50. Henry James, *The Golden Bowl* (New York: Everyman's Library, 1992 [1904]), 315 (hereafter cited internally as *GB*); *Wings of the Dove* (New York: Penguin, 1986), 89, 153.

51. Georges Poulet, *Studies in Human Time*, ed. Elliott Coleman (Baltimore, MA: Johns Hopkins University Press, 1956), 350; Peter Rawlings, "Grammars of Time in Henry James," *Modern Language Review* 98.2 (2003): 274.

52. See Françoise Dastur, "Phenomenology of the Event: Waiting and Surprise," *Hypatia* 15.4 (2000): 178–89.

53. Samuel Coleridge, *The Complete Works of Samuel Taylor Coleridge*, vol. 7, ed. W. G. T. Shedd (New York: Harper and Brothers, 1884), 212–13.

54. Bill Brown, *A Sense of Things: The Object Matter of American Literature* (Chicago: University of Chicago Press, 2003), 166.

55. Henry James, *The Ivory Tower*, ed. Percy Lubbock (London: Collins, 1917), 268; *WII*, 788.

56. Massumi, *Semblance and Event*, 13, 31; *Politics of Affect* (Cambridge, UK: Polity, 2015), 207; *Semblance and Event*, 7, 14.

57. Massumi, *Semblance and Event*, 33.

58. Richardson, *Natural History*, 145.

59. See Richard Poirier's "The Reinstatement of the Vague" in *Poetry and Pragmatism*, 129–170.

60. William James quotes Emerson's phrase "the conduct of life" in *The Varieties of Religious Experience* (1902): "The great point in the conduct of life is to get the heavenly forces on one's side by opening one's own mind to their influx" (*WII*, 103).

61. William James, *The Letters of William James*, vol. 2, ed. Henry James III (Boston: Atlantic Monthly, 1920), 122.

62. Critics often assume a division of labor between the James brothers: William conveyed a theory of consciousness without style and Henry stylistically represented the stream of consciousness without theoretical contribution. Joan Richardson persuasively argues that while William did not experiment within the unit of the sentence, the expansive scope of his work pushed "larger

syntactic boundaries" with a style that reflected "the processual nature of the changing habits of mind," *American Experience*, 131. I join Ross Posnock and Sharon Cameron in contesting the critical commonplace that Henry simply "conveys" his brother's psychological models with hyperperceptive protagonists who serve as "accurate representations" of the processes of consciousness and perception that William formulates, as Judith Ryan observes in *The Vanishing Subject: Early Psychology and Literary Modernism* (Chicago: University of Chicago Press, 1991), 76. See Posnock, *Trial of Curiosity*; and Sharon Cameron, *Thinking in Henry James* (Chicago: University of Chicago Press, 1989).

63. Henry James, *Literary Criticism*, vol. 1, *Essays, English and American Writers* (New York: Library of America, 1984), 254.

64. Henry James, *Henry James: Autobiography*, ed. Frederick W. Dupee (New York: Criterion Books, 1956), 359.

65. James, *Literary Criticism*, 271, 265, 270, 271. Tellingly, Henry James's early-career focus on Emerson's life rather than Emerson's writing is guided by his reading of Elliot Cabot's biography, *The Life of Emerson* (1887), which he reviewed for *Macmillan's Magazine* in 1888. Henry's early assessment of Emerson as an idealist figure of transcendental wonder aligns with a canonical tradition of what Posnock has termed "Emersonianism": "the cultural appropriation and mythologizing" that simplified "the actual complexities and tensions in Emerson's notion of self-reliance" to mean romantic individualism and idealism (*Trial*, 304n10). James goes on to give a more nuanced account of Emerson's connection to Transcendentalism and the Concord School in *The American Scene* (1904–1905), which considers Emerson's literary merit in ways largely absent from James's early critical writing.

66. James, *Literary Criticism*, 262, 250.

67. James, *Literary Criticism*, 252, 250.

68. James, *Literary Criticism*, 252.

69. James, *Letters of William James*, 190.

70. James, *Letters of William James*, 190.

71. James, *Letters of William James*, 191.

72. Henry James and William James, *William and Henry James: Selected Letters*, ed. Ignas K. Skrupskelis and Elizabeth M. Berkeley (Charlottesville: University of Virginia Press, 1997), 429.

73. James and James, *Selected Letters*, 426.

74. James and James, *Selected Letters*, 427, 425.

75. See F. O. Matthiessen, *Henry James: The Major Phase* (New York: Oxford University Press, 1944).

76. Emerson, "Works and Days," 525. See Edmund Wilson, ed., *The Shock of Recognition: The Development of Literature in the United States Recorded by the Men Who Made It* (Garden City, NY: Doubleday, 1943).

77. James, *Literary Criticism*, 269.

78. Adam Frank offers a lucid account of Tomkins's theory of affects in "Some Affective Bases for Guilt": "Tomkins proposed that humans and other animals have evolved affect systems that are distinct from both the drives and cognition. Humans, according to Tomkins, are born with eight or nine innate affects that act as the primary motives: the negative ones, fear-terror, distress-grief, anger-rage, shame-humiliation, and contempt-disgust; the positive ones, interest-excitement and enjoyment-joy; and the reorienting affect of surprise-startle. These are at once individual and shared; individual in that they are experienced in or on an individual physiology, and shared in that they take place primarily on the skin and musculature of the face and in the tones of the voice and are communicated both to the self and to others, or sometimes to the self as an other" (13).

79. Tomkins, *Affect*, 273.

80. Tomkins, *Affect*, 273. Tomkins's system of affects is defined by a "freedom to combine"; see "What Are Affects?," in *Shame and Its Sisters: A Silvan Tomkins Reader*, ed. Eve Kosofsky Sedgwick and Adam Frank (Durham, NC: Duke University Press, 1995), 45. This freedom defines not only the relationship between the different affects but also between the different "systems" that constitute the central assembly. Since the affect system "provides the primary motives of human beings," this freedom is necessary to explain the potentially infinite range of human motivators ("What Are Affects?," 36). Each Tomkinsian affect exists on a continuum of intensity designated by a hyphen, as in the case of "surprise-startle." The "feeling tone" of "surprise" is neutral, but shades toward "mildly negative" as one tips the intensity scale toward "startle" (*Affect*, 273). The tendency toward negative feeling increases in proportion with the increased rapidity and density of neural firing in response to the sudden stimuli that triggered a surprise-startle response in the first place. An intense startle is more likely to combine with negatively charged affects, such as fear or distress, whereas less intense surprises tend to combine with neutral or positive affects, such as interest or enjoyment.

81. Paul Ekman and Wallace V. Friesen, *Unmasking the Face: A Guide to Recognizing Emotions from Facial Expressions* (Englewood Cliffs, NJ: Spectrum, 1975), 35.

82. Both Tomkins and Ekman draw on Charles Darwin's 1859 account of surprise in *The Expressions of the Emotions in Man and Animals* (New York: Oxford University Press, 1998). In the characteristic face of Darwinian surprise, the mouth opens as the jaw relaxes and drops because energy is being siphoned

from unused sensory apparatuses (i.e., taste and vocalization), which momentarily slacken or halt in order to concentrate the energy around the more immediately vital apparatuses of visual and aural attention. Darwin outlines a continuum of surprise: "Attention, if sudden and close, graduates into surprise; and this into astonishment; and this into stupefied amazement" (278). Tomkins amends the Darwinian model based on his observation that surprise initiates attention rather than the other way around. See Tomkins, *Affect*, 273, 279; Darwin, *Expressions*, 278–89; and Ekman, *Unmasking* 37–45.

83. Barbara Kryk-Kastovsky, "Surprise, Surprise: The Iconicity-Conventionality Scale of Emotions," in *The Language of Emotions: Conceptualization, Expression, and Theoretical Foundation*, ed. Susanne Niemeier and René Dirven (Philadelphia: John Benjamins, 1997), 158.

84. Kryk-Kastovsky, "Surprise, Surprise," 163.

85. Meredith Osmond, "The Prepositions We Use in the Construal of Emotions: Why Do We Say Fed Up With and Tired Of?," in *The Language of Emotions: Conceptualization, Expression, and Theoretical Foundation*, ed. Susanne Niemeier and René Dirven (Amsterdam: John Benjamins, 1997), 114.

86. I have not included a discussion of *The Wings of the Dove* in this chapter because J. Hillis Miller has already discussed with great acuity the two sites where surprise is most forcefully felt in the third novel from James's late phase: in faces and in the prosopopeic apostrophe "Oh!" See "Lying against Death: *The Wings of the Dove*," in *Literature as Conduct: Speech Acts in Henry James* (New York: Fordham University Press, 2005), 151–227.

87. Coleridge, *Complete Works*, 212–13.

88. From the time Descartes first counted surprise among the primary "passions" in his 1649 treatise, *Les passions de l'âme* (*The Passions of the Soul*), controversies have cropped up around its duration and strength, its negative or positive charge, and its enabling or inhibiting relationship to perception; even the status of surprise as an emotion, affect, or reflex has been fiercely contested. For example, while Tomkins holds the full surprise-startle range of experience to be properly affective, Ekman claims that the briefer "startle reactions" are largely instinctive. See Paul Ekman, Wallace V. Friesen, and Ronald C. Simons, "Is the Startle Reaction an Emotion?," *Journal of Personality and Social Psychology* 49.5 (1985): 1416–26.

89. René Descartes, "The Passions of the Soul," in *The Philosophical Writings of Descartes*, vol. 1, trans. John Cottingham, Robert Stoothoff, and Dugald Murdoch (New York: Cambridge University Press, 1985), 350, 353.

90. Descartes, "Passions," 353.

91. Descartes, "Passions," 354.

92. Descartes, "Passions," 354.
93. Descartes, "Passions," 350, 354.
94. Descartes, "Passions," 356.
95. Descartes, "Passions," 355.
96. Christopher R. Miller situates Cartesian surprise within a longer intellectual history in the chapter of *Surprise* titled "From Aristotle to Emotion Theory," 16–37.
97. Fisher, *Wonder*, 1, 20.
98. Henry James, *Theory of Fiction*, ed. James E. Miller (Lincoln: University of Nebraska Press, 1972), 294.
99. Just as the term surprise first designated an unexpected military attack, "interval" has martial etymological roots. The Latin word "*intervallum*" literally means a "space between palisades or ramparts" [inter (between) + vallum (rampart)]. "Interval, n.," *OED Online*, accessed January 10, 2010, <www.oed.com/view/Entry/98410>. Both a zone of contact and of separation, the interval represents an indeterminate region between exposed vulnerability and shielding fortification, between offensive action and a protective reaction.
100. Tomkins, *Affect*, 337.
101. Tomkins, *Affect*, 338.
102. Tomkins, *Affect*, 355.

3 Nella Larsen's Novel Weather

1. The word "something" (in the sense of "something else") appears on pages 7, 10, 11, 14, 18, 21, 40, 47, 50, 54, 56, 83, 87, 91, 95, 118, and 134 of *Quicksand*.
2. Sianne Ngai, *Ugly Feelings* (Cambridge, MA: Harvard University Press, 2005), 179; Linda Dittmar, "When Privilege Is No Protection: The Woman Artist in *Quicksand* and *The House of Mirth*," in *Writing the Woman Artist: Essays on Poetics, Politics, and Portraiture*, ed. Suzanne W. Jones (Philadelphia: University of Pennsylvania Press, 1991), 145.
3. Larsen's biographer George Hutchinson summarizes the novel's critical reception in the wake of its publication: "People tried to fit it into patterns to which they were accustomed and, not always satisfied with the fit, found the novel wanting"; see *In Search of Nella Larsen: A Biography of the Color Line* (Cambridge, MA: Harvard University Press, 2006), 283. Hutchinson quotes one reviewer who complains in May of 1928: "The motivation of this character is not always convincingly explained; the intention of the book is not even always clear" (282). Further, "the character is not quite of one pattern . . . There is no continuity of development, no wholeness here," as Edna Lou Walton plaints in her review of *Quicksand*, published in *Opportunity* 6.7 (July 1928):

212–13; reprinted in *The Critics and the Harlem Renaissance*, ed. Cary D. Wintz (New York: Garland, 1996), 192. The novel is "the story of [Helga's] inner life," so "outer events are for the most part of secondary importance," yet *Quicksand* is still condemned for being "too subjective, too fragmentary, too much of a psychological study," per a third review, quoted in Claudia Tate, "Desire and Death in *Quicksand*," *American Literary History* 7.2 (1995): 238. For another vexed reviewer: "The author seems to be wandering around lost, as lost as her leading character who ends up doing such an unexpected and unexplainable thing that I was forced to re-read the book, wondering, if in my eagerness to reach the end, I had perhaps skipped a hundred pages or so . . . When she does fall on the dark side the reader has lost all interest and sympathy, nor can he believe that such a thing has really happened"; quoted in Keguro Macharia, "Queering Helga Crane: Black Nativism in Nella Larsen's *Quicksand*," *Modern Fiction Studies* 57.2 (2011): 266. Critics have continued to express frustration at the apparently unmotivated movements of Larsen's protagonist and plot. Barbara Johnson encapsulates a number of complaints when she observes that "psychological causation is missing" from *Quicksand*; see "The Quicksands of the Self: Nella Larsen and Heinz Kohut," in *The Feminist Difference: Literature, Psychoanalysis, Race, and Gender* (Cambridge, MA: Harvard University Press, 2000), 42. Sianne Ngai thematizes readers' widespread irritation with the novel alongside Helga's own irritability in her chapter on Larsen in *Ugly Feelings*, 174–208.

4. W. E. B. Du Bois, *The Souls of Black Folk* (New York: Oxford University Press, 2007 [1903]), 8. For example, "readers then and now have indeed read the novel as a dramatization of racial double consciousness, in the form of the all-too-familiar topos of the tragic mulatto," as Johnson writes in "Quicksands of the Self," 37. Hutchinson offers a helpful discussion of Du Bois's review of *Quicksand*, which he deemed a representation of a life that is "but darkened, not obliterated by the shadow of the Veil"; quoted in *In Search of Nella Larsen*, 284. Both Johnson and Judith Butler register an acute irony in Du Bois's praise for *Quicksand*'s resistance to racialized representations of sexual exoticism. In Butler's reading, the final fates suffered by Larsen's heroines – Helga's social death in an oppressive marriage and the strange murder-suicide that closes her next novel, *Passing* (1929) – reflect the high cost of Du Bois's project of "racial uplift" for black women who do not conform to his ideals of African American upward mobility achieved by reproducing the gendered norms of the bourgeois family; see "Passing, Queering: Nella Larsen's Psychoanalytic Challenge," in *Female Subjects in Black and White: Race, Psychoanalysis, Feminism*, ed. Elizabeth Abel, Barbara Christian, and Helene Moglen (Berkeley: University of California Press, 1997), 275–76.

5. Du Bois, *Souls*, 3.

6. Hazel V. Carby, *Reconstructing Womanhood: The Emergence of the Afro-American Woman Novelist* (New York: Oxford University Press, 1987), 166.

7. Carby, *Reconstructing Womanhood*, 169; Johnson, "Quicksands of the Self," 56. Johnson has argued that Helga embodies a psychic wound resulting from her impossible inscription into the social order (55). Similarly, Butler shows how Larsen's heroines suffer psychic splitting under the pressures of "vectors of power such as gender and race," and argues that readers must "rethink social regulation" in ways that make it possible "to articulate the psyche politically" (279).

8. Carby, *Reconstructing Womanhood*, 169.

9. *EL*, 943; Cavell, *Transcendental Etudes*, 199.

10. *EL*, 965; Eduardo Cadava, "The Guano of History," in *The Other Emerson*, 106; *EL*, 627. Scholars who have elaborated Du Bois's extended engagement with Emerson's writing have generally read *The Souls of Black Folk* (1903) as a corrective to the Concord sage's inadequate account of the location of the racialized subject in the world. See, for example, Anita Haya Patterson, *From Emerson to King: Democracy, Race, and the Politics of Protest* (New York: Oxford University Press, 1997); Adolph L. Reed, *W. E. B. Du Bois and American Political Thought: Fabianism and the Color Line* (New York: Oxford University Press, 1997); and Shamoon Zamir, *Dark Voices: W. E. B. Du Bois and American Thought, 1888–1903* (Chicago: University of Chicago Press, 1995). Arguments regarding Emerson's racial blind spots or his outright racism often rest on a fundamental misreading of "Fate," where Emerson is taken to endorse a discourse of racist determinism, which he is in fact "ventriloquizing" for the purpose of critique, as Cadava argues in "Guano," 121. Cadava makes the case that Emerson's essay stages rather than sanctions proslavery propaganda: "The entire essay can be read as an evocation and analysis of the various kinds of discourses that throughout history . . . have worked to enable one race to live, as Emerson tells us, 'at the expense of other races'" ("Guano," 111). See also Cavell's argument that "Fate" is centrally concerned with the abolition of slavery, in *Transcendental Etudes*, 194–212.

11. Du Bois, *Souls*, 8; *EL*, 205.

12. Here I echo Frantz Fanon's evocative phrase, "an atmosphere of certain uncertainty," which I will go on to discuss; see *Black Skin, White Masks*, trans. Charles Lam Markmann (New York: Grove Press, 1967), 110–11.

13. William Empson, *Seven Types of Ambiguity* (New York: New Directions, 1966 [1930]), 17.

14. Empson, *Seven Types*, 17, 7.

15. Cleanth Brooks and Robert Penn Warren, *Understanding Poetry* (New York: Holt, Rinehart and Winston, 1960 [1938]), 552.
16. Cleanth Brooks and Robert Penn Warren, *Understanding Fiction* (New York: Appleton-Century-Crofts, 1943), 575.
17. Brooks and Warren, *Understanding Fiction*, 601.
18. Empson, *Seven Types*, 17.
19. For instance, in a recent study, Hans Ulrich Gumbrecht claims that a practice of "reading for *Stimmung*" – translated as atmosphere and mood – offers a new "ontology of literature"; see *Atmosphere, Mood, Stimmung: On a Hidden Potential of Literature* (Stanford, CA: Stanford University Press, 2012), 2. Observing that the German word encompasses both "atmosphere" and "mood," then using the terms interchangeably, Gumbrecht nevertheless insists on the "singular quality" of "every atmosphere and every mood." Even as he locates atmosphere at the center of literary study, Gumbrecht echoes Empson's contention that a critic can only "gesture towards this singularity"; "it can never be defined absolutely by language" (14–15).
20. Mikel Dufrenne, *The Phenomenology of Aesthetic Experience*, trans. Edward S. Casey (Evanston, IL: Northwestern University Press, 1973), 542.
21. For example, Teresa Brennan poses the following question to open *The Transmission of Affect* (Ithaca, NY: Cornell University Press, 2004): "Is there anyone who has not, at least once, walked into a room and 'felt the atmosphere?'" (1). She then trades the term "atmosphere" for "affect" without marking any difference between them. Brennan's index has an entry for "atmospheric affects," but the book itself makes no direct references to atmosphere beyond her opening gambit (217).
22. Emerson's career-long commitment to tracing temperamental moods and weather suggests powerful continuities between internal and external registers of atmospheric change. However, Emerson scholars have generally treated these phenomena separately. Eduardo Cadava's *Climates of History* demonstrates how Emerson's climatic figures shape his discourses of war, race, and slavery. Drawing on meteorological terms to engage with the charged political climate of his time, Emerson aligns the transformative potential of nature with the revolutionary forces of emancipation. Emerson's representations of weather and moods converge where his understanding of the unpredictable movements of history intersect with his conception of the instability of personhood. Sharon Cameron's work on what she calls "Emerson's impersonal" in "The Way of Life by Abandonment" shows how his emphasis on the transience of moods erodes the commonplace idea that mental states are personal and reside "within." Cameron extends this conception of impersonality through a longer literary line but stops short of investigating the racialized implications of this urge to efface the bounds of personhood. Arsić's *On Leaving* draws on the work of both

these critics and offers a starting point for examining how Emerson's epistemologies of weather and moods inflect each other (see note 26).

23. Butler, "Passing, Queering," 267.

24. Frederick William Rudler, "Amber (Resin)," ed. Hugh Chisolm, *Encyclopedia Britannica*, 11th ed. (Cambridge, UK: Cambridge, UK University Press, 1911), 793.

25. Naxos is modeled after Tuskegee Institute, where Larsen taught in the nursing school from 1915–1916, arriving just after its founder Booker T. Washington's death. At Tuskegee, Washington aimed to produce a black working class who would spur economic uplift by returning to their rural communities equipped to teach and train a class of farmers, tradesmen, and manual laborers. Du Bois was an early supporter of Washington but came to critique his emphasis on economic equality over civic and cultural equality.

26. Arsić describes the conjoining of Emersonian moods and weather like this in *On Leaving*: "[Emerson's] moods and perceptions inhabit us as so many atmospheric events . . . as if coming to us from outside, registering changes in the weather" (145). My understanding of *Quicksand* as a series of "atmospheric events" is indebted to her reading of Emerson.

27. In the same way that a character who moves like a cloud eludes definition, the mutable weather sign has long challenged philosophical and meteorological designation. For example, in Descartes's 1637 "Discourse on Meteorology," ungraspable mists, vapors, and exhalations skew the senses and confound judgment. See "Discourse and Essays," in *The Philosophical Writings of Descartes*, vol. 1, 109–75. For Descartes, a cloud's suspension between form and formlessness undermined the meteorological laws he had worked to establish. A century and a half later, the meteorologist Luke Howard – sometimes simply referred to as "the namer of clouds" – responded to clouds' amorphousness with a nomenclature (still in use today) capable of denoting moment-by-moment modification. Fueled by ongoing processes of vaporous exchange, clouds, he discerned, might at any time pass into new fleeting formations; the layered haze of *stratus* clouds could heap into cottony *cumulus* forms or thin into wispy *cirrus* strands. See Howard's 1803 essay *On the Modifications of Clouds* (Cambridge, UK: Cambridge University Press, 2011). Though their theories and approaches diverged widely, both Descartes and Howard sought a language that would register infinitely variable processes of condensation and dispersal. In tracing the contours of a narrative subject who fluctuates between congealed and dispersed forms, and whose only constant is volatility, Larsen faces a similar set of challenges.

28. For a sampling of cloud references in Emerson's essays, see *EL*, 15, 206, 242, 245, 305, 331, 451, 484, 553, 974.

29. Arsić, *On Leaving*, 146.

30. Arsić, *On Leaving*, 146.
31. Laura Doyle, *Freedom's Empire: Race and the Rise of the Novel in Atlantic Modernity, 1640–1940* (Durham, NC: Duke University Press, 2008), 401.
32. Fanon, *Black Skin, White Masks*, 110.
33. Fanon, *Black Skin, White Masks*, 110–11.
34. Fanon, *Black Skin, White Masks*, 112.
35. Fanon, *Black Skin, White Masks*, 109.
36. Fanon, *Black Skin, White Masks*, 116.
37. Du Bois, *Souls*, 3; *Q*, 63, 64.
38. Arsić, *On Leaving*, 316.
39. Cavell argues something similar when he analyzes the previously referenced line from "Fate": "We should be crushed by the atmosphere, but for the reaction of the air within the body" (Emerson quoted in Cavell, *Transcendental Etudes*, 201). As Cavell continues, "the ideas that are in the air are our life's breath; they become our words; slavery is supported by some of them and might have crushed the rest of them; uncrushed, they live in opposition" (201).
40. *Q*, 88, 83; Du Bois, *Souls*, 8.
41. Cavell, *Transcendental Etudes*, 165; Arsić, *On Leaving*, 31.
42. Cavell, *Transcendental Etudes*, 121.
43. Coming out of the nineteenth-century sentimentalist tradition, the figure of the "tragic mulatta" upholds a feminine ideal of ladylike chastity until she is subject to a sudden fall into impurity. At the other extreme is the primitivist strain of modernism that relies on racist, exotic stereotypes of black female sexuality. My contention is that Larsen invokes these tropes only to baffle an either/or choice between equally inadequate literary representations of black women. On the wider tradition of the tragic mulatto and mulatta narrative, see Werner Sollors, *Neither Black Nor White and Yet Both: Thematic Explorations of Interracial Literature* (Cambridge, MA: Harvard University Press, 1999).
44. According to Farah Griffin, the northbound journey of the migration narrative "is marked by four pivotal moments: (1) an event that propels the action northward, (2) a detailed representation of the initial confrontation with the urban landscape, (3) an illustration of the migrant's attempts to negotiate that landscape and his or her resistance to the negative effects of urbanization, and (4) a vision of the possibilities or limitations of the Northern, Western, or Midwestern city and the South;" see *Who Set You Flowin'?: The African-American Migration Narrative* (New York: Oxford University Press, 1996), 3.
45. "The ties of race ensnare the nearly illegible Helga in the plainly readable plot of return," as Posnock writes in *Color and Culture: Black Writers and the*

Making of the Modern Intellectual (Cambridge, MA: Harvard University Press, 1998), 80.

46. The novel opens with Helga's rejection of the normative stability promised by marriage into a "first family" of nearby Atlanta, who deemed it presumptuous "to be anything but inconspicuous and conformable" (*Q,* 8). Such an arrangement would require that she pair the "veil" she was born under with another self-effacing "Vayle" – the family name of her ex-fiancé from Naxos. In Copenhagen, Helga refuses a second proposal, this time from a famous Danish artist who she had previously yearned for.

47. Laura E. Tanner, "Intimate Geography: The Body, Race, and Space in Larsen's *Quicksand,*" *Texas Studies in Literature and Language* 51.2 (2009): 180. Tanner notes how many of *Quicksand's* readers have puzzled over its "apparently inexplicable conclusion" (180), echoing Jeffrey Gray's observation that "criticism of *Quicksand* has seldom failed to mention the problem of its ending"; see "Essence and the Mulatto Traveler: Europe as Embodiment in Nella Larsen's *Quicksand,*" *Novel* 27.3 (1994): 267.

48. Deborah E. McDowell, "Introduction," in Nella Larsen's *Quicksand and Passing,* xi.

49. Mary Esteve, *The Aesthetics and Politics of the Crowd in American Literature* (New York: Cambridge University Press, 2003), 168. Esteve couples *Quicksand's* description of clouds with Larsen's expressed impatience with the process of ending her novel in order to argue that Larsen is "ventur[ing] toward the limits of her writerly experience" (167) in the novel's final pages, which proceed with an "'endless lack of purpose'" (Larsen quoted in *Aesthetics and Politics,* 168).

50. Ngai, *Ugly Feelings,* 190; Tate, "Desire and Death," 240. Critics unwilling to resign the novel's "abrupt and contradictory" conclusion to Larsen's incompetence at endings generally have taken a psychological or psychoanalytic approach to explaining the perceived break between the concluding sequence and what comes before (McDowell, "Introduction," xii). See, for example, McDowell's argument that Larsen's apparent "concessions to that dominant ideology of romance – marriage and motherhood" are signs of black bourgeois sexual repression (xii). Thadious Davis makes a similar argument in his biography, *Nella Larsen, Novelist of the Harlem Renaissance: A Woman's Life Unveiled* (Baton Rouge: Louisiana State University Press, 1994), 267–69. In Claudia Tate's Lacanian reading, it is the death drive that propels Helga to her "tragic" end ("Desire and Death," 240). Several critics have explained Helga's final descent by diagnosing her psychosis, neuroses, and narcissism. On psychosis in *Quicksand,* see Bill Hardwig, "'A Lack Somewhere': Lacan, Psychoanalysis, and *Quicksand,*" *Soundings* 80.4 (1997): 573–89; on

neurosis, see Robert Bone, *The Negro Novel in America* (New Haven, CT: Yale University Press, 1965); on narcissism, see Johnson, "Quicksands of the Self."

51. Davis, *Nella Larsen*, 176.
52. Gary Saul Morson, *Narrative and Freedom: The Shadows of Time* (New Haven, CT: Yale University Press, 1994), 47. Foreshadowing, Morson explains, depends on an asymmetry between the knowledge of protagonist and reader, but also between the protagonist and author: "The fact that the story is already written and the structure already determined . . . makes such a sign [the storm] possible, and so foreshadowing is an infallible reminder of the author's essential surplus. It establishes the merely illusory nature of what the character experiences as open temporality" (48).
53. Morson, *Narrative and Freedom*, 48.
54. Morson, *Narrative and Freedom*, 49.
55. My thinking has been shaped here by Isabelle Stengers's discussion of William James's pragmatic investment in "choices which engage and expose" in "William James: An Ethics of Thought?," *Radical Philosophy* 157 (2009): 9–17. A pragmatic ethics of thinking, according to Stengers, treats every thought as "an affirmation that there is something to think and that it can be thought" (12). To think is thus to affirm that "'life is worth living,' to decide to live against the real possibility of suicide" that James struggled with on a daily basis (11).
56. I am indebted to the organizing distinction Arden Reed draws between weather as "repetition" and "difference" in *Romantic Weather: The Climates of Coleridge and Baudelaire* (Providence, RI: Brown University Press, 1983), 8–9.
57. Ezek. 34:26, *King James Bible*.
58. Johnson, "Quicksands of the Self," 48.
59. James's lectures on *Pragmatism* outline his method for weighing "the practical value" or the "cash-value" of ideas and actions.
60. Cavell, *Transcendental Etudes*, 193.
61. Arsić, *On Leaving*, 31.
62. See, for example, Carby, *Reconstructing Womanhood*, 138; and Tate, "Desire and Death," 234. While we don't witness Helga's physical death, she suffers a social and spiritual death in the South. *Passing* ends even more abruptly and ambiguously with the protagonist's fall from an open window.
63. McDowell, "Introduction," xi.
64. Nancy K. Miller, "Emphasis Added: Plots and Plausibilities in Women's Fiction," in *Narrative Dynamics: Essays on Time, Plot, Closure, and Frame*, ed. Brian Richardson (Columbus: Ohio State University Press, 2002), 119.
65. Miller, "Emphasis Added," 122.

66. Susan Stanford Friedman, "*Lyric Subversion of Narrative: Virginia Woolf and the Tyranny of Plot*," in *Reading Narrative: Form, Ethics, Ideology*, ed. James Phelan (Columbus: Ohio State University Press, 1989), 163.

67. Miller, "Emphasis Added," 123.

68. Arthur P. Davis, *From the Dark Tower: Afro-American Writers, 1900–1960* (Washington, DC: Howard University Press, 1974), 96.

69. Several pieces published in the science journal *Nature* index a century-long history of debunking the "unnecessary mystery" around quicksand, beginning with a piece by Charles E. S. Phillips titled "Electrical and Other Properties of Sand," *Nature* 84 (August 25, 1910): 255–61. A letter to the editor by the British scientist Arnulph Mallock (published the year before *Quicksand*) likewise works to dispel the "many superstitions" that obscure the nature of "real quicksands"; see "The Consistence of Mixtures of True Fluid and of a Fluid with Solid Particles," *Nature* 120 (October 29, 1927): 620. Though scientists discovered over a hundred years ago that "quicksand can't suck you under," they "have not tired of disproving the myth" observes Roxanne Khamsi in "Quicksand Can't Suck You Under," *Nature* (September 28, 2005) <www.nature.com/news/2005/050926/full/new s050926-9.html>.

4 Gertrude Stein's Grammars of Attention

1. Gertrude Stein, "Many Many Women," in *Matisse, Picasso, and Gertrude Stein: With Two Shorter Stories* (Mineola, NY: Dover, 2000 [1933]), 133.

2. Gertrude Stein, *Narration* (Chicago: University of Chicago Press, 2010 [1935]), 13. Hereafter cited internally as *N*.

3. For discussions of Steinian sentences and paragraphs as organic forms of life, see Meyer, *Irresistible Dictation* and Richardson's chapter on Stein in *Natural History*, 232–52.

4. Gertrude Stein, *The Autobiography of Alice B. Toklas* (New York: Vintage, 1990 [1933]), 119.

5. Ulla E. Dydo with William Rice, *Gertrude Stein: The Language That Rises, 1923–1934* (Evanston, IL: Northwestern University Press, 2003), 9.

6. Dydo, *Language That Rises*, 595.

7. See Richard Bridgman, *Gertrude Stein in Pieces* (New York: Oxford University Press, 1971); Gertrude Stein, *A Primer for the Gradual Understanding of Gertrude Stein*, ed. Robert B. Haas (Los Angeles: Black Sparrow Press, 1971); and Donald Sutherland, *Gertrude Stein, a Biography of Her Work* (New Haven, CT: Yale University Press, 1951).

8. Jonathan Crary, *Suspensions of Perception: Attention, Spectacle, and Modern Culture* (Cambridge, MA: MIT Press, 2001), 4.

9. Crary, *Suspensions of Perception*, 1. Simmel equated the inability to pay attention with an incapacity for emotional investments in people and things. He memorably labels this state of perceptual and affective unresponsiveness the "blasé attitude [*Blasiertheit*]" in "The Metropolis and Mental Life," in *The Sociology of Georg Simmel*, trans. Kurt Wolff (New York: Free Press, 1950), 414–15. In a like manner, Kracauer labels the affective consequence of modernity's overstimulated, under-attentive state as boredom – a persistent inability to take an interest in the world – in his 1924 essay "Boredom"; see *The Mass Ornament: Weimar Essays*, trans. Thomas Y. Levin (Cambridge, MA: Harvard University Press, 1995 [1924]), 331–34.

10. Walter Benjamin, "The Work of Art in the Age of Mechanical Reproduction," in *Illuminations*, 240; Benjamin quoted in Crary, *Suspensions of Perception*, 1.

11. Benjamin, "Mechanical Reproduction," 239.

12. Crary, *Suspensions of Perception*, 14.

13. Crary, *Suspensions of Perception*, 1.

14. Crary, *Suspensions of Perception*, 4.

15. Crary, *Suspensions of Perception*, 2.

16. Crary, *Suspensions of Perception*, 51.

17. Crary, *Suspensions of Perception*, 2. See for instance, Crary's footnote on Deweyan attention (49n111) and his discussions of Jamesian attention (42–43 and 60–63).

18. Stein, *Autobiography*, 96. Stein published her findings from experimental work carried out with Leon Solomon under the supervision of Hugo Münsterberg in "Normal Motor Automatism," *Psychological Review* 3 (1896): 492–512. In this article Stein and Solomon argue "that habits of attention are reflexes of the complete character of the individual" (*WL*, 84). Critics who have elaborated the relationship between James's psychology and Stein's early theories of composition include Jennifer Ashton, "Gertrude Stein for Anyone," *ELH* 64.1 (1997): 289–331; Ronald B. Levinson, "Gertrude Stein, William James, and Grammar," *American Journal of Psychology* 54 (1941): 124–28; Meyer, *Irresistible Dictation*; Lisa Ruddick, *Reading Gertrude Stein: Body, Text, Gnosis* (Ithaca, NY: Cornell University Press, 1990); and Ryan, *Vanishing Subject*.

19. John Dewey, "The Theory of Emotion," in *The Early Works of John Dewey, 1882–1898*, vol. 4, ed. Jo Ann Boydston (Carbondale: Southern Illinois University Press, 1971), 175n20.

20. The "best writers" are the ones "who feel writing the most," as Stein contends in "Pictures," in *Writings, 1932–1946* (New York: Library of America, 1998), 243.

21. Stein quoted in Thornton Wilder's "Introduction," in Gertrude Stein's *Four in America* (New Haven, CT: Yale University Press, 1947), xi.

22. Gertrude Stein, *How to Write* (New York: Dover, 1975 [1931]), 66. Hereafter cited internally as *HTW*.

23. Mark Goble, *Beautiful Circuits: Modernism and the Mediated Life* (New York: Columbia University Press, 2010), 127.

24. For Frank, Stein's phrase "the compositional aspect of affect in perception" indexes her fundamental recognition that feelings direct (or disperse) our attention. See Adam Frank, "Thinking Confusion: On the Compositional Aspect of Affect," in *Transferential Poetics: From Poe to Warhol* (New York: Fordham University Press, 2014), 24–46.

25. Frank, "Thinking Confusion," 24–25.

26. Joan Retallack, *Gertrude Stein: Selections* (Berkeley: California University Press, 2008), 75.

27. Thornton Wilder uses this phrase in his introductions to *Four in America* (xiv) and *The Geographical History of America; or, The Relation of Human Nature to the Human Mind* (New York: Random House, 1936), 12.

28. Wilder, "Introduction," xiv.

29. Dydo, *Language That Rises*, 396.

30. Gertrude Stein, *How Writing Is Written: Vol. II of the Previously Uncollected Writings of Gertrude Stein*, ed. Robert B. Haas (Los Angeles: Black Sparrow Press, 1974), 155.

31. The first installment of *Autobiography* appeared in *Atlantic Monthly* in May of 1933, but the book was published as a whole in September of that year.

32. Stein, *How Writing Is Written*, 66; Simmel, "Metropolis and Mental Life," 410.

33. Crary, *Suspensions of Perception*, 2.

34. Gertrude Stein, *Everybody's Autobiography* (Cambridge, MA: Exact Change, 1993 [1937]), 66.

35. For work that attends to the nuances of Stein's transitional work in the wake of *Autobiography*, see Katherine Biers, "Gertrude Stein Talking," in *Virtual Modernism: Writing and Technology in the Progressive Era* (Minneapolis: University of Minnesota Press, 2013), 173–98.

36. Wilder, "Introduction," xi.

37. Stein, *How Writing Is Written*, 63 (emphasis added). "And Now" was first published in *Vanity Fair* in September of 1934. Excerpts were later incorporated into *Everybody's Autobiography* (1937), the sequel Stein finally wrote four years after the first *Autobiography*.

38. Further variations on Stein's "I am I" statement will reappear in her lectures, but also as a recurring motto in her examinations of "the relation of human nature and the human mind and identity" in *Everybody's Autobiography* and

The Geographical History of America, as well as in a piece called "Identity a Poem" (1935), which is comprised of fragments from the latter work (*WL*, 146).

39. *Four in America* was written in late winter or early spring of 1934, but Stein was planning and making reference to it the previous summer.

40. In *Autobiography*, for example, Stein is compared to "a general of either of both sides" and "a general [who] would never lose a battle" (19, 108). For more on Stein and generals, see Charles Caramello's chapter "Generals James and Stein" in, *Henry James, Gertrude Stein, and the Biographical Act* (Chapel Hill: University of North Carolina Press, 1996) 169–200.

41. An early reviewer of *Four in America* describes it as Stein's investigation of "how each of her representative Americans would have expressed his genius if he had been in some very different relation to the problems of human experience" (quoted in Caramello, *Biographical Act*, 174).

42. In Dydo's summation, these studies present "a great welter of confusing ideas" and can be read as "preparations for the clarity she reaches in the lectures," *Language That Rises*, 616–17.

43. Stein had in fact given lectures before this tour, but none matched the scale and scope of the series she planned to deliver to American audiences.

44. Sherwood Anderson and Gertrude Stein, *Sherwood Anderson/Gertrude Stein: Correspondence and Personal Essays*, ed. Ray Lewis White (Chapel Hill: University of North Carolina Press, 1972), 85.

45. Stein quoted in Dydo, *Language That Rises*, 610.

46. *Q. E. D.* was completed the year after the release of *The Wings of the Dove* in October of 1903 (but only published posthumously in 1950). Beyond quoting Kate Croy directly, Stein's first novella also draws upon James's triangular structure of character relations, and upon his depiction of those characters' consciousnesses. Stein's title could also conceivably be a nod to a quote from *Roderick Hudson*, James's first novel to depict the love triangle that would recur throughout his oeuvre: "'*Quod erat demonstradum!* cried Rowland. 'I think you know the Latin,'" *Roderick Hudson* (Cambridge, UK: The Riverside Press, 1917 [1875]), 470. For a fuller account of the novella's indebtedness to Henry James, see Michaela Giesenkirchen, "Adding Up William and Henry: The Psychodynamic Geometry of *Q. E. D.*," *American Literary Realism* 43.2 (2011): 112–32.

47. Stein, *How Writing Is Written*, 66.

48. My understanding of Stein's "open feeling" is informed by Sianne Ngai's reading of *The Making of Americans* in *Ugly Feelings*, 261, 283.

49. Stein, *Making of Americans*, 296.

50. Stein's fraught relationship with war has been well documented by such critics as Madelyn Detloff, *The Persistence of Modernism: Loss and Mourning in the*

Twentieth Century (Cambridge, UK: Cambridge University Press, 2009); Janet Malcolm, "Gertrude Stein's War: The Years in Occupied France," *New Yorker* (June 2, 2003): 58–81; Liesl Olson, *Modernism and the Ordinary* (New York: Oxford University Press, 2009); Schoenbach, *Pragmatic Modernism*; John Whittier-Ferguson, "The Liberation of Gertrude Stein: War and Writing," *Modernism/modernity* 8.3 (2001): 405–28; and Barbara Will, "Lost in Translation: Stein's Vichy Collaboration," *Modernism/ modernity* 11.4 (2004): 651–68. Stein returns to the unsettling analogy between writing and war throughout her career; to cite just two examples, she characterizes her lengthy struggle to be published as full of lively conflict that infuses her writing with interest: "Wars are interesting because there is a back and forth every minute in a war"; see "George Washington," in *Four in America*, 50. Looking back on *Four in America* in *Everybody's Autobiography*, Stein characterizes the project in similarly military terms: "That is what war is and dancing it is forward and back, when one is out walking one wants not to go back the way they came but in dancing and in war it is forward and back. That is what I tried to say in *Four in America*" (109).

51. Henry James, *Collected Travel Writings: Great Britain and America* (New York: Library of America, 1993), 689.

52. Stein, *Autobiography*, 78; "Forerunner, n.," *OED Online*, accessed April 13, 2013, <www.oed.com/view/Entry/73142>.

53. Stein, "George Washington," 51, 60.

54. James embarked upon his tour shortly after Stein moved to Europe.

55. I borrow this phrase from Alex Zwerdling's *Improvised Europeans: American Literary Expatriates and the Siege of London* (New York: Basic Books, 1994). For Stein's thoughts on her expatriatism, see *Geographical History*; "George Washington"; and "Thoughts on an American Contemporary Feeling," *Creative Art* 10.2 (1932): 129.

56. The introduction to Heather O'Donnell's dissertation, "The Natives Return: Henry James and Gertrude Stein in America" (Yale University, 2003), helpfully outlines some parallels between their return journeys. As she describes, at crucial points of their careers, both writers were similarly compelled to reflect on how their own expatriatism and reputation for difficulty could potentially alienate American audiences. Likewise, each somewhat reluctantly came to admit a vested interest in the public opinion of their home country and the massive market to be tapped there. Ultimately, James and Stein each took advantage of the publicity generated by the prospect of their return journeys in order to reinforce their place in a literary tradition they feared might otherwise remember them only for a single work or a one-dimensional personality. Though James had enjoyed success beyond *Daisy Miller* (1878), the early novella he was best known for, his later, much denser, novels of consciousness had failed to find a wide audience. A revised

section of O'Donnell's dissertation is published as "'My Own Funny Little Lecture Boom': Henry James's American Performance," *Henry James Review* 24.2 (2003): 133–45.

57. James and James, *Selected Letters*, 420.
58. James, *Travel Writings*, 358.
59. James, *Travel Writings*, 358, 359. My reading of this opening scene is indebted to Posnock's account of it in *The Trial of Curiosity*, 88–89.
60. Meyer, *Irresistible Dictation*, 137–38. Meyer further claims that Emerson's "lords of life" shaped Stein's work "even more thoroughly" than they did Emerson's own work (141). Among these "lords of life," "Surprise" is Stein's chief force of unsettlement.
61. Stein, *Autobiography*, 78.
62. *WL*, 56; Karin Cope, *Passionate Collaborations: Learning to Live with Gertrude Stein* (Victoria, BC: ELS Editions, 2005), 11.
63. Stein, "Pictures," 225, 226.
64. Stein, "Pictures," 235.
65. Stein, "Pictures," 236. My interpretation of this passage is informed by Brian Glavey's reading of it in *The Wallflower Avant-garde: Modernism, Sexuality, and Queer Ekphrasis* (New York: Oxford University Press, 2016), 42.
66. Gertrude Stein, *Picasso* (London: Dover, 1984), 16.
67. Quoted in Steven Meyer, "Gertrude Stein," in *Modernism and the New Criticism: The Cambridge History of Literary Criticism*, vol. 7, ed. Arthur Walton Litz, Louis Menand, and Lawrence Rainey (Cambridge, UK: Cambridge University Press, 2000), 107.
68. Fröller quoted in Retallack, *Gertrude Stein*, 3. As far as I can tell, "Dita Fröller" is an alter ego of Retallack – perhaps her vision of Stein's ideal reader – who provides apt epigraphs for her *Gertrude Stein* reader (3, 29) and for *The Poethical Wager* (Berkeley: University of California Press, 2003), 1, 34. Tellingly, Retallack quotes Fröller in the epigraph of a 2007 poem titled "THEREINVENTIONOFTRUTH," *How2* 3.1 (2007), <www.asu.edu/pip ercwcenter/how2journal/vol_3_no_1/letters/retallackreinvention.html>. Fröller is cited nowhere outside of Retallack's work, and the titles attributed to her – "Stein Stein Stein Stein Stein" and "Autobio: A Littered Aria," from "*New Old World Marvels*, Washington, DC, and Paris: Pre-Post-Eros Editions" – have been "forthcoming" for a number of years now.

Coda

1. John Cage, *I-VI* (Middleton, CT: Wesleyan University Press, 1990), 1.
2. Retallack describes both Stein's and Cage's work in terms of their "geometries of attention," an organizing refrain throughout *The Poethical Wager*. This coda

was catalyzed by some of the generative connections she draws with this felicitous phrase.

3. John Cage, *Empty Words: Writings '73-'78* (Middleton, CT: Wesleyan University Press, 1979), 65.

4. Cage quoted in Richard Kostelanetz, *Conversing with Cage* (New York: Routledge, 2003), 114.

5. Cage quoted in Kostelanetz, *Conversing with Cage*, 216.

6. Retallack, *Poethical Wager*, 175.

7. Cage quoted in Kyle Gann, *No Such Thing as Silence: John Cage's 4'33"* (New Haven, CT: Yale University Press, 2010), 4.

8. Retallack, *Poethical Wager*, xxxiii.

9. Wilder, "Introduction," xiv.

10. Dewey, *Democracy and Education*, 192.

11. Black Mountain College, "Prospectus," in *Education: Documents of Contemporary Art*, ed. Felicity Allen (Cambridge, MA: MIT Press, 2011), 36.

12. Cage quoted in Retallack, *Poethical Wager*, 175.

13. Black Mountain College, "Prospectus," 37.

14. Posnock, "Reading Poirier," 27, 26.

15. Dewey, *Experience and Education*, 35. For more on The Club, see Valerie Hellstein's dissertation, "Grounding the Social Aesthetics of Abstract Expressionism: A New Intellectual History of The Club" (SUNY at Stony Brook, 2010).

16. John Cage, interview by Holly E. Martin, "The Asian Factor in John Cage's Aesthetics: Interview from 1976," *Black Mountain College Studies Journal* 4 (2013), <www.blackmountainstudiesjournal.org/volume-iv-9–16/holly-mar tin-the-asian-factor-in-john-cages-aesthetics>.

17. Dewey, *Democracy and Education*, 44; *Experience and Education*, 25.

18. The school's interdisciplinary ethos provided Cage with ample opportunities for collaboration across visual, literary, and performing arts, which spurred his increasingly adventurous forays into alternate media. The lecture form that Cage begins to develop after his first summer at the college will ultimately become the backbone of his multimedia "events" or "happenings." The first "happening," titled "Theater Piece No. 1" (also known as "Black Mountain Piece") took place during Black Mountain's summer session in August 1952, just a few weeks before *4'33"* premiered in Woodstock. For more on "Theater Piece No. 1," see Eva Díaz, *The Experimenters: Chance and Design at Black Mountain College* (Chicago: University of Chicago Press, 2015), 78–83.

19. The foreword to *Silence* asserts that "Lecture on Nothing" employs the same "rhythmic structure" as his *Sonatas and Interludes* (which Cage performed as part of a recital at Black Mountain during the spring of 1948). Cage gives a

detailed account of their shared structure in his preface to the "Lecture" (*S*, 109).

20. Cage, "Interview from 1976."
21. As Marjorie Perloff observes, Cage's discipline of "non-intentionality" forces him "to break with ego, habit, self-indulgence"; see *Radical Artifice: Writing Poetry in the Age of Media* (Chicago: University of Chicago Press, 1994), 150.
22. Posnock, "Reading Poirier," 169.
23. Joan Retallack suggests that Cage first considered the relationship between his work and Dewey's *Art as Experience* after he heard Retallack deliver a paper that "placed Cage's work within the American pragmatist aesthetic" in May 1989 at the Strathmore Hall Arts Center Cage-Fest in Rockville, Maryland. She recalls: "Cage thanked me for the essay, saying with great emotion, 'With what you say about Dewey it all makes sense'"; see "Introduction: Conversations in Retrospect," in *MusiCage: Cage Muses on Words, Art, Music*, ed. Joan Retallack (Hanover, NH: Wesleyan University Press, 1996), xxiv.
24. Dewey, *Art as Experience*, 259.
25. Black Mountain College, "Prospectus," 37.
26. Rauschenberg quoted in Gann, *No Such Thing*, 157. Rauschenberg taught at Black Mountain at the same time as Cage, who admired Rauschenberg's "empty canvases" (while noting that the "canvas is never empty") (*S*, 103). Cage saw Rauschenberg's explorations of emptiness as a precursor and analogue of his own investigations of "structured silence": "The white paintings came first; my silent piece came later" (*S*, 98). On Cage's relationship to Rauschenberg at Black Mountain, see Gann, *No Such Thing*, 155–60.

Bibliography

Agamben, Giorgio, *Infancy and History: The Destruction of Experience*, trans. Liz Heron (London: Verso, 2005).

Altieri, Charles, *The Particulars of Rapture: An Aesthetics of the Affects* (Ithaca, NY: Cornell University Press, 2003).

Anderson, Sherwood, and Gertrude Stein, *Sherwood Anderson/Gertrude Stein: Correspondence and Personal Essays*, ed. Ray Lewis White (Chapel Hill: University of North Carolina Press, 1972).

Armstrong, Paul, *The Challenge of Bewilderment: Understanding and Representation in James, Conrad, and Ford* (Ithaca, NY: Cornell University Press, 1987).

Arsić, Branka, *On Leaving: A Reading in Emerson* (Cambridge, MA: Harvard University Press, 2010).

Arsić, Branka, and Cary Wolfe, eds., *The Other Emerson* (Minneapolis: University of Minnesota Press, 2010).

Ashton, Jennifer, "Gertrude Stein for Anyone," *ELH* 64.1 (1997): 289–331.

Baldwin, Thomas, "Philosophy," in *Proust in Context*, ed. Adam Watt (Oxford: Oxford University Press, 2013) 75–82.

Baudelaire, Charles, *Baudelaire: Correspondance, tome II, 1860–1866* (Paris: Gallimard, 1973).

   Intimate Journals, trans. Christopher Isherwood (Mineola, NY: Dover, 2006 [1947]).

   Journaux intimes: Fusées; Mon coeur mis à nu (Paris: Les Éditions G. Crès et Cie, 1920).

   "The Life and Work of Eugène Delacroix," in *The Painter of Modern Life and Other Essays*, ed. and trans. Jonathan Mayne (London: Phaidon, 2003) 42–69.

   "The Painter of Modern Life," in *Baudelaire: Selected Writings on Art and Artists*, ed. Patrick Edward Charvet (New York: Cambridge University Press, 1981) 390–435.

   Paris Spleen, trans. Louise Varese (New York: New Directions, 1970).

   "Salon of 1846," in *Baudelaire: Selected Writings on Art and Artists*, ed. and trans. Patrick Edward Charvet (New York: Penguin, 1981) 47–107.

   "Salon de 1859," in *Oeuvres complètes de Charles Baudelaire: Curiosités esthétiques* (Paris: Michel Lévy frères, 1868) 245–358.

Benjamin, Walter, "On Some Motifs in Baudelaire," in *Illuminations*, trans. Harry Zohn (New York: Schocken, 1969) 155–96.

"The Work of Art in the Age of Mechanical Reproduction," in *Illuminations*, trans. Harry Zohn (New York: Schocken, 1969) 217–53.

Bentley, Nancy, *Frantic Panoramas: American Literature and Mass Culture* (Philadelphia: University of Pennsylvania Press, 2009).

Bercovitch, Sacvan, *The American Jeremiad* (Madison: University of Wisconsin Press, 2012 [1978]).

The Puritan Origins of the American Self (New Haven, CT: Yale University Press, 2011 [1975]).

Bersani, Leo, *Baudelaire and Freud* (Berkeley: University of California Press, 1977).

Bersani, Leo and Adam Phillips, *Intimacies* (Chicago: University of Chicago, 2008).

Biers, Katherine, "Gertrude Stein Talking," in *Virtual Modernism: Writing and Technology in the Progressive Era* (Minneapolis: University of Minnesota Press, 2013) 173–98.

Black Mountain College, "Prospectus," in *Education: Documents of Contemporary Art*, ed. Felicity Allen (Cambridge, MA: MIT Press, 2011) 36–38.

Blackmur, Richard P., "Introduction," in *The Art of the Novel: Critical Prefaces by Henry James* (New York: Charles Scribner's Sons, 1962) vii–xxxix.

Bloom, Harold, *Wallace Stevens: The Poems of Our Climate* (Ithaca, NY: Cornell University Press, 1980).

Bone, Robert, *The Negro Novel in America* (New Haven, CT: Yale University Press, 1965).

Brennan, Teresa, *The Transmission of Affect* (Ithaca, NY: Cornell University Press, 2004).

Bridgman, Richard, *Gertrude Stein in Pieces* (New York: Oxford University Press, 1971).

Brodwin, Stanley, "Emerson's Version of Plotinus: The Flight to Beauty," *Journal of the History of Ideas* 35 (1974): 465–83.

Brooks, Cleanth, "The Language of Paradox," in *The Well Wrought Urn* (London: Dennis Dobson, 1947) 3–20.

Brooks, Cleanth, and Robert Penn Warren, *Understanding Fiction* (New York: Appleton-Century-Crofts, 1943).

Understanding Poetry (New York: Holt, Rinehart, and Winston, 1960 [1938]).

Brooks, Peter, "The Turn of *The American*," in *New Essays on* The American, ed. Martha Banta (New York: Cambridge University Press, 1987) 43–67.

Brower, Reuben A., "Reading in Slow Motion," in *In Defense of Reading: A Reader's Approach to Literary Criticism*, ed. Richard Poirier and Reuben A. Brower (New York: Dutton, 1962) 3–21.

Brown, Bill, *A Sense of Things: The Object Matter of American Literature* (Chicago: University of Chicago Press, 2003).

Brown, Lee Rust, *The Emerson Museum: Practical Romanticism and the Pursuit of the Whole* (Cambridge, MA: Harvard University Press, 1997).

Buck-Morss, Susan, "Aesthetics and Anaesthetics: Walter Benjamin's Artwork Essay Reconsidered," *October* 62 (1992): 3–41.

Buell, Lawrence, *Emerson* (Cambridge, MA: Harvard University Press, 2003).

Butler, Judith, "Passing, Queering: Nella Larsen's Psychoanalytic Challenge," in *Female Subjects in Black and White: Race, Psychoanalysis, Feminism*, ed. Elizabeth Abel, Barbara Christian, and Helene Moglen (Berkeley: University of California Press, 1997) 266–84.

Cadava, Eduardo, *Emerson and the Climates of History* (Stanford, CA: Stanford University Press, 1997).

"The Guano of History," in *The Other Emerson*, ed. Branka Arsić and Cary Wolfe (Minneapolis: University of Minnesota Press, 2010) 101–29.

Cage, John, *I-VI* (Middleton, CT: Wesleyan University Press, 1990).

"The Asian Factor in John Cage's Aesthetics: Interview from 1976," by Holly E. Martin, *Black Mountain College Studies Journal* 4 (2013). <www.blackmoun tainstudiesjournal.org/volume-iv-9–16/holly-martin-the-asian-factor-in-joh n-cages-aesthetics>.

Empty Words: Writings, '73–'78 (Middleton, CT: Wesleyan University Press, 1979).

Silence: Lectures and Writings by John Cage (Middleton, CT: Wesleyan University Press, 1961).

Cameron, Sharon, *Thinking in Henry James* (Chicago: University of Chicago Press, 1989).

"The Way of Life by Abandonment: Emerson's Impersonal," in *Impersonality: Seven Essays* (Chicago: University of Chicago Press, 2007) 79–107.

Caramello, Charles, *Henry James, Gertrude Stein, and the Biographical Act* (Chapel Hill: University of North Carolina Press, 1996).

Carby, Hazel V., *Reconstructing Womanhood: The Emergence of the Afro-American Woman Novelist* (New York: Oxford University Press, 1987).

Carpenter, F. I., *Emerson and Asia* (Cambridge, MA: Harvard University Press, 1968 [1930]).

Carter, Everett, "The Emersonian Proust," *Comparative Literature Studies* 29.1 (1992): 39–53.

Caruth, Cathy, *Trauma: Explorations in Memory* (Baltimore, MA: Johns Hopkins University Press, 1995).

Cavell, Stanley, *Emerson's Transcendental Etudes* (Stanford, CA: Stanford University Press, 2003).

Clune, Michael, *Writing Against Time* (Stanford, CA: Stanford University Press, 2013).

Cohn, Dorrit, "'First Shock of Complete Perception': The Opening Episode of *The Golden Bowl*, Volume 2," *Henry James Review* 22.1 (2009): 1–9.

Coleridge, Samuel, *The Complete Works of Samuel Taylor Coleridge*, vol. 7, ed. W. G. T. Shedd (New York: Harper and Brothers, 1884).

Commager, Henry Steele, *The American Mind: An Interpretation of American Thought and Character Since the 1880's* (New Haven, CT: Yale University Press, 1950).

Cope, Karin, *Passionate Collaborations: Learning to Live with Gertrude Stein* (Victoria, BC: ELS Editions, 2005).

Copleston, Frederick, *A History of Philosophy*, vol. 1, *Greece and Rome* (New York: Image Books, 1993 [1946]).

Crane, Gregg, "Intuition: The 'Unseen Thread' Connecting Emerson and James," *Modern Intellectual History* 10.1 (2013): 57–86.

Crary, Jonathan, *Suspensions of Perception: Attention, Spectacle, and Modern Culture* (Cambridge, MA: MIT Press, 2001).

Dames, Nicholas, "Wave-Theories and Affective Physiologies: The Cognitive Strain in Victorian Novel Theories," *Victorian Studies* 46.2 (2004): 206–16.

Darwin, Charles, *The Expressions of the Emotions in Man and Animals* (New York: Oxford University Press, 1998).

Dastur, Françoise, "Phenomenology of the Event: Waiting and Surprise," *Hypatia* 15.4 (2000): 178–89.

Davis, Arthur P., *From the Dark Tower: Afro-American Writers, 1900–1960* (Washington, DC: Howard University Press, 1974).

Davis, Thadious M., *Nella Larsen, Novelist of the Harlem Renaissance: A Woman's Life Unveiled* (Baton Rouge: Louisiana State University Press, 1994).

Delbanco, Andrew, *The Puritan Ordeal* (Cambridge, MA: Harvard University Press, 1989).

Demos, Virginia E., "Silvan Tomkins's Theory of Emotion," in *Reinterpreting the Legacy of William James*, ed. Margaret E. Donnelly (Washington, DC: American Psychological Association, 1992) 211–29.

Descartes, René, "Discourse and Essays," in *The Philosophical Writings of Descartes*, vol. 1, trans. John Cottingham, Robert Stoothoff, and Dugald Murdoch (New York: Cambridge University Press, 1985) 109–75.

"The Passions of the Soul," in *The Philosophical Writings of Descartes*, vol. 1, trans. John Cottingham, Robert Stoothoff, and Dugald Murdoch (New York: Cambridge University Press, 1985) 325–404.

Descombes, Vincent, *Proust: Philosophy of the Novel*, trans. Catherine Chance Macksey (Stanford, CA: Stanford University Press, 1992).

Detloff, Madelyn, *The Persistence of Modernism: Loss and Mourning in the Twentieth Century* (Cambridge, UK: Cambridge University Press, 2009).

Dewey, John, *Art as Experience* (New York: Penguin, 2005 [1934]).

Democracy and Education, 1916: The Middle Works of John Dewey, 1899–1924, vol. 9, ed. Jo Ann Boydston. (Carbondale: Southern Illinois University Press, 2008).

"Emerson: The Philosopher of Democracy," *International Journal of Ethics* 13.4 (1903): 405–13.

Experience and Education (New York: Simon and Schuster, 1938).

Psychology (New York: Harper and Brothers, 1890).

"The Theory of Emotion," in *The Early Works of John Dewey, 1882–1898*, vol. 4, ed. Jo Ann Boydston (Carbondale: Southern Illinois University Press, 1971 [1894]) 152–88.

Díaz, Eva, *The Experimenters: Chance and Design at Black Mountain College* (Chicago: University of Chicago Press, 2015).

Dickstein, Morris, "The Rise and Fall of 'Practical' Criticism: From I. A. Richards to Barthes and Derrida," in *Theory's Empire: An Anthology of Dissent*, ed. Daphne Patal and Wilfrido Corral (New York: Columbia University Press, 2005) 60–77.

Dickstein, Morris, ed., *The Revival of Pragmatism* (Durham, NC: Duke University Press, 1998).

Dittmar, Linda, "When Privilege Is No Protection: The Woman Artist in *Quicksand* and *The House of Mirth*," in *Writing the Woman Artist: Essays on Poetics, Politics, and Portraiture*, ed. Suzanne W. Jones (Philadelphia: University of Pennsylvania Press, 1991) 133–54.

Doyle, Laura, *Freedom's Empire: Race and the Rise of the Novel in Atlantic Modernity, 1640–1940* (Durham, NC: Duke University Press, 2008).

Du Bois, W. E. B., *The Souls of Black Folk* (New York: Oxford University Press, 2007 [1903]).

Dufrenne, Mikel, *The Phenomenology of Aesthetic Experience*, trans. Edward S. Casey (Evanston, IL: Northwestern University Press, 1973).

Dunston, Susan L., "Ethics," in *Emerson in Context*, ed. Wesley T. Mott (New York: Cambridge University Press, 2014) 171–79.

Dydo, Ulla E., *Gertrude Stein: The Language That Rises, 1923–1934*, (Evanston, IL: Northwestern University Press, 2003).

Edel, Leon, "Afterword," in *Henry James's The American* (New York: Signet Classics, 1963) 331–38.

Ekman, Paul, and Wallace V. Friesen, *Unmasking the Face: A Guide to Recognizing Emotions from Facial Expressions* (Englewood Cliffs, NJ: Spectrum, 1975).

Ekman, Paul, Wallace V. Friesen, and Ronald C. Simons, "Is the Startle Reaction an Emotion?," *Journal of Personality and Social Psychology* 49.5 (1985): 1416–26.

Ellison, Julie, *Emerson's Romantic Style* (Princeton, NJ: Princeton University Press, 1984).

Emerson, Ralph Waldo, *The Early Lectures of Ralph Waldo Emerson, 1833–1836*, ed. Stephen Whicher and Robert Spiller (Cambridge, MA: Harvard University Press, 1951).

Emerson in His Journals, ed. Joel Porte (Cambridge, MA: Harvard University Press, 1982).

Essays and Lectures (New York: Library of America, 1983).

Journals and Miscellaneous Notebooks of Ralph Waldo Emerson, vol. 4, *1832–1834*, ed. Alfred R. Ferguson (Cambridge, MA: Harvard University Press, 1964).

Journals and Miscellaneous Notebooks of Ralph Waldo Emerson, vol. 5, *1835–1838*, ed. Merton M. Sealts (Cambridge, MA: Harvard University Press, 1965).

Journals and Miscellaneous Notebooks of Ralph Waldo Emerson, vol. 7, *1838–1842*, ed. A. W. Plumstead and Harrison Hayford (Cambridge, MA: Harvard University Press, 1969).

Journals and Miscellaneous Notebooks of Ralph Waldo Emerson, vol. 8, *1841–1843*, ed. William H. Gilman and J. E. Parsons (Cambridge, MA: Harvard University Press, 1970).

The Later Lectures of Ralph Waldo Emerson, vol. 1, *1843–1854*, ed. Ronald A. Bosco and Joel Myerson (Athens: University of Georgia Press, 2010).

The Later Lectures of Ralph Waldo Emerson, vol. 2, *1855–1871*, ed. Ronald A. Bosco and Joel Myerson (Athens: University of Georgia Press, 2010).

The Topical Notebooks of Ralph Waldo Emerson, vol. 2, ed. Susan Sutton Smith (Columbia: University of Missouri Press, 1993).

"Works and Days," in *Ralph Waldo Emerson: The Major Prose*, ed. Ronald A. Bosco and Joel Myerson (Cambridge, MA: Harvard University Press, 2015) 517–35.

Empson, William, *Seven Types of Ambiguity* (New York: New Directions, 1966 [1930]).

Esteve, Mary, *The Aesthetics and Politics of the Crowd in American Literature* (New York: Cambridge University Press, 2003).

Fanon, Frantz, *Black Skin, White Masks*, trans. Charles Lam Markmann (New York: Grove Press, 1967).

Fisher, Philip, *Wonder, the Rainbow, and the Aesthetics of Rare Experiences* (Cambridge, MA: Harvard University Press, 1998).

"Forerunner, n.," *OED Online*, accessed April 13, 2013, <www.oed.com/view/En try/73142>.

Fraisse, Luc, *L'éclectise philosophique de Marcel Proust* (Paris: Presses Universitaires Paris-Sorbonne, 2013).

Frank, Adam, "Some Affective Bases for Guilt: Tomkins, Freud, Object Relations," *English Studies in Canada* 32.1 (2006): 11–25.

"Thinking Confusion: On the Compositional Aspect of Affect," in *Transferential Poetics: From Poe to Warhol* (New York: Fordham University Press, 2014) 24–46.

Freud, Sigmund, *Beyond the Pleasure Principle* (New York: Dover, 2015 [1920]).

Friedman, Susan Stanford, "Lyric Subversion of Narrative: Virginia Woolf and the Tyranny of Plot," in *Reading Narrative: Form, Ethics, Ideology*, ed. James Phelan (Columbus: Ohio State University Press, 1989) 162–85.

Gann, Kyle, *No Such Thing as Silence: John Cage's 4'33"* (New Haven, CT: Yale University Press, 2010).

Gaskill, Nicholas, "What Difference Can Pragmatism Make for Literary Study?," *American Literary History* 24.2 (2012): 374–89.

Genette, Gérard, *Narrative Discourse: An Essay in Method* (Ithaca, NY: Cornell University Press, 1980).

Giesenkirchen, Michaela, "Adding Up William and Henry: The Psychodynamic Geometry of *Q. E. D.*," *American Literary Realism* 43.2 (2011): 112–32.

Gilman, Margaret, "Baudelaire and Emerson," *Romantic Review* 34.3 (1943): 211–22.

Glavey, Brian. *The Wallflower Avant-garde: Modernism, Sexuality, and Queer Ekphrasis* (New York: Oxford University Press, 2016).

Goble, Mark, *Beautiful Circuits: Modernism and the Mediated Life* (New York: Columbia University Press, 2010).

Gray, Jeffrey, "Essence and the Mulatto Traveler: Europe as Embodiment in Nella Larsen's *Quicksand*," *Novel* 27.3 (1994): 257–70.

Griffin, Farrah, *Who Set You Flowin'?: The African-American Migration Narrative* (New York: Oxford University Press, 1996).

Grimstad, Paul, *Experience and Experimental Writing: Literary Pragmatism from Emerson to the Jameses* (New York: Oxford University Press, 2013).

Gumbrecht, Hans Ulrich, *Atmosphere, Mood, Stimmung: On a Hidden Potential of Literature* (Stanford, CA: Stanford University Press, 2012).

Hadot, Pierre, *Plotinus, or, the Simplicity of Vision*, trans. Michael Chase (Chicago: University of Chicago Press, 1998).

Hansen, Miriam Bratu, *Cinema and Experience: Siegfried Kracauer, Walter Benjamin, and Theodor W. Adorno* (Berkeley: University of California Press, 2012).

Hardwig, Bill, "'A Lack Somewhere': Lacan, Psychoanalysis, and *Quicksand*," *Soundings* 80.4 (1997): 573–89.

Harrison, J. S., *The Teachers of Emerson* (New York: Haskell House, 1966 [1910]).

Hellstein, Valerie, "Grounding the Social Aesthetics of Abstract Expressionism: A New Intellectual History of The Club," PhD diss. (SUNY at Stony Brook, 2010).

Howard, Luke, *On the Modifications of Clouds* (Cambridge, UK: Cambridge University Press, 2011 [1803]).

Howe, Irving, *The American Newness: Culture and Politics in the Age of Emerson* (Cambridge, MA: Harvard University Press, 1986).

Howells, Bernard, "'La vaporisation du moi': Baudelaire's *Journaux intimes*," *French Studies* 42.4 (1988): 424–42.

Hutchinson, George, *In Search of Nella Larsen: A Biography of the Color Line* (Cambridge, MA: Harvard University Press, 2006).

"Innovate, v.," *OED Online*, accessed August 7, 2015, <www.oed.com/Entry/96310>.

"Interval, n.," *OED Online*, accessed January 10, 2010, <www.oed.com/view/Entry/98410>.

Isherwood, Christopher, "Translator's Preface," in Charles Baudelaire's *Intimate Journals*, trans. Christopher Isherwood (Mineola, NY: Dover, 2006) 5–12.

James, Henry, *The Ambassadors* (New York: Norton, 1964 [1903]).

    The American (London: Macmillan, 1878).

    "Anthony Trollope," *The Century Magazine* 26.3 (July 1883): 384–94.

    The Art of the Novel: Critical Prefaces by Henry James (New York: Charles Scribner's Sons, 1962).

    Collected Travel Writings: Great Britain and America (New York: Library of America, 1993).

    The Golden Bowl (New York: Everyman's Library, 1992 [1904]).

    Henry James: Autobiography, ed. Frederick W. Dupee (New York: Criterion Books, 1956).

    The Ivory Tower, ed. Percy Lubbock (London: Collins, 1917).

Literary Criticism, vol. 1, *Essays, English and American Writers* (New York: Library of America, 1984).

Theory of Fiction, ed. James E. Miller (Lincoln: University of Nebraska Press, 1972).

The Wings of the Dove (New York: Penguin, 1986 [1902]).

James, Henry, and William James, *William and Henry James: Selected Letters*, ed. Ignas K. Skrupskelis and Elizabeth M. Berkeley (Charlottesville: University of Virginia Press, 1997).

James, William, *The Letters of William James*, vol. 2, ed. Henry James III (Boston: Atlantic Monthly, 1920).

"The Physical Basis of Emotion," *Psychological Review* 101.2 (1894): 205–10.

The Principles of Psychology, vol. 1 (New York: Dover, 1950 [1890]).

The Principles of Psychology, vol. 2 (New York: Dover, 1950 [1890]).

"What Is an Emotion?," *Mind* 9.34 (1884): 188–205.

Writings, 1902–1910 (New York: Library of America, 1987).

Writings, 1878–1899 (New York: Library of America, 1992).

Jay, Martin, *Songs of Experience: Modern American and European Variations on a Universal Theme* (Berkeley: University of California Press, 2005).

Johnson, Barbara, "The Quicksands of the Self: Nella Larsen and Heinz Kohut," in *The Feminist Difference: Literature, Psychoanalysis, Race, and Gender* (Cambridge, MA: Harvard University Press, 2000) 37–60.

Khamsi, Roxanne, "Quicksand Can't Suck You Under," *Nature* (September 28, 2005). <www.nature.com/news/2005/050926/full/news050926-9.html>.

Kohan, Kevin, "James and the Originary Scene," *Henry James Review* 22.3 (2001): 229–38.

Kostelanetz, Richard, *Conversing with Cage* (New York: Routledge, 2003).

Kracauer, Siegfried, *The Mass Ornament: Weimar Essays*, trans. Thomas Y. Levin (Cambridge, MA: Harvard University Press, 1995 [1924]).

Kryk-Kastovsky, Barbara, "Surprise, Surprise: The Iconicity-Conventionality Scale of Emotions," in *The Language of Emotions: Conceptualization, Expression, and Theoretical Foundation*, ed. Susanne Niemeier and René Dirven (Philadelphia: John Benjamins, 1997) 155–69.

Landy, Joshua, *Philosophy as Fiction: Self, Deception, and Knowledge in Proust* (New York: Oxford University Press, 2004).

Larsen, Nella, *Quicksand and Passing*, ed. Deborah McDowell (New Brunswick, NJ: Rutgers University Press, 2004).

Levinson, Ronald B., "Gertrude Stein, William James, and Grammar," *American Journal of Psychology* 54 (1941): 124–28.

Looby, Christopher, "Scholar and Exegete: A Tribute to Sacvan Bercovitch, MLA Honored Scholar of Early American Literature, 2002," *Early American Literature* 39.1 (2002): 1–9.

Looby, Christopher, and Cindy Weinstein, "Introduction," in *American Literature's Aesthetic Dimensions*, ed. Christopher Looby and Cindy Weinstein (New York: Columbia University Press, 2012) 1–34.

Lubbock, Percy, *The Craft of Fiction* (New York: Peter Smith, 1947 [1921]).

Macharia, Keguro, "Queering Helga Crane: Black Nativism in Nella Larsen's *Quicksand*," *Modern Fiction Studies* 57.2 (2011): 254–75.

Malcolm, Janet, "Gertrude Stein's War: The Years in Occupied France," *New Yorker*, (June 2, 2003): 58–81.

Mallock, A., "The Consistence of Mixtures of True Fluid and of a Fluid with Solid Particles," *Nature* 120 (October 29, 1927): 619–20.

Marchi, Dudley M. "Baudelaire's America—Contrary Affinities," *Yearbook of General and Comparative Literature* 47 (2000): 37–52.

Massumi, Brian, "The Autonomy of Affect," in *Deleuze: A Critical Reader*, ed. Paul Patton (Oxford: Blackwell, 1996): 217–39.

"Navigating Movements: A Conversation with Brian Massumi," by Mary Zournazi, in *Hope: New Philosophies for Change*, ed. Mary Zournazi (New York: Routledge, 2002) 210–43.

Parables for the Virtual (Durham, NC: Duke University Press, 2002).

Politics of Affect (Cambridge, UK: Polity, 2015).

Semblance and Event (Cambridge, MA: MIT Press, 2011).

Matthiessen, F. O., *Henry James: The Major Phase* (New York: Oxford University Press, 1944).

McDowell, Deborah E., "Introduction," in Nella Larsen's *Quicksand and Passing*, ed. Deborah E. McDowell (New Brunswick, NJ: Rutgers University Press, 1986) ix–xxxv.

Meyer, Steven, "Gertrude Stein," in *Modernism and the New Criticism: The Cambridge History of Literary Criticism*, vol. 7, ed. Arthur Walton Litz, Louis Menand, and Lawrence Rainey (Cambridge, UK: Cambridge University Press, 2000) 93–121.

Irresistible Dictation: Gertrude Stein and the Correlations of Writing and Science (Stanford, CA: Stanford University Press, 2001).

Miller, Christopher R., *Surprise: The Poetics of the Unexpected from Milton to Austen* (Ithaca, NY: Cornell University Press, 2015).

Miller, J. Hillis, "Lying against Death: *The Wings of the Dove*," in *Literature as Conduct: Speech Acts in Henry James* (New York: Fordham University Press, 2005) 151–227.

Miller, Nancy K., "Emphasis Added: Plots and Plausibilities in Women's Fiction," in *Narrative Dynamics: Essays on Time, Plot, Closure, and Frame*, ed. Brian Richardson (Columbus: Ohio State University Press, 2002) 110–29.

Moretti, Franco, "Homo Palpitans," in *Signs Taken for Wonders: On the Sociology of Literary Forms* (New York: Verso, 2005) 109–29.

Morson, Gary Saul, *Narrative and Freedom: The Shadows of Time* (New Haven, CT: Yale University Press, 1994).

Mossé-Bastide, Rose-Marie, *Bergson et Plotin* (Paris: Presses Universitaires de France, 1959).

Murphy, Michael, *Proust and America* (Liverpool: Liverpool University Press, 2007).

New, Elisa, *The Line's Eye: Poetic Experience, American Sight* (Cambridge, MA: Harvard University Press, 1998).

Ngai, Sianne, *Ugly Feelings* (Cambridge, MA: Harvard University Press, 2005).

North, Michael, "The Making of 'Make It New,'" *Guernica* (August 15, 2013). <www.guernicamag.com/the-making-of-making-it-new/>.

Nussbaum, Martha C., "Exactly and Responsibly: A Defense of Ethical Criticism," *Philosophy and Literature* 22.2 (1998): 343–65.

O'Donnell, Heather, "'My Own Funny Little Lecture Boom': Henry James's American Performance," *Henry James Review* 24.2 (2003): 133–45.

"The Natives Return: Henry James and Gertrude Stein in America," PhD diss. (Yale University, 2003).

Olson, Liesl, *Modernism and the Ordinary* (New York: Oxford University Press, 2009).

Osmond, Meredith, "The Prepositions We Use in the Construal of Emotions: Why Do We Say Fed Up With and Tired Of?," in *The Language of Emotions: Conceptualization, Expression, and Theoretical Foundation*, ed. Susanne Niemeier and René Dirven (Amsterdam: John Benjamins, 1997) 111–33.

Patterson, Anita Haya, *From Emerson to King: Democracy, Race, and the Politics of Protest* (New York: Oxford University Press, 1997).

Perloff, Marjorie, *Radical Artifice: Writing Poetry in the Age of Media* (Chicago: University of Chicago Press, 1994).

Phillips, Charles E. S., "Electrical and Other Properties of Sand," *Nature* 84 (August 25, 1910): 255–61.

Plotinus, *Enneads*, 9 vols., trans. A. H. Armstrong, *Loeb Classical Library* (Cambridge, MA: Harvard University Press, 2014).

An Essay on the Beautiful, trans. Thomas Taylor (London: printed for the author, 1792).

Five Books of Plotinus, trans. Thomas Taylor (London: printed for Edward Jeffrey, 1794).

Select Works of Plotinus, trans. Thomas Taylor (London: Black and Son, 1817).

Poirier, Richard, *The Comic Sense of Henry James: A Study of the Early Novels* (New York: Oxford University Press, 1960).

Poetry and Pragmatism (Cambridge, MA: Harvard University Press, 1992).

"Poetry, Pragmatism, and American Literature: An Interview with Richard Poirier," by Giorgio Mariani, *College Hill Review* 5 (2010). <www.collegehill review.com/005/0050201.html>.

The Renewal of Literature (New Haven, CT: Yale University Press, 1988).

Posnock, Ross, *Color and Culture: Black Writers and the Making of the Modern Intellectual* (Cambridge, MA: Harvard University Press, 1998).

"'Don't Think, but Look!': W. G. Sebald, Wittgenstein, and Cosmopolitan Poverty," *Representations* 112.1 (2010): 112–39.

"I'm Not There," *Daedalus* 143.1 (2013): 85–95.

"Reading Poirier Pragmatically," *Yale Review* 80 (1992): 156–69

Renunciation: Acts of Abandonment by Writers, Philosophers, and Artists (Cambridge, MA: Harvard University Press, 2016).

The Trial of Curiosity: Henry James, William James, and the Challenge of Modernity (New York: Oxford University Press, 1991).

Poulet, Georges, "Phenomenology of Reading," *New Literary History* 1.1 (1969): 53–68.

Studies in Human Time, ed. Elliott Coleman (Baltimore, MA: Johns Hopkins University Press, 1956).

Proust, Marcel, "Contre Sainte-Beuve," in *Marcel Proust: On Art and Literature, 1896–1919*, trans. Sylvia Townsend Warner (New York: Caroll and Graf, 1997) 19–276.

Finding Time Again, trans. Ian Patterson (London: Penguin, 2003).

The Guermantes Way, trans. Mark Treharne (London: Penguin, 2003).

On Reading, trans. Jean Autret and William Burford (London: Souvenir Press, 1972).

Remembrance of Things Past, vol. 2, *The Captive*, trans. C. K. Scott Moncrieff (New York: Random House, 1932).

The Way by Swann's, trans. Lydia Davis (London: Penguin, 2003).

Puckett, Kent, "Before and Afterwardsness in Henry James," in *Narrative Middles: Navigating the Nineteenth-Century Novel*, ed. Caroline Levine and Mario Ortiz-Robles (Columbus: Ohio State University Press, 2011).

Rappe, Sara, *Reading Neoplatonism: Non-discursive Thinking in the Texts of Plotinus, Proclus, and Damascius* (New York: Cambridge University Press, 2000).

Rawlings, Peter, "Grammars of Time in Henry James," *Modern Language Review* 98.2 (2003): 273–84.

Reed, Adolph L., *W. E. B. Du Bois and American Political Thought: Fabianism and the Color Line* (New York: Oxford University Press, 1997).

Reed, Arden, *Romantic Weather: The Climates of Coleridge and Baudelaire* (Providence, RI: Brown University Press, 1983).

Retallack, Joan, *Gertrude Stein: Selections* (Berkeley: California University Press, 2008).

"Introduction: Conversations in Retrospect," in *MusiCage: Cage Muses on Words, Art, Music*, ed. Joan Retallack (Hanover, NH: Wesleyan University Press, 1996) xiii–xliii.

The Poethical Wager (Berkeley: University of California Press, 2003).

"THEREINVENTIONOFTRUTH," *How2* 3.1 (2007). <www.asu.edu/piper cwcenter/how2journal/vol_3_no_1/letters/retallackreinvention.html>.

Richardson, Joan, *A Natural History of Pragmatism: The Fact of Feeling from Jonathan Edwards to Gertrude Stein* (New York: Cambridge University Press, 2007).

Pragmatism and American Experience: An Introduction (New York: Cambridge University Press, 2014).

Richardson, Robert, *Emerson: The Mind on Fire* (Berkeley: University of California Press, 1995).

First We Read, Then We Write: Emerson on the Creative Process (Iowa City: University of Iowa Press, 2009).

Robinson, David M., *Emerson and the Conduct of Life: Pragmatism and Ethical Purpose in the Later Work* (New York: Cambridge University Press, 1993).

Ruddick, Lisa, *Reading Gertrude Stein: Body, Text, Gnosis* (Ithaca, NY: Cornell University Press, 1990).

Rudler, Frederick William, "Amber (resin)," in *Encyclopedia Britannica*, 11th ed., ed. Hugh Chisolm (Cambridge, UK: Cambridge University Press, 1911).

Ryan, Judith, *The Vanishing Subject: Early Psychology and Literary Modernism* (Chicago: University of Chicago Press, 1991).

Sartre, Jean-Paul, *Baudelaire*, trans. Martin Turnell (New York: New Directions, 1967).

Schoenbach, Lisi, *Pragmatic Modernism* (New York: Oxford University Press, 2012).

Sedgwick, Eve Kosofsky, *Touching Feeling: Affect, Pedagogy, Performativity* (Durham, NC: Duke University Press, 2013).

The Weather in Proust (Durham, NC: Duke University Press, 2011).

Sedgwick, Eve Kosofsky, and Adam Frank, "Shame in the Cybernetic Fold: Reading Silvan Tomkins," in *Shame and Its Sisters: A Silvan Tomkins Reader* (Durham, NC: Duke University Press, 1995) 1–28.

Silverman, Kaja, "Too Early/Too Late: Subjectivity and the Primal Scene in Henry James," *Novel* 21.2/3 (1988): 147–73.

Simmel, Georg, "The Metropolis and Mental Life," in *The Sociology of Georg Simmel*, trans. Kurt Wolff (New York: Free Press, 1950) 409–24.

Smith, George, "The Last Phase: Henry James and the Psycho-Painterly Style," *Henry James Review* 30.1 (2009): 62–67.

Sollors, Werner, *Neither Black Nor White and Yet Both: Thematic Explorations of Interracial Literature* (Cambridge, MA: Harvard University Press, 1999).

Stein, Gertrude, *The Autobiography of Alice B. Toklas* (New York: Vintage, 1990 [1933]).

Everybody's Autobiography (Cambridge, MA: Exact Change, 1993 [1937]).

The Geographical History of America; or, The Relation of Human Nature to the Human Mind (New York: Random House, 1936).

"George Washington," in *Four in America* (New Haven, CT: Yale University Press, 1947) 161–221.

How to Write (New York: Dover, 1975 [1931]).

How Writing Is Written: Vol. 2 of the Previously Uncollected Writings of Gertrude Stein, ed. Robert B. Haas (Los Angeles: Black Sparrow Press, 1974).

The Making of Americans (Normal, IL: Dalkey Archive Press, 1995 [1925]).

"Many Many Women," in *Matisse, Picasso, and Gertrude Stein: With Two Shorter Stories* (Mineola, NY: Dover, 2000) 117–198.

Narration (Chicago: University of Chicago Press, 2010 [1935]).

Picasso (London: Dover, 1984 [1938]).

"Pictures," in *Writings, 1932–1946* (New York: Library of America, 1998), 224–43.

A Primer for the Gradual Understanding of Gertrude Stein, ed. Robert B. Haas (Los Angeles: Black Sparrow Press, 1971).

"Thoughts on an American Contemporary Feeling," *Creative Art* 10.2 (1932): 129.

Writings and Lectures, 1911–1945, ed. Patricia Meyerowitz (London: Peter Owen, 1967).

Stein, Gertrude, and Leon Solomon, "Normal Motor Automatism," *Psychological Review* 3 (1896): 492–512.

Stengers, Isabelle, "William James: An Ethics of Thought?," *Radical Philosophy* 157 (2009): 9–17.

"Surprise, n.," *OED Online*, accessed July 3, 2009, <www.oed.com /view/Entry/ 194999>.

Sutherland, Donald, *Gertrude Stein, a Biography of Her Work* (New Haven, CT: Yale University Press, 1951).

Tadié, Jean-Yves, *Marcel Proust* (New York: Viking, 2000).

Tanner, Laura E., "Intimate Geography: The Body, Race, and Space in Larsen's *Quicksand*," *Texas Studies in Literature and Language* 51.2 (2009): 179–202.

Tate, Claudia, "Desire and Death in *Quicksand*," *American Literary History* 7.2 (1995): 234–60.

Terada, Rei, *Feeling in Theory: Emotion after the "Death of the Subject"* (Cambridge, MA: Harvard University Press, 2001).

Thrailkill, Jane, *Affecting Fictions: Mind, Body, and Emotion in American Literary Realism* (Cambridge, MA: Harvard University Press, 2007).

Tomkins, Silvan S., *Affect Imagery Consciousness,* vol. 1, *The Positive Affects* (New York: Springer, 1962).

"What Are Affects?," in *Shame and Its Sisters: A Silvan Tomkins Reader,* ed. Eve Kosofsky Sedgwick and Adam Frank (Durham, NC: Duke University Press, 1995) 33–74.

Veeder, William, "James and the Consolations of Time," *Henry James Review* 17.3 (1996): 230–41.

Virtanen, Reino, "Proust and Emerson," *Symposium* 6.1 (1952): 123–39.

Walton, Edna Lou, "Review of *Quicksand*," in *Opportunity* 6.7 (July 1928): 212–13. Reprinted in *The Critics and the Harlem Renaissance*, ed. Cary D. Wintz (New York: Garland, 1996).

Watt, Adam, Reading in Proust's *A la recherche*: 'le délire de la lecture' (Oxford: Oxford University Press, 2009).

Wellek, René, *History of Modern Criticism, 1750–1950*, vol. 8, *French, Italian, and Spanish Criticism, 1900–1950* (New Haven, CT: Yale University Press, 1992).

Whittier-Ferguson, John, "The Liberation of Gertrude Stein: War and Writing," *Modernism/modernity* 8.3 (2001): 405–28.

Wilder, Thornton, "Introduction," in Gertrude Stein's *Four in America* (New Haven, CT: Yale University Press, 1947) v–xxvii.

Will, Barbara, "Lost in Translation: Stein's Vichy Collaboration," *Modernism/modernity* 11.4 (2004): 651–68.

Wilson, Edmund, ed. *The Shock of Recognition: The Development of Literature in the United States Recorded by the Men Who Made It* (Garden City, NY: Doubleday, 1943).

Yeazell, Ruth Bernard, *Language and Knowledge in the Late Novels of Henry James* (Chicago: Chicago University Press, 1976).

Zamir, Shamoon, *Dark Voices: W. E. B. Du Bois and American Thought, 1888–1903* (Chicago: University of Chicago Press, 1995).

Zwerdling, Alex, *Improvised Europeans: American Literary Expatriates and the Siege of London* (New York: Basic Books, 1994).

Index